The
Complete Guide
— to —
PRESSURE
CANNING

The Complete Guide
— to —
PRESSURE CANNING

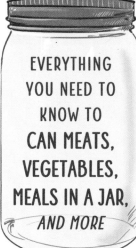

EVERYTHING
YOU NEED TO
KNOW TO
CAN MEATS,
VEGETABLES,
MEALS IN A JAR,
AND MORE

DIANE DEVEREAUX
The Canning Diva®

Illustrations by **AMBER DAY**

ROCKRIDGE
PRESS

I DEDICATE THIS BOOK TO MY TWO BEAUTIFUL CHILDREN—
CALEB AND AUDREY—MY LOVING FAMILY, AND TO THE CHERISHED
MEMORY OF MY LOYAL GARDEN COMPANION, KALA GIRL

CONTENTS

Introduction *xi*

PART ONE: CANNING 101

PART TWO: THE RECIPES

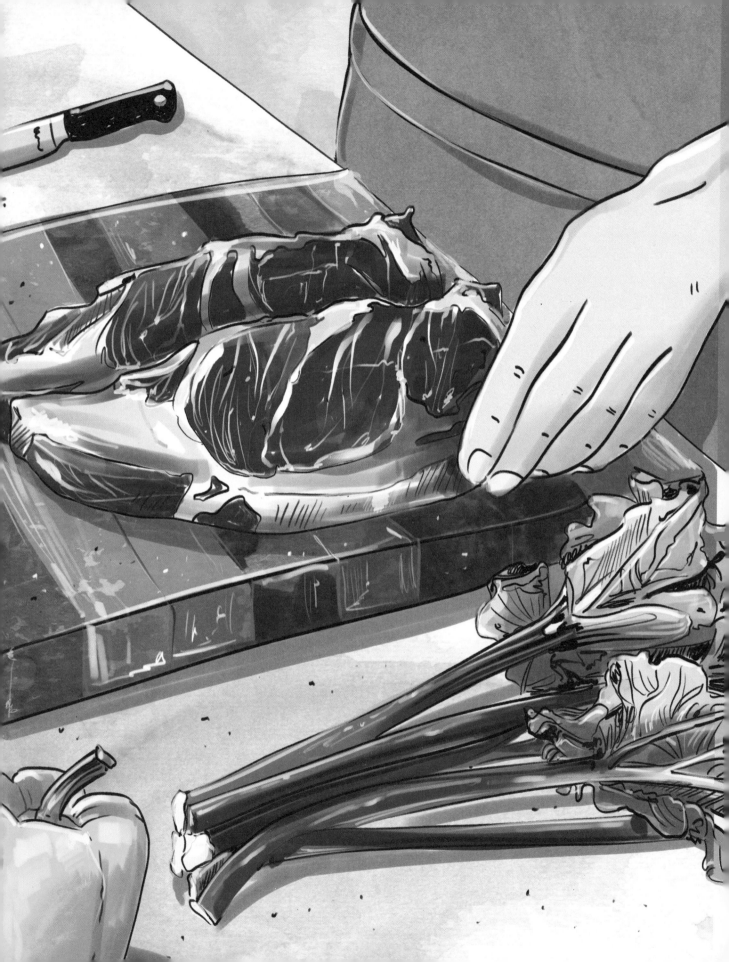

INTRODUCTION

I AM SO EXCITED TO BRING TO YOU the first complete guide to pressure canning. Many canning cookbooks spend countless pages detailing simplistic water bath recipes, yet fall short when it comes to pressure canning. *The Complete Guide to Pressure Canning* is a sensible road map focusing solely on how to safely use a pressure canner and how to safely preserve low-acid foods. Scared? Don't be.

The Complete Guide to Pressure Canning demonstrates a pressure canner's ease-of-use, demystifies the science and math used to safely preserve low-acid foods, and offers delicious recipes for readers of all skill levels, whether you are new to canning or have home canned all your life. Explore a whole new world of food preservation with step-by-step instruction, easy at-a-glance charts, two in-depth practice recipes, and much more.

Feel confident knowing you are in good hands with me, The Canning Diva®, as I have been canning since I was a teenager and have successfully taught this time-honored craft for over a decade. I have taken great joy in debunking the many fears and negative stereotypes often associated with pressure canning. In this complete guide, I detail the various components of a pressure canner, teach the vital roles acid, time, and temperature play in preservation, and dive deeper into forgotten foods like canned meat and fish.

Personally, pressure canning has opened the doors to so many fun recipes I otherwise would not have been able to preserve. Soups, stews, and meals in a jar are just a sampling. What's more exciting is witnessing over time how my pantry became less likely to harbor an aluminum can. The majority of what my family consumes is preserved in mason jars by my very own two hands. Kitchen staples like stocks and broths, colorful vegetables, and legumes in every shape and size now line my pantry shelf. It is quite pleasing and cost-saving to shop in my pantry *first*, rather than the grocery store.

If you have a busy, on-the-go lifestyle or desire to be prepared in times of disaster, pressure canning can help you stay one step ahead. With two active kids, I love knowing I can have a healthy meal on the table in less than 20 minutes, and my stock of pressure-canned meals in a jar keeps me from swinging by the fast food drive-thru on particularly hectic weeknights. Think of *The Complete Guide to Pressure Canning* as your own personal guide to reducing time in the kitchen. Just "heat and eat," as I like to say.

Are you ready to become a pressure canning expert? Let's get started!

1

CANNING 101

CHAPTER ONE

CANNING FUNDAMENTALS

WELCOME TO HOME CANNING and preserving! In this chapter, you will learn the fundamentals of home canning, with the primary focus on pressure canning. The best way to understand how to safely preserve food in jars for long-term storage is to gain knowledge of the math and science behind the craft. But don't worry—you don't need a degree in science to understand the material covered in the following pages. My approach is more holistic, offering a full overview of the canning process. We begin with the history of canning, then dive into the three main pillars of food preservation, and end with a discussion of the overall concept of preserving food in jars to give you the knowledge you need to pressure can with confidence in your home kitchen.

A Brief History of Canning

Canning, or jarring, dates back to the Napoleonic War era starting in 1803. In a nutshell, Napoleon was losing the war on the front line because his men were without food. "An army travels on its stomach," Napoleon famously said. By the time fresh foods made it to the front line, they would be rotten and inedible, leaving his men to pillage or purchase whatever the native country offered as a food source.

Napoleon put it to his people, through the Society for the Encouragement of Industry: whoever could find a way to preserve large quantities of foods to sustain their soldiers would receive a 12,000-franc reward. Nicolas Appert, a chef, confectioner, and distiller, collected the prize in 1810, after he spent 14 years exploring how food cooked within a glass jar would not spoil unless exposed to oxygen. He developed a method of jar sealing and successfully preserved soups, fruits, vegetables, juices, dairy products, marmalades, jellies, and syrups. With his award money, he developed the first commercial cannery, the House of Appert, which operated from 1812 to 1933.

Fast-forward 50 years or so, and Louis Pasteur discovered how time, temperature, and acidic value can play a vital role in protecting us from harmful microorganisms in our foods. It was Pasteur who was able to prove why food spoils and why beer and wine sour due to microorganisms. He therefore invented pasteurization. Pasteurization destroys microorganisms by a process of heating beverages and foods, then allowing them to cool. One of the best ways to destroy germs is with boiling water—a process still used to this day.

Modern scientists have expanded upon these discoveries. Advancements in technology allow us to get water and air hotter than boiling water temperature—this process is known as pressure canning. This, combined with standard safety methods, has permitted households to preserve sustainable food sources long-term.

Why I Love Pressure Canning

Pressure canning opens the doors to so many recipe possibilities. Here are some of the reasons I love pressure canning:

It saves time. While there is an initial time investment in prepping and cooking food, the countless hours I have saved by having a ready-made meal in a jar or by using a home-canned meal starter from my pantry more than make up for it.

It's a great way to extend good deals. As smart consumers, we all take advantage of supply and demand. When there's a bumper harvest, or meat goes on sale at our local grocer, we may purchase more at a lower price. We all love the satisfaction of getting a good deal, but without a way to extend such savings, we produce waste. Pressure canning allows us to stock up on such cost savings and preserve these foods for years, far longer than freezing or refrigeration.

It helps save money. I have found that certain kitchen staples, such as chicken and beef stock, can be created in large quantities for far less than what they cost at the grocery store.

I always know what's in my food. I know what I put into every single jar, because I either grew it myself or purchased it from a source I trust. I know what I am putting into my body and into the precious bodies of my loved ones.

It reduces garden waste. Water bathing is a suitable means of preservation; however, it is limited to high-acid foods. If you do not take the leap into pressure canning and your garden yields far more than expected, so much will go to waste. With pressure canning, you may preserve all sorts of vegetables in water without worry.

It makes me feel good. There is nothing better than seeing my pantry full of spaghetti sauce, a variety of soups and stews, Chicken Potpie Filling (page 162), and chicken and beef stocks—all made possible by pressure canning.

Canning 101

Home canning is such an amazing craft—a lost art that I am having a blast bringing back. I often say I am bridging the generational gap for so many who wanted to learn but never had the opportunity to do so. This gap also fueled the onslaught of fear and misinformation that has long prevented many newcomers from attempting to learn. My role as

The Canning Diva® is to take the fear out of home canning, teach safe canning practices, and create useful recipes that families will enjoy creating and eating for years to come! So how do I remove fear and quash the misinformation? Through education.

HOW CANNING PREVENTS FOOD SPOILAGE

Living microorganisms (bacteria, yeast, and mold) are a natural part of our existence. They are all around us, including in the air we breathe. Some have health benefits that have led us to produce lifesaving antibiotics (like penicillin) and other medicines, yet others can cause foods to spoil or lead to serious illness. When working with food in the kitchen, we must concern ourselves with harmful pathogenic microorganisms like staphylococcus and salmonella, which cause food-borne illnesses, and we must learn how to prevent them from invading our food source.

With any living thing, certain conditions are required for optimal growth. The perfect environment for harmful pathogenic microorganisms is moist, between 60°F and 90°F, and has available free oxygen. However, while those are prime conditions, microorganisms can grow in temperatures as low as 40°F and as high as 140°F. So be mindful of those leftovers you kept sitting out on the countertop . . . there is a reason we push to get them refrigerated, below 40°F, as soon as possible.

So how does canning prevent harmful microorganisms from invading our food? With proper food preparation, like scrubbing the exterior of root crops, knowledge of a recipe's overall pH, and the application of high heat and adequate processing times, dangerous bacteria will not survive in a sealed jar of food. Let's take a closer look at common food spoilers:

Bacteria

One of the most predominate bacterium associated with home canning is *Clostridium botulinum,* known to produce a toxin that causes a disease called botulism. While some harmful microorganisms require oxygen to grow and multiply, this particular bacterium requires an anaerobic environment, or an environment without free oxygen. This makes a sealed jar of food a perfect environment—but it's only perfect if the bacterium is present to begin with. That is why it is imperative to thoroughly wash vegetables and properly handle meat and fish when canning. Also, following proper processing methods is key to killing this harmful bacterium in the event that it escapes thorough cleaning and makes its way into the jar.

Enzymes

Enzymes are natural proteins found in plants and animals that speed up chemical reactions. They are also responsible for the ripening of fruits and vegetables. Ironically, the enzymes that make our food ready to eat are the same enzymes that cause our food to spoil if not eaten within a suitable time frame. Why? These enzymes stay active even after produce is harvested and meat is slaughtered. So how do we prevent our food from spoiling? We expose it to acid and/or high heat.

Molds and Yeasts

Molds are microscopic fungi that live on plant and animal matter. There are thousands of species that produce spores. Spores float through the air undetected and can also be transported by water and insects. A poorly sealed jar is the perfect place for spores to take root and grow. The roots may be difficult to see, as they may start very deep within the food, but the mold is visible as it grows and produces streaks of colors and then fuzz. Yeast spores grow on food much in the same way mold spores do, preferring acidic and sugary foods, like pickles and jam.

When preparing fruits and vegetables to preserve, discard any foods with fuzzy mold or slimy goo. You cannot just cut off the mold or try to wash off the slime. Mold and yeast are impervious to acid. The only way to destroy mold spores and yeast when canning is to expose them to high heat for a specific period of time.

UNDERSTANDING THE THREE PILLARS OF CANNING

In order to understand how to process your recipes safely, you first must understand the vital roles the three pillars of canning—acidic value (or pH), time, and temperature—play in home canning and food preservation. It is due to these three pillars that home canning has stayed relevant and safe for centuries.

Acidic Value

Food naturally has a pH value. Sometimes that value is neutral (7) or alkaline (above 7), and other times a food's value can be highly acidic (below 7). On the pH scale, numbers demonstrate the acidic value—the higher the number on the scale, the lower the acidic value (numbers 4.6 to 8), whereas the lower the number, the higher the acidic value (numbers 1 to 4.6). For those of you who maintain pools or hot tubs, it is the same pH scale of acid and alkalinity.

TOMATOES: A SPECIAL CASE

———————✣———————

Pressure canning may be used for recipes that hover in and out of the sensitive 4.6 pH area, or as a way to speed up processing times of high-acid recipes. For example, although you may safely water bathe whole tomatoes, which generally have a pH of 4.3 to 4.9, it takes upwards of 85 minutes to process them at a boiling water temperature. Using a pressure canner, you can achieve the same results in 25 minutes. Even if you take into account the heating up, venting, and cooling down required when pressure canning, you still have less time invested compared to water bathing, not to mention you retain a higher nutritional value because the food is exposed to high heat for a shorter time.

When it comes to the acidic value of food, please do not confuse an acidic pH value with flavor. Let me ask you, what do you think has more acidity: a sweet strawberry or a hot habanero pepper? For those of you who answered hot pepper, you may be surprised to know that, in fact, a strawberry is more acidic (3.5 pH) than a habanero pepper (5.8 pH). Spicy or hot *tasting* foods do not necessarily have higher acidic value on the pH scale.

The reason the food's acidic value matters is that, without the presence of acid, harmful bacteria will grow. Another major factor to consider with respect to acidic pH value is the sum of all foods in one recipe, not just the main ingredient. Take, for instance, salsa. Although the main ingredient is tomatoes, which generally have a high acidity and a pH value of 4.3 to 4.9, it is the sum of all ingredients that counts most in home canning. Once you start adding onions, jalapeños, cilantro, corn, and black beans, you now have diluted, or neutralized, the salsa's overall acidic value. When this happens, you have two choices: You can increase the acid by adding vinegar, lemon, or lime juice, making it suitable for water bathing; or you can keep the recipe as is and pressure can it because of its overall low acid content.

Time and Temperature

Time and temperature are particularly important in the processing stage of canning. The recipe's overall acidic value dictates the proper processing method: either water bath or pressure canning. Each method is defined by its temperature output. The typical water bathing temperature is 212°F, while the temperature of pressure canning is upwards of 250°F. The length of time necessary to safely process a recipe is dictated by the foods' acidic values and the temperature required to adequately process it.

Foods such as root crops and meat are considered low acid because they have a pH of 4.6 or higher, so we must rely on time and temperature

to safely kill harmful bacteria during processing. When canning low-acid foods, the temperature required to kill harmful bacteria, yeast, and mold ranges from 240°F to 250°F, depending on your elevation. Such high temperatures can only be achieved when using a pressure canner, not a water bather. Pressure canning is the only safe method for processing low-acid foods because it will get foods hot enough for long enough, making food safe for long-term storage.

CANNING METHODS

There are two methods of processing home-canned goods. One is water bathing, reserved for high-acid recipes with a pH of 4.6 and lower; the other is pressure canning, reserved for low-acid

---

"BUT GRANDMA NEVER KILLED ANYONE"

———— ❄ ————

There have been water bath recipes for low-acid foods in circulation for decades. And while many people have had success, others have gotten very sick. How can this happen? Take, for instance, the process of canning chicken using a water bather. The chicken is raw packed into jars, then placed in a water bath and covered with three inches of water. Now, to successfully kill harmful microorganisms, the chicken must be exposed to a consistent 212°F for three full hours.

But here's where it gets tricky: Water easily evaporates at the boiling point (212°F). During the next three hours, additional water must be added to the water bath to keep the jars covered, and the newly added water cannot cause the overall water temperature to dip below 212°F, ever, at the risk of introducing harmful bacteria.

Why would you struggle to accomplish such a task when there is a much safer, quicker alternative? Take advantage of the knowledge gained through scientific research and advancements in technology, and use a pressure canner instead for low-acid foods.

recipes with a pH of 4.6 or higher. In this book, we are solely focusing on pressure canning, but I will also cover a basic explanation of water bathing and how it compares to pressure canning.

Pressure Canning

We now know that adding acid to low-acid foods assists in killing harmful bacteria, but what if adding acid to a recipe isn't an option? I really have no desire to pickle my chicken. To make low-acid foods safe for long-term storage, we must rely solely on time and temperature to kill harmful bacteria. In this case, we must exceed boiling water temperatures.

A pressure canner reaches temperatures upwards of 250°F, which is a high temperature attained by air pressure. Unlike water bathing, in pressure canning you are not relying on the temperature of the water to preserve your food in jars; instead, you are relying on the temperature of the air inside the pressure canner. Without the ability to reach temperatures higher than 240°F, we would not be able to safely preserve soups, stews, chili, meats, and many delicious vegetables.

Water Bathing

Water bathing is the most popular form of processing for many canners.

Water bath canning is for acidic foods such as jams, salsas, and pickles that only require a boiling water temperature (212°F) to safely kill harmful bacteria. Water bathing requires a large stockpot or canner and a jar rack to prevent jars from clanking into each other and cracking. Water completely covers every jar and is heated to a full rolling boil to ensure that you have attained 212°F. Jars are then processed for the specific amount of time indicated in the recipe.

Because only high-acid foods can be processed in a hot water bath, we can rely on the temperature of boiling water to safely preserve the food. This means, however, that the jars must be adequately covered with water and the water must be at a full rolling boil for the entire processing time to ensure that the required 212°F temperature penetrates the contents of each jar. If any of the jars are exposed to air (not covered by water), it is likely that harmful bacteria will grow in the portion of exposed food. It is not recommended to water bathe low-acid foods because, given the length of time required to do so safely (upwards of 3 hours), it is very tricky to ensure that each jar stays covered with water and the water is kept at a consistent 212°F for the full length of processing.

ADJUSTING FOR ALTITUDE

It takes longer for water to boil at a higher altitude because the air pressure is lower. Further, water evaporates faster but gases expand more. For those of you living in higher altitudes, chances are

PRESSURE CANNING ALTITUDE CHART		
Altitude in Feet	**Dial-Gauge Canner**	**Weighted-Gauge Canner**
0–1000	10	10
1001–2000	11	15
2001–4000	12	15
4001–6000	13	15
6001–8000	14	15
8001–10,000	15	15

you have already learned to adjust your cooking and baking recipes. When pressure canning, the total processing time per recipe remains the same but the pounds of pressure must be adjusted based on the number of feet you are above sea level. Use this simple chart to make adjustments for either a dial-gauge or weighted-gauge pressure canner (see page 6).

If you are not sure of your altitude, see the Altitudes of Cities in the United States and Canada (page 195).

What Can I Pressure Can?

Often I will say, "Food is art, and canning is my way of preserving art." Actually, I say it so much that I had it trademarked. I fell in love with pressure canning because of the amazing foods I can safely preserve this way. Here is a short list of foods you may safely pressure can:

- Broths and stocks
- Casseroles
- Fish
- Fruits and chutneys
- Legumes and beans
- Meat
- Poultry and water fowl
- Ready-made meals
- Soups, stews, and chilis
- Tomatoes and sauces
- Vegetables
- Wild game

What Shouldn't I Pressure Can?

While pressure canning opens the doors to many recipe possibilities, there are still a handful of foods that either are unsafe to preserve or just don't taste good after pressure canning. Here's my list of what *not* to pressure can:

- Dense foods like mashed potatoes are not recommended because the heat cannot adequately penetrate through the center, putting the food at risk for microorganism growth. It is recommended that potatoes, pumpkin, and squash be cubed and covered in water for canning. They may be mashed prior to using/eating.

- Milk and milk-based creams are not recommended for home canning because there hasn't been enough research by our states' extension programs to publish a "seal of

THE TRUTH ABOUT CANNING FAT

———— ·✽· ————

Some foods on the elusive "do not can list" are there not because you cannot can them, but because no one has taken the time to explain the correct way to preserve them.

For instance, several websites state that you should not can fat. Written this way, it is quite misleading. I would hate to see anyone use a less marbled cut of meat when making Beef Burgundy (page 158) because they are scared into thinking fat is bad or unsafe for home canning. What should be said is this: Canning recipes with excessive fat or grease may prevent a lid from sealing.

To prevent lid failures when canning recipes with a higher fat content, start by giving each jar a generous 1¼ inches of headspace. Next, dip a clean washcloth in warm water, wring it dry, and then dip it in vinegar. Wipe each jar rim and screw thread using the prepared washcloth. Allowing more space in each jar will help prevent foods from encroaching on the jar rim. Using vinegar naturally cuts through grease, fat, sugary substances, and mineral residue. Further, vinegar naturally kills bacteria, so wiping your rim is a last line of defense prior to processing and sealing.

approval." So why do we see evaporated and condensed milk sold in cans at the store?

- – Milks (and creams) are commercially canned in aluminum. The pasteurization process heats milk to 275°F, which exceeds what we can achieve in our home kitchen via pressure canning.

- – Commercial canneries purposely, and drastically, reduce the temperature of the milk when canning to avoid it lingering in the temperature danger zone of 60°F to 90°F, preventing the growth of pathogenic microorganisms. This is also something we are unable to achieve in our home kitchen because our containment source is a glass jar. Glass cannot handle a vast swing in temperature without breaking, fracturing, or shattering.

- Delicate, soft-skinned fruits and berries, such as strawberries, turn brown in color and become mushy in a pressure canner. The exposure to high temperature is often too much for a delicate berry; therefore, the integrity of the food breaks down, and it becomes mushy and brown in color. These color and texture changes don't make the foods inedible, but they are certainly unappealing.

How Does Canning Affect Nutrients?

Exposing any food to heat causes some nutrient loss, but how much loss depends on the food itself, the temperature used to cook it, and the length of cooking time. While some vitamins and phytonutrients are lost when foods are exposed to heat, heating does not damage protein, fiber, and minerals in the same way.

Some vitamins are quite heat sensitive, like vitamin C, so any exposure to heat will cause the vitamin to escape the food. Further, it isn't just heat that does the damage, it is the length of exposure to heat that will cause an excessive nutrient depletion. Thiamine, niacin, and folate are destroyed significantly by excessive exposure to heat and/or water.

On the other hand, exposing certain foods to heat makes certain nutrients more available to our bodies. For this reason, it is best to keep in mind that not all vitamins are affected negatively by heat during cooking or canning. For example, the total carotenoid content in carrots and similar vegetables actually increases after boiling.

NUTRITIONAL BENEFITS OF PRESSURE CANNING

Heat isn't all bad when it comes to nutrients in your food. Heating foods has its advantages, such as killing harmful microorganisms, increasing digestibility, and increasing the availably of certain phytonutrients. Here are a few ways pressure canning can enhance the nutritional value of your food:

It Makes Certain Foods Edible

Broad beans, white kidney beans, and red kidney beans contain toxins that make them unsafe to eat in their raw state. Therefore, these beans must be cooked for a great length of time to be deemed safe. In this case, cooking or pressure canning beans is the only way to safely prepare these foods so our bodies may benefit from their protein, fiber, and mineral content.

It Helps Foods Retain Nutrients

The beauty of pressure canning is that you preserve the entire recipe. You start by creating a recipe in a stockpot and then transfer all the contents to a jar. Soups and meals in a jar are great examples of nutrient retention, as in these cases all the nutrients that typically escape the food during cooking are retained within the jar.

It Cooks Foods Faster for Shorter Heating Times

Another major benefit to preserving with a pressure canner versus a water bather is that the foods are exposed to high heat for shorter amounts of time. Shorter cooking times using a higher temperature means food retains more of its nutrients due to less heat exposure.

VITAMIN LOSS OF WATER-SOLUBLE VITAMINS BY COOKING METHOD	
Method	% of Vitamin B and C loss
Boiling	35–60%
Poaching	< boiling
Steaming	10–25%
Pressure canning	5–10%
Microwave cooking	5–25%
Roasting	10–47%
Stewing and Braising	10–12%
Grilling	10–12%
Baking	10–12%
Frying	7–10%

NO SUGAR, NO SALT? NO PROBLEM!

As you have learned in this chapter, it is the recipe's overall acidic value and processing time and temperature that accomplish long-term preservation when canning foods.

A popular canning misconception is that salt is the preserver. With the exception of creating brine for pickling recipes, salt is merely for flavor in pressure canning. Take, for instance, home-canned green beans in water. Many recipes include ¼ teaspoon salt per jar as an ingredient. Anyone with a low-sodium diet knows that adding salt would be counterproductive to their health; however, many recipes fail to tell you that the salt is optional.

Another popular misconception is that the sugar in jam recipes is what preserves the jam. This couldn't be further from the truth. What we know to be true is that a plethora of sugar will help the jam gel when exposed to heat; however, who wants to ingest upwards of 7 cups sugar for every batch of strawberry jam? For diabetics and those watching their sugar intake, this is a huge deterrent to creating and consuming home-canned jams. Thankfully, low-sugar jam recipes are available using far less sugar and relying on ClearJel® to gel the jam.

STABILITY OF VITAMINS					
Vitamin	Acid: low pH	Alkali: high pH	Heat > 158°F	Light	O$_2$
WATER-SOLUBLE VITAMINS					
C	No effect	Very sensitive	Very sensitive	Very sensitive	Very sensitive
B6	No effect	No effect	Sensitive	Very sensitive	No effect
FAT-SOLUBLE VITAMINS					
A	No effect	No effect	No effect	Very sensitive	Very sensitive
D	No effect	Sensitive	No effect	Sensitive	Very sensitive
E	No effect	No effect	No effect	Sensitive	Very sensitive

CHAPTER TWO

THE PRESSURE CANNER'S KITCHEN

SUPPLIES, BASIC INSTRUCTIONS, AND SAFETY

IN THIS CHAPTER, I'LL HELP SET YOU UP for success, detailing the tools and equipment you need, comparing and contrasting the various types of pressure canners on the market, and walking you through the basic functions of a pressure canner. Do you have a pressure canner that was passed down from your grandma, or did you find a good deal at an estate sale? I cover what to look for and how to improve secondhand canners. Throughout this chapter, I've also included some professional tips to give you a thorough understanding of how to safely operate each type of pressure canner and explain how each canner may operate slightly differently but still produces the same results.

Essential Tools and Equipment

It amazes me how far the world of technology has advanced since I was a kid! Even something as simple and inexpensive as a magnetic lid grabber makes adding a lid to a jar so much safer. It used to be such a struggle to get a sterilized lid out of boiling water with only a set of tongs and a pot holder. Canning and food preservation is about practicality, so here is a quick list of the tools you need for efficient and safe pressure canning at home:

Pressure Canner: Size matters. A tall, 23-quart canner, or larger, allows for double-stacking jars using a second canning rack, which may be purchased separately. A 15.5-quart canner is the smallest pressure canner available for home canning. It yields 7 quarts or 8 pints, depending on the manufacturer and jar type used. There are two types of pressure canners: weighted gauge and dial gauge. Some pressure canners may also double as water bathers.

Jars: Jars come in multiple sizes, including pint and quart with two different mouth opening sizes—regular and wide mouth. Wash new jars with warm soapy water or in the dishwasher.

If your used jars have been stored clean, a simple rinse with warm water will suffice. If you plan to hot pack your recipe, keep your clean jars in a sink of warm water or keep them room temperature on the countertop. Jars may be cleaned and reused indefinitely as long as they are free from cracks and chips.

Lids and Rings: Canning lids, unless they are specifically sold as reusable, can only be used once for canning. You can find reusable lids and seals on the market, but they are considerably more expensive. You can reuse the rings indefinitely as long as they are free of excessive rust.

Although some manufacturers now state that it is not necessary to boil their lids prior to use, I still boil them, since the lids will come in direct contact with my food, and the quality of the lid determines whether the food can be safely stored long-term. Without a good-sealing lid, my energy, time, and food is wasted.

Headspace Measuring and Air Bubble Remover Tool: This is your best friend when you're canning. It's an inexpensive tool with measurements on one end and a flat tip to remove air bubbles on the other. It ensures the proper amount of free space in each jar for food expansion and contraction during processing and vacuum sealing.

Widemouthed Jar Funnel: Save additional work cleaning residue off each jar rim by getting all the food in the jar the first time. Using a funnel means you waste less food and time and helps maximize jar space.

Magnetic Lid Grabber: Get lids out of boiling water safely by using this tool to magnetically grab one jar lid at a time. This is another handy tool Grandma would have loved to have back in the day!

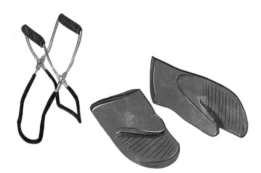

Waterproof, Heat-Resistant Canning Mitts or Jar Grabber: Dish towels and pot holders conduct heat when wet, but a waterproof mitt or a jar grabber keeps your hands safe from burns. These tools help you maintain dexterity when handling wet, boiling-hot jars.

Large Slotted Spoon and Ladle: While many jars can be filled using a ladle, a slotted spoon helps balance the ratio of liquids to solids in each jar, which is essential to maximizing jar space.

Dish towels and Cutting Boards: Granite and stoneware countertops are naturally cool. If you put scalding hot glass jars directly on granite or stoneware, they may fracture, crack, or shatter. Keep processed hot jars away from direct contact with cool granite or stoneware countertops by placing them on a cutting board covered with dish towels. Doing so prior to filling jars prevents the countertop surface from decreasing the temperature of warm glass jars. The cutting boards elevate jars off cold countertops and dish towels soak up water.

UNDERSTANDING THE IMPORTANCE OF HEADSPACE

The key to getting a lid to seal is twofold: you need a clean jar rim surface and properly measured headspace. Over- or under-filling jars prevents a good lid seal, which is why allowing proper headspace is crucial for long-term storage.

Headspace is defined as the unfilled space inside a jar, above the food and below the lid. Typically, canning recipes specify leaving ¼ inch of headspace for jams and jellies; ½ inch for fruits, salsas, chutneys, and tomatoes; and 1 to 1¼ inches for low-acid foods processed in a pressure canner.

This unfilled space allows foods to expand during processing and contract when cooling to form a vacuum seal. The extent of expansion is determined by the air content in the food and the processing temperature. Air expands greatly when heated to high temperatures. The higher the temperature, the greater the expansion, and therefore, the greater the headspace required.

In many pressure canning recipes you will see the phrase a *generous inch of headspace* used to describe the unfilled space inside a jar. Because our headspace measuring tool stops measuring at 1 inch, we guesstimate an additional ¼ inch to create the generous inch. This additional space is required because the foods expand a bit more than expected during testing.

Clean Terrycloth Washcloth: Reserve a separate washcloth for each recipe to wipe jar rims and screw threads when canning. While any material will work, terrycloth is the best for absorbing moisture and capturing residue during cleaning.

Distilled White Vinegar: Vinegar is a canning and kitchen staple that naturally kills bacteria. Wet a washcloth in warm water, wring it out so it's just damp, and then dip it in vinegar prior to wiping jar rims and screw threads. Add 1 ounce (2 tablespoons) vinegar to the water in your pressure canner prior to processing. The vinegar prevents mineral deposits from forming on your glass jars.

Timer: Have a reliable timer in the kitchen to properly track cooking and processing times.

Permanent Marker: After lids have sealed and jars have been cleaned, label each lid with the recipe or food and the month and year it was preserved.

Helpful Nonessentials

Here is a short list of additional tools you may use to make your canning experience more enjoyable:

Apron: Protects your clothing from food splatters in the kitchen. Personally, I like wearing an apron with pockets, so I can keep my weighted gauge or counterweight and permanent marker handy when they are not in use.

Jar Labels: While all you really need is a permanent marker to label your jars, colorful adhesive labels can be a fun addition to your canning supplies, especially if you plan to give away your creations as gifts. Adhering labels to the lids rather than the glass jars will make for easier clean-up and removal.

Plastic or Silicone Spatula: Removing air bubbles trapped in each jar is essential to maximizing jar space and getting a good lid seal. A spatula, the handle of a wooden spoon, and even a chopstick are good tools to have handy while canning.

Buying a Pressure Canner

A pressure canner, although scary to many, is actually a simple appliance. It is designed to create the pressure necessary to achieve the high temperatures required to safely process low-acid foods. While there are several manufacturers and two different types of pressure canners available, the vessel itself is the same no matter which brand or style you choose.

Pressure canners made before the 1970s were heavy-walled kettles with clamp-on or turn-on lids and a single vent pipe. These canners relied on a weighted gauge to jiggle, making an audible sound to signify proper processing. Many of these earlier canners are still in use today. Since the 1970s, redesigns of pressure canners have resulted in lightweight, thin-walled kettles, mostly with turn-on lids and locking brackets. Many pressure canners have gaskets or rubber sealing rings to prevent steam from escaping, but some rely on a tight metal-to-metal seal with the use of clamping mechanisms. Newer pressure canners have a visual indicator in the form of a dial gauge. When buying a pressure canner, look for the Underwriters Laboratories approval of safety symbol (UL) to be sure that the canner meets all modern safety standards.

GETTING ACQUAINTED WITH PRESSURE CANNERS

There are two main types of pressure canners on the market: weighted gauge and dial gauge. There even is a combination of the two, where the pressure canner gives you a dial gauge and a weighted gauge so you have both audible and visual indicators. Despite the slight difference in how pressure is monitored, there are many common attributes to a pressure canner.

Parts of a Pressure Canner

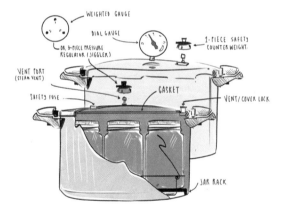

Vent Pipe. The vent pipe is the primary pressure relief valve, which releases pressure in excess of 15 pounds. The vent pipe is on the lid of every canner. Before every use, hold the lid up to the light and look through the vent pipe to ensure it is not clogged. If it is clogged, use a steady flow of water and a bottle brush (if required) to gently free any debris. Every pressure canner must vent steam from the vent pipe prior to gaining pressure.

Safety Fuse or Overpressure Plug. Located on the lid of the pressure canner, the safety fuse is a rubber plug or thin metal insert designed to vent excess pressure from the canner. To keep the fuse working properly, avoid picking or scrubbing it aggressively when you clean your pressure canner.

Tight-Fitting Lid. A tight-fitting lid is an essential component that keeps the pressure contained within the canner. To accomplish a tight seal to increase pressure, some canner lids have a rubber seal and locking bracket, while others simply use multiple screw and clamp-locking mechanisms. Each manufacturer gives instructions on how to properly adhere the lid to the canner.

Weighted Gauge (a.k.a. Jiggler), Counterweight. Commonly referred to as a jiggler, the weighted gauge that sits loosely on top of the vent pipe is what indicates the pressure within weighted-gauge canners. When a weighted-gauge canner reaches the correct level of pressure, the jiggler rocks in a designated pattern/frequency (as specified in the manufacturer's instructions). Dial-gauge canners have counterweights instead of weighted gauges. Both sit loosely atop the vent pipe to prevent steam from escaping, which builds pressure and temperature within the canner.

Flat Canning Rack. The canning rack sits on the bottom of the canner to elevate the glass jars off the heat source, preventing the jar bottoms from cracking due to the high heat. For tall pressure canners with a 23-quart or more capacity, it is safe to double-stack jars using a second flat canning rack, which separates the jars and gives the top row a flat surface to rest on. If a second flat rack is not used, the top jars will not be stable and may rattle, tip, fall, and most likely crack.

Locking Mechanisms. While individual manufacturers may have devised their own ways to safely secure the lid to the vessel, all canners have a locking mechanism. Some are in the form of brackets adhered to the side wall of the vessel and lid; others are actual clamps that tighten the lid to the vessel. New canners now have an indicator that indicates when the lid is locked and the canner is able to gain pressure.

TYPES OF PRESSURE CANNERS

Weighted-Gauge Pressure Canner

A weighted-gauge pressure canner simply relies on a locking lid and a weighted gauge to indicate the internal pressure. This special weighted gauge, or jiggler, has three notched holes, for different pounds of pressure per square inch (PSI). Some manufacturers require the user to modify the gauge based on the PSI required in the recipe. This is called a 3-piece weighted gauge. Essentially you are given a spindle which represents 5 PSI and two individual weights each representing 5 PSI. The recipe will indicate the PSI required to safely process the food.

This is an audible form of pressure indication—the jiggler rocks on top of the vent pipe, making a "ticking" noise when metal gently hits metal. The higher the internal pressure of the canner, the faster the jiggler rocks. Once the weighted gauge is rocking in a consistent pattern (check your user's manual for the rocking pattern specific to your model), set your timer to the recipe's processing time.

Pros:

- This type of canner does not have to be monitored as closely as the dial-gauge canner; as long as you can hear the weight rocking steadily, you know it is maintaining the correct amount of pressure.
- Weighted gauges do not have to be checked each year for accuracy and rarely need to be replaced.

Cons:

- If your house is noisy, it might be difficult to hear the jiggler well enough to be sure

that the canner is maintaining the correct amount of pressure throughout processing.

Dial-Gauge Pressure Canner

Unlike the weighted-gauge pressure canner, the dial-gauge pressure canner has a dial on the lid that indicates the pounds of pressure, or PSI, inside the locked canner. Some manufacturers of dial-gauge canners offer testing units that you can use to check the accuracy of the gauge. Testing your gauge periodically not only keeps your canner in optimal working condition, it also ensures that your food is safe. Another resource to test your dial gauge is your local university extension program. On most pressure canners, the dial gauge is replaceable.

Pros:

- You can determine the pressure level of your canner at a glance.
- Dial-gauge canners are ideal for those living at high altitudes, as they can be adjusted to reach more precise levels of pressure.

Cons:

- Many manufacturers suggest that you check your dial gauge once a year, as they may lose accuracy.
- These types of canners must be monitored regularly during processing to ensure that the correct pressure is maintained.

An important safety feature on most dial-gauge pressure canners is a safety release plug. A rubber overpressure plug on the canner lid will automatically pop out and release steam in the event the canner exceeds a safe level of pressure, above 20 PSI. Please note that if the overpressure plug releases hot air rapidly from within the canner, the glass jars will likely break inside the canner.

There are also dual-gauge pressure canners with both weighted and dial gauges on the canner lid, offering users both visual and audible pressure indicators.

WHICH TYPE OF PRESSURE CANNER SHOULD I BUY?

This is a personal preference and may also be driven by budget. There is no wrong answer when purchasing a UL Certified pressure canner. There are many reasons to purchase a particular pressure canner over another. Many of us prefer a visual reference when monitoring the pressure, while others like knowing that, once the weighted gauge is set on top of the vent pipe, they do not need to continually monitor their canner during processing.

You might choose the canner based on price or availability. Do you have a hand-me-down canner from your grandmother or did you pick one up for a great price at an estate sale? Awesome! Pressure canners are built to last and are often passed down from generation to generation. I would never pass up the opportunity to get a good deal. I would, however, recommend contacting the manufacturer so you may purchase replacement parts to ensure your used canner operates properly and safely.

WHAT DO I DO IF I HAVE AN INDUCTION COOKTOP OR STOVE?

The Problem: For a pot or pan to work on induction cooktops, the base must be comprised of a ferrous metal; otherwise, it will not conduct heat. You may test to see if your pot or pan will work on induction by holding a magnet to the base. If the magnet sticks, it will work on induction. Pressure canners are mainly comprised of aluminum or nonmagnetic stainless steel. For this reason, pressure canners will not work on induction.

The Solution: Purchase a high-performance butane gas range that has either a single or double burner. They work perfectly on your kitchen countertop and are also portable. I use a single butane burner for indoor canning classes and demonstrations, when giving culinary presentations, and when cooking recipes on TV.

Four Questions to Help You Choose the Perfect Pressure Canner:

1. **What is my stove-top surface?** For those of you with glass flat-top stoves, it is important you know the weight limit for the glass surface and/or the individual burner. The stove manufacturer has this information. There are aluminum pressure canners on the market, which are lighter weight than most. Also, it may mean you have to purchase a smaller, 15.5-quart canner instead of the classic 23-quart size.

2. **How much do I intend to preserve?** When I set aside the time to pressure can, I want to yield as many jars as I possibly can in one session. For this reason, I preserve in pints so I can double-stack them in my 23-quart pressure canner for a 16-pint yield. Others might want the ability to preserve as many quarts as possible in one session, so they would opt for a 41.5-quart canner that yields 32 pints or 19 quarts at a time. For some, having the standard output of 7 quarts or 8 pints is sufficient each time they pressure can, so a 15.5-quart canner is just right.

3. **What is my budget?** The amount you are able to invest can be a huge deciding factor. Though I would have loved to pressure can 32 pints at a time, my budget only stretched to a canner that could produce 16 pints per canning session. New pressure canners cost anywhere from $75 to $500, depending on a variety of factors. Do some comparison shopping to find the right canner for your budget.

4. **What is considered too much care and maintenance?** Many manufacturers suggest that the dial gauge be tested annually to ensure that it stays in optimal working condition. This may be a nuisance to some who may not have a state extension program close by or don't wish to purchase a testing kit. For this reason, you may choose to purchase a weighted-gauge canner.

Regardless of the style of canner, I always tell home canners to purchase a second weighted gauge or counterweight. Without this crucial part, the canner will not work, but if one weight is lost or damaged, you will have a spare waiting in the wings. Personally, I use dial-gauge canners—six of them, to be exact. My home is loud and active with kids and dogs and people coming and going, so I cannot rely on an audible noise to ensure that my canner is working properly.

With so many different options on the market, it can be overwhelming to buy a new pressure canner, especially if you're new to the scene. Here is a handy comparison of the top three pressure canner brands you'll encounter (see below).

THREE POPULAR PRESSURE CANNER BRANDS: A BUYER'S GUIDE

Features	Brands		
	ALL AMERICAN	**MIRRO**	**PRESTO**
Thick lined walls, heavier weight	X		
Thinner walls, lighter weight		X	X
Dial gauge (pressure can be monitored visually)	X		X
Weighted gauge (pressure can be monitored audibly)	X	X	X
Lid-locking mechanism	X	X	X
Overpressure safety plug to avoid canner increasing pressure past 25 PSI			X
Replacement parts available for purchase	X	X	X
Dial-gauge pressure testing kit available for purchase			X

WHY DO I HAVE TO LET MY PRESSURE CANNER SIT AFTER PROCESSING?

I am often asked why it is necessary to let a pressure canner rest and naturally return to 0 PSI after processing. You don't have to do it when pressure *cooking* a meal, so why do you have to when pressure canning? Unlike pressure cooking a pot roast to serve that evening for supper, when pressure canning, we are preserving food in glass jars, and it's actually more about cooling down than reducing the pressure. Let me give you a quick scenario.

Whether waiting tables at a restaurant or serving dinner at home, you just finished pouring the last bit of hot coffee from a glass coffeepot into your guest's mug. After doing so, you immediately head to the kitchen, proceed to the sink, and run ice cold tap water into the hot glass pot. What just happened to the glass pot? Well, hopefully the glass just cracked and didn't shatter everywhere, but in the end, the glass coffeepot is now broken and no longer usable. Worse, the glass may stay intact, but the swing in temperature from very hot to very cold produced small stress fractures in the glass, damaging its integrity and making it susceptible to breaking the next time it is used.

The premise is the same with home canning. Because we use glass jars, we must be mindful of rapid temperature fluctuations that cause the glass to fracture, crack, or even shatter. Letting your pressure canner release heat naturally prevents your glass jars from breaking. I use this cooling-down time to clean up my kitchen and prepare countertop space to cool jars once they are removed from the canner.

CHAPTER THREE

YOUR FIRST BATCHES

IN THE FIRST TWO CHAPTERS, I discussed the fundamentals of canning, how a pressure canner works, how to use a pressure canner to safely preserve food, and the important features of both dial-gauge and weighted-gauge pressure canners. In this chapter, I take you from start to finish using two simple reference recipes. I touch on every step in the canning process so you have the tools and tips necessary to duplicate any recipe in your home kitchen. In addition to the tips, there is a pressure canning problem solver to help you troubleshoot any issues with your pressure-canned batches. This chapter also covers how to properly store your home-canned goods and includes a seasonal produce guide to help you plan your canning calendar.

Before You Begin

For those of you who are new to the art of pressure canning, I highly suggest selecting a day when you can devote 4 to 6 hours to the process, depending on the recipe, and remaining in your kitchen for the entire time. There will come a time when you will pressure can more spontaneously, like when your garden produces an unexpected harvest, but you don't want your first time to be rushed in any way.

PREPARE YOUR PRESSURE CANNER

For those of you taking your pressure canner out of the box for the first time, follow your manufacturer's manual for proper installation of the dial gauge, vent pipe, any gaskets, etc. If you are installing any replacement parts onto a used canner for the first time, follow the manufacturer's guidelines for installation.

For those of you who may also use your pressure canner to create meals (pressure cooking), make sure that every attachable part is secured tightly to the vessel and, most importantly, inspect and clear out the vent pipe before every canning session.

To inspect your vent pipe, hold the lid up to the light and look through the vent hole. If you cannot see light through the vent hole, it is clogged, and you must clean it and remove any food debris before proceeding. Use a steady flow of water and a bottle brush (if required) to gently free any debris. After cleaning, reinspect the vent pipe to ensure that you can see clearly through the hole.

PREPARE YOUR KITCHEN AND GATHER TOOLS AND EQUIPMENT

After inspecting your pressure canner to ensure that it will work properly, give your kitchen counter a good cleaning, set up a jar-cooling area—I use one or two large cutting boards topped with clean dish towels—and assemble your utensils and supplies. Here is a list of essential pressure canning equipment you will want to have handy:

- ❑ Pressure canner
- ❑ Clean jars, lids, and rings
- ❑ Headspace measuring and air bubble remover tool
- ❑ Widemouthed funnel
- ❑ Magnetic lid grabber
- ❑ Heatproof, water-resistant canning mitts
- ❑ Large slotted spoon and ladle
- ❑ Clean terrycloth washcloth(s)
- ❑ Distilled white vinegar
- ❑ Timer
- ❑ Permanent marker

Pressure Canning Reference Recipes

While this cookbook contains a number of exciting pressure canning recipes, it is best for newcomers to practice a recipe or two before diving into more complex recipes. Here you'll find two practice recipes, one for canning a vegetable in water, and one for canning a meat in water. Both recipes allow you to practice proper pressure canning methods and the required steps to safely preserve low-acid foods, and each one gives you a point of reference to reflect back upon.

CREATE NEW TRADITIONS WITH A CANNING PARTY

———— ❖ ————

I love getting friends and family together for a canning party. We bring cocktails and snacks and set aside 6 hours to crank out as many jars of home-canned goods as possible—all the while chatting, laughing, and catching up on life. There is no rule that says you must do this alone! Many hands make light work, and you can divide up the yummy jars of goodness after they've been processed.

GREEN BEANS

MAKES APPROXIMATELY 9 QUARTS OR 18 PINTS

PREP: 30 MIN • CANNER: 1 HR • PROCESSING: 25 MIN/20 MIN • TOTAL: 1 HR 55 MIN/ 1 HR 50 MIN

These simple green beans are easy to preserve and amazing to eat! Packed full of nutrients, they make a delicious side dish for any meal. When purchased in bulk, fresh green beans will fill dozens of quart jars. To serve, simply heat in a pan on your stove top, add a bit of butter, and season with a dash of salt and pepper.

10 pounds fresh green beans

9 teaspoons canning salt (optional)

Distilled white vinegar, for wiping jars

1. Inspect all your jars to ensure the rims do not have any chips or cracks. Be sure lids are new and rings are free from rust. Prepare the jars by washing them in hot, soapy water or in the dishwasher. Let the jars rest in hot water in the sink while you prep the beans and get everything else set up.

2. Rinse the green beans in a colander, being sure to remove any shriveled, soft, or rust-colored green beans. Snip or cut off the stems, keeping the bean tips intact. Cut the beans into bite-size pieces, about 2 inches long.

3. Fill a 16-quart stockpot with 20 cups of hot water and bring to a boil. Once the water is at a boil, cover the pot, reduce the heat, and keep it at a simmer.

4. Place the jar lids and rings in a smaller pot and cover them with water; place the pot over high heat. When the water comes to a rolling boil, set a timer for 5 minutes. When the timer goes off, shut off the burner. ➡

5. Place two large cutting boards on the counter next to the stove and cover them with clean dish towels. Place the warm, clean jars on the prepared cutting boards.

6. If using salt for flavor, add 1 teaspoon salt to each quart and ½ teaspoon to each pint. Pack the green beans into the jars, leaving 1 inch of headspace. (This is called raw pack because the beans are not cooked before processing.) Using a wooden spoon, gently tamp down the beans, making sure they adequately fill the jar so you won't have any large pockets of air that affect the bean-to-water ratio. Use your headspace measuring tool to be sure the beans are below the 1-inch mark in each jar.

7. Remove the lid from the stockpot and ladle the simmering water over the green beans, being sure to keep 1 inch of headspace. If you run out of hot water, boil 5 more cups of water and cover the remaining beans with the newly boiled water. Lightly tap the filled jars on the cutting board to release trapped air bubbles, and use your air bubble remover tool to release any trapped air along the sides of the jar and in the center of the beans.

8. Fill a small bowl with distilled white vinegar. To prepare each jar, wet a clean terrycloth washcloth in warm water and wring it dry with your hands. Dip a tip or portion of the washcloth into the white vinegar. Wipe the rim of the jar and its screw thread with the washcloth. Dip a clean corner of the same washcloth in the vinegar, and then wipe the jar rim and screw thread a second time. Using a magnetic lid grabber, remove one jar lid from the pot of hot water. Without touching the interior side of the lid, set the lid on top of the jar rim. Using your hands, screw the ring onto the jar and gently tighten it. (Don't screw it on so tight that it is difficult to unscrew again.) For cleanliness, it is important that you complete this process one jar at a time.

9. Remove the pots from the stove and place the pressure canner on a burner. Fill the canner with the required amount of hot water, according to the manufacturer's instructions. (Some canners have a notch inside the canner to indicate the water level for canning.) Add 2 tablespoons distilled white vinegar to the water. (This will prevent mineral deposits from forming on your glass jars.)

10. Place jars inside the canner on top of the flat canning rack. If your canner allows you to double-stack pints, place a second flat canning rack on top of the jars inside the canner and proceed to stack additional pints on the second flat canning rack. Secure the lid on the pressure canner and lock it into place.

11. Turn the burner under the pressure canner to high heat. In about 15 minutes, the vent pipe should start spitting a bit of water and some steam. Wait until the vent pipe shoots a steady flow of steam, whether very visible or not, and then set your timer for 10 minutes.

12. **In a weighted-gauge pressure canner:** After the steam has vented for 10 minutes, place the 10-PSI weight on the vent pipe. The weight will begin to rock as the canner beings to increase in pressure. Once it is rocking consistently, set your timer for 25 minutes for quarts and 20 minutes for pints. If the weighted gauge begins rocking too vigorously, reduce the burner heat slightly to achieve a consistent rocking pattern.

13. **In a dial-gauge pressure canner:** After the steam has vented for 10 minutes, place a counterweight on the vent pipe. When the

dial gauge reads 11 PSI, set your timer to 25 minutes for quarts and 20 minutes for pints. Throughout the processing time, use your burner knob to decrease or increase the heat output as necessary. If the pressure exceeds 13 PSI, reduce the heat slightly to keep the dial between 11 and 12 PSI. Do not let the PSI drop below the required amount. If this does happen, increase the heat to achieve the required PSI and reset the timer for the full processing time.

14. As soon as the timer goes off, turn off the burner. Do NOT touch the pressure canner. Do NOT remove the weighted gauge or counterweight. The pressure in the canner must return to 0 PSI naturally. Allow the canner to rest, undisturbed, for 30 minutes or until the locking mechanism releases. Carefully remove the weighted gauge or counterweight, and then remove the canning lid, keeping your face and hands away from the hot steam that will escape the canner. Allow the jars to cool for another 5 minutes before removing them from the canner using waterproof canning mitts or a jar grabber. Place the hot jars on the towel-covered cutting boards. (Make sure the jars are not exposed to cold drafts, especially if you are canning in winter.)

15. After the jars have cooled for 2 to 3 hours, check the lids to see if they have sealed. Press down on the center of each lid with your finger—if it stays concave and does not pop back up, the lid is sealed. If it pops back up, the lid is not sealed; place the jar in the refrigerator and eat the contents within 1 week. If multiple lids have not sealed, you can reboil the water, refill the jars, and process again.

16. Let the jars cool at room temperature for 12 hours or overnight, then remove the rings. Using warm, soapy water, wash the outside of each jar and rinse well. Wash the rings in warm, soapy water or in the dishwasher and store for future use. Do NOT screw the rings back onto the jars. Dry the jars and use a permanent marker to label the lid of each one with the date and recipe name.

17. Store the jars in your pantry or in another dark place at a temperature between 50°F and 70°F.

Ingredient Tip: It will take 10 pounds whole, uncut green beans to yield approximately 9 quarts or 18 pints of cut green beans.

RAW PACK VS. HOT PACK

Raw packing is the practice of filling jars tightly with unheated food, hence the term "raw." Doing so will cause some foods, especially fruit, to float in the jar after they are processed. Raw packing is more suitable for vegetables processed in a pressure canner and pickled foods processed in a water bather. When raw packing, the juice, syrup, brine, or water to be added to the foods should be heated to a boil before adding it to the jars. This practice helps remove trapped air from the food's tissue, therefore shrinking the food and preventing it from floating in the jar.

Hot packing is the practice of heating food to boiling, simmering 2 to 5 minutes, and then promptly transferring the cooked food to the jars before canning. Many fresh foods contain upwards of 30 percent air and 80 percent water. Hot packing essentially preshrinks foods and is the best way to remove trapped air and excess water. It is also a suitable way to blend the variety of flavors within a recipe. Hot packing permits more food to be placed into each jar; if foods are not preshrunk, the likelihood of there being a higher water content in the food may mean you will get less food per jar.

CHICKEN BREASTS

MAKES APPROXIMATELY 7 QUARTS OR 14 PINTS

PREP: 30 MIN • CANNER: 1 HR 35 MIN • PROCESSING: 1 HR 30 MIN/1 HR 15 MIN • TOTAL: 3 HR 35 MIN/3 HR 20 MIN

Having canned chicken on hand will make quick, healthy meals easy! Simply reheat using a stove top, add seasonings and create meals like chicken quesadillas, chicken curry soup, chicken tacos, enchiladas and chicken alfredo. Home-canned chicken is even great to take camping! The possibilities are endless!

14 to 16 large boneless, skinless chicken breasts, raw
Distilled white vinegar, for wiping jars

1. Inspect all your jars to ensure the rims do not have any chips or cracks. Be sure lids are new and rings are free from rust. Prepare the jars by washing them in hot, soapy water or in the dishwasher.

2. Place the jar lids and rings in a small pot and cover them with water; place the pot over high heat. When the water comes to a rolling boil, set a timer for 5 minutes. When the timer goes off, shut off the burner.

3. Place two large cutting boards on the counter next to the stove and cover them with clean dish towels. Place the clean jars on the prepared cutting boards.

4. Remove excess fat from each chicken breast and cut into 2-inch chunks. Raw-pack the chicken chunks into the clean jars, leaving 1 inch of headspace. Using the air bubble remover tool, maneuver the chicken pieces so they are as tightly packed as possible. Press and fill any crevices with more chicken. Repeat until all the chicken has been added to the jars. Water is not required here, as the chicken will make its own broth, however it will not

fully cover all of the chicken. If you wish to have more broth in each jar, pour in enough cold water to cover, leaving 1 inch of headspace. Use your headspace measuring tool to be sure all chicken pieces are below the 1-inch mark. Remove any excess air bubbles and adjust the water or chicken level as needed to keep the 1 inch of headspace.

5. Fill a small bowl with distilled white vinegar. To prepare each jar, wet a clean terrycloth washcloth in warm water and wring it dry with your hands. Dip a tip or portion of the washcloth into the white vinegar. Wipe the rim of the jar and its screw thread with the washcloth. Dip a clean corner of the same washcloth in the vinegar, and then wipe the jar rim and screw thread a second time. Using a magnetic lid grabber, remove one jar lid from the pot of hot water. Without touching the interior side of the lid, set the lid on top of the jar rim. Using your hands, screw the ring onto the jar and gently tighten it. (Don't screw it on so tight that it is difficult to unscrew again.) For cleanliness, it is important that you complete this process one jar at a time.

6. Remove any pots from the stove and place the pressure canner on a burner. Fill the canner with the required amount of cool water, according to the manufacturer's instructions. (Some canners have a notch inside the canner to indicate the water level for canning.) Add 2 tablespoons distilled white vinegar to the water. (This will prevent mineral deposits from forming on your glass jars.)

7. Place jars inside the canner on top of the flat canning rack. If your canner allows you to double-stack pints, place a second flat canning rack on top of the jars inside the canner and proceed to stack additional pints on the second flat canning rack. Secure the lid on the pressure canner and lock it into place.

8. Because the jars, food and water are cool in temperature, start with the burner on medium and allow the contents to heat gradually for 20 minutes, then increase the heat to medium-high. Within 15 minutes, the vent pipe should start spitting a bit of water and some steam. Wait until the vent pipe shoots a steady flow of steam, and then set your timer for 10 minutes.

9. **In a weighted-gauge pressure canner:** After the steam has vented for 10 minutes, place the 10-PSI weight on the vent pipe. The weight (a.k.a. jiggler) will begin to rock as the canner beings to increase in pressure. Once it is rocking consistently, set your timer for 1 hour 30 minutes for quarts or 1 hour 15 minutes for pints. If the weighted gauge begins rocking too vigorously, reduce the burner heat slightly to achieve a consistent rocking pattern.

10. **In a dial-gauge pressure canner:** After the steam has vented for 10 minutes, place the counterweight on the vent pipe. When the dial gauge reads 11 PSI, set your timer for 1 hour 30 minutes for quarts or 1 hour 15 minutes for pints. Throughout the processing time, use your burner knob to decrease or increase the heat output as necessary. If the pressure exceeds 13 PSI, reduce the heat slightly to keep the dial between 11 and 12 PSI. Do NOT let the PSI drop below the required amount. If this does happen, increase the heat until you achieve the required PSI and reset the timer for the full processing time. ➡

11. As soon as the timer goes off, turn off the burner. Do NOT touch the pressure canner. Do NOT remove the weighted gauge or counterweight. The pressure in the canner must return to 0 PSI naturally. Allow the canner to rest, undisturbed, for 30 minutes or until the locking mechanism releases. Carefully remove the weighted gauge or counterweight, and then remove the canning lid, keeping your face and hands away from the hot steam that will escape the canner. Allow the jars to cool for another 5 minutes before removing them from the canner using waterproof canning mitts or a jar grabber. Place the hot jars on the towel-covered cutting boards. (Make sure the jars are not exposed to cold drafts, especially if you are canning in winter.)

12. After the jars have cooled for 2 to 3 hours, check the lids to see if they have sealed. Press down on the center of each lid with your finger—if it stays concave and does not pop back up, the lid is sealed. If it pops back up, the lid is not sealed; place the jar in the refrigerator and eat the contents within 1 week. If multiple lids have not sealed, you can refill the jars and process again.

13. Let the jars cool at room temperature for 12 hours or overnight, then remove the rings. Using warm, soapy water, wash the outside of each jar and rinse well. Wash the rings in warm, soapy water or in the dishwasher and store for future use. Do NOT screw the rings back onto the jars. Dry the jars and use a permanent marker to label the lid of each one with the date and recipe name.

14. Store the jars in your pantry or in another dark place at a temperature between 50°F and 70°F.

DO I REALLY NEED TO VENT MY PRESSURE CANNER FOR 10 MINUTES?

It is vitally important to allow steam to escape from the canner for 10 minutes before placing the weighted gauge or counterweight on the vent pipe. Venting ensures that all air is exhausted from the canner and the jars. It eliminates any air pockets in the jars of food that would cause an uneven transfer of heat. Do not exceed 10 minutes of venting unless the recipe specifically says to do so. Do not ever let the pressure canner run dry, or it will crack the jars.

Top 10 Rules of Pressure Canning

1. Always keep your vent pipe clean and free from debris.

2. Vinegar is your friend. Use it to clean the jar rims and screw threads, and add 2 tablespoons to the canner water prior to processing to keep the jars clean and free of mineral deposits.

3. Always let your canner vent for 10 minutes before placing the weighted gauge or counter-weight on the vent pipe.

4. Always let your canner's PSI drop to 0 naturally before taking off the lid.

5. Protect your face and hands from steam when removing the canner lid after processing.

6. After processing and removing the canner lid, let your jars sit for a minimum of 5 minutes before removing them from the canner.

7. Use a reliable timer. We get busy in the kitchen. Trying to keep track of the time by simply watching the clock and relying on memory can be a costly mistake.

8. Do not set your timer until your pressure canner reaches the required PSI.

9. Do not place hot food in a cold jar or place hot jars on cold surfaces. Treat your glass jars as you would a glass coffeepot; avoid drastic temperature swings.

10. Do not let the PSI dip below the required level specified in the recipe. If this happens, you will need to achieve the required PSI and restart the timer for the full required processing time.

TIPS FOR SUCCESSFUL PRESSURE CANNING

————— ❖ —————

1. **Maintain the correct pressure.** When using a dial-gauge pressure canner, keeping the pressure exactly at the specified PSI is quite difficult. It is okay to keep your canner 2 or 3 PSI higher than the required temperature, but do not let the pressure go higher than 4 PSI above the specified pressure level for the recipe, or the liquid will siphon out of the jars.

2. **Know your altitude.** Because foods take longer to cook in higher elevations, it is imperative that you know your altitude prior to canning so you can make the proper adjustments to temperature and processing time. Use the handy Pressure Canning Altitude Chart (page 6) to ensure that you adjust your PSI correctly.

3. **Set aside dedicated time to create and can a recipe.** Sometimes, I start canning early in the morning so I still have the rest of my day to enjoy other activities. Other times, I pressure can after dinner because I intentionally created a large batch of food. For instance, I might make a double batch of chili to feed the family and put the rest into quart jars for canning.

4. **Designate an area in your home to store your canning supplies.** Staying organized is the best way to have everything at the ready, preventing you from scrambling for something when you need it the most.

5. **Stock up on weighted gauges and/or counterweights.** Purchase a second weighted gauge (a.k.a. jiggler) if you have a weighted-gauge canner, or a second counterweight, if you have a dial-gauge canner, and keep it in a safe place with your canning supplies. It is a lifesaver in the event that you lose the weight that came with your pressure canner. Without this simple, inexpensive tool, your pressure canner will not work.

Pressure Canning Problem Solver

As with any cooking project, sometimes things just don't work out quite right. Here are some of the most common problems, what causes them, and how to fix them next time.

PRESSURE CANNING PROBLEM SOLVER		
PROBLEM	**REASON/CAUSE**	**SOLUTION/PREVENTION**
Liquid loss in jar *This is not a sign of spoilage; do not open the lid to replace the liquid. If more than half the liquid is lost, refrigerate the jar and eat within a week.*	The pressure may have increased or decreased too rapidly during processing. The weighted gauge, or jiggler, may have rocked too vigorously during processing. Jars may have been overfilled.	Monitor the heat output of your stove's burner to keep the PSI consistent throughout processing. Do not leave your kitchen for long periods of time. Maximizing jar space is important; however keeping the required headspace is essential. Use a headspace measuring tool—do not eyeball it.
Food is darker at top of jar	Air was left within the jar, which caused oxidation and dried out the food.	While the food is safe to eat, it is unattractive. You may choose to remove the oxidized food prior to heating and eating. Prevent this from happening by using recommended headspace and preventing liquid loss during processing.
Food floating in canner water	Siphoning may have occurred due to a rapid increase or decrease in pressure. The bottom of a glass jar may have broken during processing. Small fractures can form on the glass jar if exposed to vast temperature swings, like the glass coffeepot scenario on page 19.	Monitor the heat output of your stove's burner to keep the PSI consistent throughout processing. Do not leave your kitchen for long periods of time. Inspect jars for cracks, chips, and fractures before using. Avoid exposing hot jars to cold temperatures when filling, processing or cleaning.
Lid seal failure *Discard food unless the unsealed lid was discovered within a few hours after removing from canner. Refrigerate jars that have not sealed 3 hours after removing from canner. Reprocess unsealed foods within 12 to 24 hours.*	Jars may have been overfilled. The rim of the jar was not cleaned with a washcloth dipped in vinegar. A rapid decrease in pressure may have occured during or after processing, causing liquid to siphon from the jar and bits of residue to block the lid from sealing. The rings may have been overtightened. The rings must be secure but loose enough to let air escape and create a vacuum seal.	Measure required headspace when filling jars. To avoid skipping a jar when wiping rims, keep track by immediately placing the sterilized lid and ring on the recently cleaned jar rim. Monitor the heat output of your stove's burner to keep the PSI consistent throughout processing. Do not leave your kitchen for long periods of time. When hand tightening rings onto the jar, after the ring is secured, lightly reverse pressure by slightly unscrewing the ring.
Glass jar breaks during processing	Canner became dry during processing. Jars packed with cold foods were immersed in boiling hot water. Jar had chips, cracks or stress fractures. Jars were placed directly on the bottom of the canner. Ring was overtightened, preventing hot air from escaping the jar.	Follow manufacturer guidelines when filling canner with required level of water. Do not deviate. Use cool water in your canner, place cold jars in canner and slowly heat using medium heat for 20 minutes before increasing temperature to begin processing. Inspect jars for cracks, chips and fractures before using. Avoid exposing hot jars to cold temperatures when filling, processing, or cleaning. Use your flat canning rack to elevate glass jars off heat source. When hand tightening rings onto the jar, after the ring is secured, lightly reverse pressure by slightly unscrewing the ring.

PRESSURE CANNING PROBLEM SOLVER *(continued)*

PROBLEM	REASON/CAUSE	SOLUTION/PREVENTION
Steam escaping from the lid of the canner	The pressure canner is not building pressure or temperature due to an air leak.	Shut off the canner, allow to cool, and inspect. If your canner lid has a gasket: Remove the rubber gasket and inspect for cracks. If no cracks are present, clean with warm soapy water, rinse, and dry. Coat with a small amount of vegetable oil. Replace the gasket, ensuring that it is properly housed in the lid. If your canner lid does not have a gasket: Unscrew the knobs and remove the lid. Lightly coat the metal rim of the vessel with cooking oil and replace the lid. Working on both sides of the lid, evenly screw the knobs, being sure to keep the lid level. Unevenly sealing the lid will cause air to escape the canner. Check to ensure that the handles, gauges, and vent pipe are all secured and nuts and bolts are properly tightened. Continued use will cause some bolts to loosen. Consult the manufacturer's user manual.
Exterior of jars have a chalky, white residue on them	Mineral deposits from hard water have attached themselves to the jar.	Use soft water. Add two tablespoons of vinegar to the canner water prior to adding jars before processing.
The lid sealed initally, then unsealed during storage *Discard the entire jar; this food is unsafe to eat!*	The food may have spoiled from under-processing.	Follow the recipe and process at the correct PSI for the full time required. If the recipe you are using does not specify the PSI and length of time to process, get a new recipe.
	There may have been a hairline crack in the jar that went undetected.	Nothing. Sometimes this happens, but thankfully it is rare.
	The humidity and temperature fluctuated too vastly in the storage area.	Store your jars with the rings off. If a lid is going to come unsealed during storage, you want to know about it. Do not let a ring produce a false-looking lid seal. Be sure to store home-canned goods in 50°F–70°F and without excessive humidity.
	Mice may be inhabiting your food storage area.	Set mousetraps or call an exterminator.

Storing Your Home-Canned Goods

After lids seal and jar contents have cooled (approximately 12 to 24 hours after canning), remove the rings and wash the jars with warm, soapy water. During processing, food particles may seep into the canning water, so the exterior of the jars may be covered with minute food particles. Washing the jars reduces the risk of mold growing on the exterior of the jars and pests sniffing them out in your pantry. Once the jars are washed and dried, it's time to store them. Here are some best practices for storing your pressure-canned goodies:

No rings! It is easier to detect a lid failure during storage when the rings are not attached to the jar. Further, if the rings are screwed on, it's easy for rust to build up between the lid and the ring, making it difficult to unscrew and leaving behind an unsightly rusty mess that may come in contact with your food.

First in, first out. Labeling the jar lid with the month and year it was canned and the name of the food preserved will help you rotate your food supplies. It is imperative to rotate foods being stored so the oldest foods are eaten first and none of your hard work goes to waste if food goes bad before it gets eaten.

Location, location, location. Store jars upright, out of direct and indirect sunlight, and in a temperature range of 50°F to 70°F. Choose a location free from humidity and without vast temperature fluctuations. If you store jars in your basement, be sure to elevate jars off dirt or cement floors to avoid excessive moisture. Also, do not stack the jars on top of each other during storage.

There are many locations throughout your home suitable for storing your canned goods. A pantry, root cellar, or kitchen closet space are all excellent. Limited on space? Store your home-canned goods in a linen or coat closet, under beds, or in a kitchen cupboard that is not often accessed, and that is not directly above a large appliance. Appliances like stoves and refrigerators emit heat, and heat rises, causing the temperature within those cupboards to be warmer than other cupboards. Over time, warmer temperatures cause the food to deteriorate quicker, putting the food at risk of being unsafe to consume.

WHAT IS THE SHELF LIFE OF HOME-CANNED FOODS?

It is recommended that we eat our home-canned goods within the first year, but no one dives deeper into why this is recommended. Here's the reason: Canned foods begin to lose nutrients after the first year of storage. Now, that doesn't mean the food goes bad or needs to be thrown out once a year has passed. As you enter year two and three, the nutritional value decreases further; however, I look at it like this: First, I know what I put into each jar. Second, if we can eat Ho Hos, Ding Dongs, and Doritos, which have limited, if any, real nutritional value, I will gladly eat the home-canned foods that have been stored into year three, even if the original nutritional value has decreased by more than half.

If you properly store your home-canned foods in a dry place at a temperature between 50°F and 70°F and out of direct and indirect sunlight, you will extend their shelf life. So long as the lid stays sealed and proper conditions are kept during storage, you may enjoy eating your home-canned goods upwards of three years. Keep in mind, some foods may lose texture and darken slightly, but these deteriorations do not affect their safety.

Saving the Seasons

Use this list of seasonally available produce to help you plan your canning calendar. Depending on your growing temperature zone, the list may vary some. Be sure to check the USDA Plant Hardiness Zone Map for region-specific information, especially if you are planning to grow your own produce for canning.

SPRING

- Asparagus
- Brussels sprouts
- Cabbage
- Collards
- English peas
- Kale
- Kohlrabi
- Leeks
- Mustard greens
- Radish
- Rhubarb
- Spinach
- Turnip

SUMMER

- Beans
- Cherries
- Corn
- Cucumber
- Eggplant
- Gourds
- Melons
- Okra
- Peaches
- Pears
- Peas
- Peppers
- Plums
- Pumpkins
- Southern peas
- Summer squash
- Sweet potatoes
- Tomatoes

FALL AND WINTER

- Apples
- Beets
- Brussels sprouts
- Carrots
- Celery
- Endive
- Potatoes
- Radicchio
- Rutabagas
- Spinach
- Squashes
- Swiss chard

2

THE RECIPES

CHAPTER FOUR

TOMATOES AND VEGETABLES

THIS CHAPTER TAKES YOU beyond water bathing so you can preserve all sorts of vegetables to enjoy as side dishes, quick meals, and much more. Everything canned in your kitchen is free from preservatives, so you can reap the nutritional benefits of fresh veggies well past their growing seasons. Feeling the weight of the winter doldrums? Open a jar of Basil Diced Tomatoes (page 47) or Tomato Chutney (page 49), and you'll be transported to your sun-drenched summer garden. Need a healthy side dish to round out a meal? Mixed Vegetables (page 58) to the rescue! Just heat, add seasoning, and serve. The possibilities are endless when you plan ahead and always have canned fresh veggies at the ready.

Tomato Canning 101

While some vegetables lose vital nutrients when exposed to high heat, tomatoes actually experience an increase in lycopene, a nutrient that devours 10 times more oxygenated free radicals in our bodies than vitamin E. Of course, heating does deplete some of the vitamin C found in tomatoes, but because we are using a pressure canner, we can process tomatoes for a shorter length of time to lessen the vitamin loss. So grab your clean jars and let's get to pressure canning these health-packed fruits in a variety of tasty ways.

WHICH TOMATO SHOULD I CHOOSE?

There is no wrong tomato—they are all delicious in a jar! What it comes down to, however, is prep time and what you prefer to grow if you have a garden.

For my canning projects, I gravitate to Roma tomatoes, also called plum or oblong tomatoes, because of their thin skin and more solid, less liquidy, center. Using a Roma saves me from having to blanch the tomato and peel the skin and keeps my recipes from having an overabundance of liquid. I also use canning tomatoes, also known as globe, round, or beefsteak tomatoes. One year in particular, I had no choice but to use canning tomatoes because there just wasn't a good harvest for Romas due to the weather. At the end of the day, choose whatever tomato you enjoy eating, growing, or using in everyday cooking.

PREPARING TOMATOES FOR CANNING

When selecting tomatoes to preserve, make sure they are firm and not overly ripe. Do not preserve bruised, overly soft tomatoes or those that show signs of mold or yeast growth. Once you've gathered your bounty, here are some basic tips for tomato canning:

Blanching

For those tomatoes with thicker skin like globe tomatoes, blanching is a great technique used to quickly remove the skin without having to peel them by hand. This technique can also be used on other soft fruits like plums and peaches.

Fill a stockpot half full with water, and bring it to a rapid boil over high heat. Use a sharp paring knife to cut out the core of each tomato, then score a 2-inch "X" on its bottom. Place the tomatoes in a metal colander or steamer basket that fits inside the stockpot. Fill a large bowl or stockpot with ice water and place it in the sink. Using heat resistant gloves, lower the colander into the boiling water, completely submerging the tomatoes. Let the water come back to a boil, then set a timer for 1 minute. When the timer goes off, immediately remove the tomatoes from the boiling water and plunge them into the bowl of ice water. Let the tomatoes chill for 1 minute, then take them out one at a time and peel off the skins.

Removing Excess Liquid

To avoid adding an excessive amount of liquid to your recipe, which likely will dilute the flavor, after you blanch and peel the tomatoes, quarter larger ones and let them rest flesh-side down in a colander in the sink. Drain your tomatoes for 30 minutes prior to chopping and adding to a recipe to remove the excess liquid. Feel free to capture and freeze this liquid if you intend to make stock, soup, or sauce in the near future.

Adding Acid

Tomatoes are higher in acid when green; as enzymes ripen tomatoes into their luscious red color, their overall acidic value decreases. With the plethora of hybrids on the market and the natural pH fluctuation as a tomato ripens, it is always safest when canning tomatoes to increase their acid by adding bottled—not fresh—lemon juice (bottled lemon juice has a much more

TOMATO ACIDIFICATION	
JAR SIZE	AMOUNT OF BOTTLED LEMON JUICE
Half-pint (8 ounces)	1½ teaspoons
Pint (16 ounces)	1 tablespoon
Quart (32 ounces)	2 tablespoons

standardized pH level). Above is a handy reference chart to help you determine how much lemon juice to add to your tomatoes before canning.

Seasoning with Spice Blends

Pressure canning tomatoes with seasonings infuses them with flavor, making for delicious, ready-made meals. When packing tomatoes into jars, add 2½ teaspoons of your favorite spice blend to every pint and 1½ tablespoons to every quart jar.

These blends can be doubled or tripled, depending on the amount you choose to set aside or use. Store spice blends in half-pint jars out of direct sunlight. Be sure to label the lid with the month, year, and spice blend name. These blends will stay vibrant for a year or longer if stored properly.

Chili Seasoning Spice Blend

MAKES APPROXIMATELY ½ CUP

2 tablespoons chili powder

2 teaspoons garlic powder

2 teaspoons onion powder

2 teaspoons red pepper flakes

2 teaspoons dried oregano

2 teaspoons paprika

2 teaspoons ground cumin

2 teaspoons coriander

1½ teaspoons coarse sea salt

1 teaspoon ground black pepper

Taco Seasoning Spice Blend

MAKES APPROXIMATELY ⅓ CUP

2 tablespoons chili powder

2 teaspoons garlic powder

2 teaspoons onion powder

2 teaspoons dried oregano

2 teaspoons paprika

1 teaspoon ground cumin

1 teaspoon coarse sea salt

1 teaspoon ground black pepper

Italian Spice Blend

MAKES APPROXIMATELY ⅓ CUP

4 teaspoons dried basil

2 teaspoons dried thyme

1 tablespoon dried oregano

2 teaspoons dried rosemary

1 teaspoon dried sage

1½ teaspoons garlic powder

½ teaspoon red pepper flakes (optional)

Asian Spice Blend

MAKES APPROXIMATELY ⅓ CUP

2 tablespoons yellow curry powder

2 teaspoons garlic powder

2 teaspoons onion powder

2 teaspoons ground ginger

1½ teaspoons coarse sea salt

1 teaspoon ground black pepper

Tomato and Vegetable Processing Charts

Use these handy charts to help you pressure can tomatoes and vegetables in water. Salt is completely optional and only for flavor. The charts indicate whether the tomato or vegetable must be raw packed or hot packed. Here are the steps to accomplish both based on your preference or the chart's indication:

Raw pack. Bring 6 cups water to a boil. Fill clean, hot jars with prepared raw tomatoes or vegetables, leaving 1 inch of headspace. Cover the tomatoes or vegetables with boiling water, leaving

TOMATO PROCESSING CHART				
TOMATO TYPE	**APPROX. QUANTITY**	**APPROX. YIELD**	**STYLE OF PACK**	**JAR SIZE**
Whole and Halved	13 pounds	9 pints	Raw and Hot	Pints
	21 pounds	7 quarts	Raw and Hot	Quarts
Diced	13 pounds	8 pints	Raw and Hot	Pints
	21 pounds	6 quarts	Raw and Hot	Quarts
Whole and Halved (no added water)	13 pounds	9 pints	Raw - No Added Water	Pints
	21 pounds	7 quarts	Raw - No Added Water	Quarts
Crushed (no added water)	13 pounds	9 pints	Raw - No Added Water	Pints
	21 pounds	7 quarts	Raw - No Added Water	Quarts
Tomato Juice	23 pounds	14 pints	Hot	Pints
	23 pounds	7 quarts	Hot	Quarts

1 inch of headspace. Remove air bubbles and add more boiling water as necessary, keeping 1 inch of headspace.

Hot pack. Place prepped tomatoes or vegetables in a large saucepan and add enough water to completely cover them. Bring to a boil over medium-high heat. Boil gently for 5 minutes. Using a slotted spoon, fill clean, hot jars with the cooked tomatoes or vegetables, leaving 1 inch of headspace. Add cooking liquid to the jars to cover the vegetables, keeping 1 inch of headspace. Remove air bubbles and add more liquid as necessary to maintain 1 inch of headspace.

JAR HEADSPACE	BOTTLED LEMON JUICE	CANNING SALT (OPTIONAL)	PROCESS TIME	PSI DIAL GAUGE*	PSI WEIGHTED GAUGE*
1 inch	1 tbsp	½ tsp	10 min	11 PSI	5 PSI
1 inch	2 tbsp	1 tsp	10 min	11 PSI	10 PSI
1 inch	1 tbsp	½ tsp	10 min	11 PSI	5 PSI
1 inch	2 tbsp	1 tsp	10 min	11 PSI	10 PSI
1 inch	1 tbsp	½ tsp	25 min	11 PSI	10 PSI
1 inch	2 tbsp	1 tsp	25 min	11 PSI	10 PSI
1 inch	1 tbsp	½ tsp	15 min	11 PSI	10 PSI
1 inch	2 tbsp	1 tsp	15 min	11 PSI	10 PSI
1 inch	1 tbsp	½ tsp	15 min	11 PSI	10 PSI
1 inch	2 tbsp	1 tsp	15 min	11 PSI	10 PSI

* For elevations above 1,000 feet, check the Pressure Canning Altitude Chart on page 6 to safely increase PSI.

VEGETABLE PROCESSING CHART

VEGETABLE TYPE	APPROX. QUANTITY	APPROX. YIELD	STYLE OF PACK	JAR SIZE
Asparagus (whole or pieces)	16 pounds	9 pints	Raw or Hot	Pints
	25 pounds	7 quarts	Raw or Hot	Quarts
Green Beans	9 pounds	9 pints	Raw or Hot	Pints
	14 pounds	7 quarts	Raw or Hot	Quarts
Carrots	11 pounds	9 pints	Raw or Hot	Pints
	18 pounds	7 quarts	Raw or Hot	Quarts
Whole Kernel Corn	20 pounds (in husk)	9 pints	Raw or Hot	Pints
	32 pounds (in husk)	7 quarts	Raw or Hot	Quarts
Mushrooms (whole or sliced)	8 pounds	9 half-pints	Hot	Half-pints
	15 pounds	9 pints	Hot	Pints
Okra (whole or 1-inch pieces) soak for 30 min in vinegar, rinse and pat dry	7 pounds	9 pints	Hot	Pints
	11 pounds	7 quarts	Hot	Quarts
Peas (shelled) boil 2 min before hot packing	20 pounds (in pods)	9 pints	Raw or Hot	Pints
	32 pounds (in pods)	7 quarts	Raw or Hot	Quarts
Potatoes (white flesh) 1–2 inches in dia. whole, large potatoes quartered or ½-inch cubes	13 pounds	9 pints	Hot	Pints
	20 pounds	7 quarts	Hot	Quarts
Peppers (stem and seeds removed) roast/broil at 400°F then peel or raw pack with skin on	4½ pounds	9 half-pints	Raw	Half-pints
	9 pounds	9 pints	Raw	Pints
Sweet Potatoes (1-inch pieces) boil 10 minutes before hot packing	11 pounds	9 pints	Hot	Pints
	18 pounds	7 quarts	Hot	Quarts
Spinach or Greens remove thick stem, blanch 1 lb. at a time for 5 min	18 pounds	9 pints	Hot	Pints
	28 pounds	7 quarts	Hot	Quarts

JAR HEADSPACE	CANNING SALT (OPTIONAL)	PROCESS TIME	PSI DIAL GAUGE*	PSI WEIGHTED GAUGE*
1 inch	½ tsp	30 min	11 PSI	10 PSI
1 inch	1 tsp	40 min	11 PSI	10 PSI
1 inch	½ tsp	20 min	11 PSI	10 PSI
1 inch	1 tsp	25 min	11 PSI	10 PSI
1 inch	½ tsp	25 min	11 PSI	10 PSI
1 inch	1 tsp	30 min	11 PSI	10 PSI
1 inch	½ tsp	55 min	11 PSI	10 PSI
1 inch	1 tsp	1 hr 25 min	11 PSI	10 PSI
1 inch	⅛ tsp	45 min	11 PSI	10 PSI
1 inch	⅛ tsp	45 min	11 PSI	10 PSI
1 inch	½ tsp	25 min	11 PSI	10 PSI
1 inch	1 tsp	40 min	11 PSI	10 PSI
1 inch	½ tsp	40 min	11 PSI	10 PSI
1 inch	1 tsp	40 min	11 PSI	10 PSI
1 inch	½ tsp	35 min	11 PSI	10 PSI
1 inch	1 tsp	40 min	11 PSI	10 PSI
1 inch	none	35 min	11 PSI	10 PSI
1 inch	none	35 min	11 PSI	10 PSI
1 inch	½ tsp	1 hr 5 min	11 PSI	10 PSI
1 inch	1 tsp	1 hr 30 min	11 PSI	10 PSI
1 inch	½ tsp	1 hr 10 min	11 PSI	10 PSI
1 inch	1 tsp	1 hr 30 min	11 PSI	10 PSI

* For elevations above 1,000 feet, check the Pressure Canning Altitude Chart on page 6 to safely increase PSI.

WHOLE OR HALVED TOMATOES

MAKES 7 QUARTS OR 14 PINTS

PREP: 20 MIN • COOK: 5 MIN • CANNER: 1 HR • PROCESSING: 25 MIN • TOTAL: 1 HR 40 MIN

Having a stock of these tomatoes on hand is great any time of year when you need to whip up a homemade spaghetti sauce or want something bright to throw into a soup or stew. For this recipe, the tomatoes are raw packed into each jar without adding water to cover the tomatoes. The tomatoes will make their own juice. I recommend using wide-mouthed jars to make raw packing easier. Be sure your clean jars are room temperature.

14 tablespoons bottled lemon juice

23 pounds canning tomatoes (45 medium), blanched, peeled, and halved or left whole

1. Add 2 tablespoons lemon juice to every clean quart jar and 1 tablespoon to every clean pint jar.

2. Raw pack whole or halved tomatoes, packed tight, leaving 1 inch of headspace. Water is not required here, as the tomatoes will make their own liquid. Use your headspace measuring tool to be sure the tomatoes are below the 1-inch mark. Remove any excess air bubbles and adjust the tomatoes as needed being sure to maintain the 1 inch of headspace.

3. Wipe the rim of each jar with a warm wet washcloth dipped in distilled white vinegar. Place a lid and ring on each jar and hand tighten.

4. Place jars in the pressure canner, lock the pressure canner lid, and bring to a boil on high heat. Let the canner vent for 10 minutes. Close the vent and continue heating to achieve 11 PSI for a dial gauge and 10 PSI for a weighted gauge. Process the quarts and pints for 25 minutes.

TOMATO JUICE

MAKES 7 QUARTS OR 14 PINTS

PREP: 20 MIN • COOK: 5 MIN • CANNER: 1 HR • PROCESSING: 15 MIN • TOTAL: 1 HR 40 MIN

Did someone say Bloody Marys? Besides the classic brunch cocktail, Tomato Juice has a lot of delicious culinary uses. Use it to poach chicken breasts or fish fillets, or to boil rice or pasta; drink it for a burst of nutrients during the dark winter months; or mix it into broths and soups for some extra oomph.

23 pounds canning tomatoes (45 medium), quartered
14 tablespoons bottled lemon juice

1. Place the tomatoes in a large stainless steel stockpot and mash with a potato masher to break down the quarters, about 1 minute. Bring to a slow boil over medium heat to avoid scorching, mixing frequently. Once the mixture is at a boil, reduce the heat and simmer for 5 minutes.

2. Working in batches, press the mixture through a straining sieve, chinois, or food mill to remove seeds, skin, and pulp. Capture all liquid in a clean stockpot.

3. Add 2 tablespoons lemon juice to every quart and 1 tablespoon to every pint jar.

4. Ladle Tomato Juice into jars, leaving 1 inch of headspace.

5. Wipe the rim of each jar with a warm wet washcloth dipped in distilled white vinegar. Place a lid and ring on each jar and hand tighten.

6. Place jars in the pressure canner, lock the pressure canner lid, and bring to a boil on high heat. Let the canner vent for 10 minutes. Close the vent and continue heating to achieve 11 PSI for a dial gauge and 10 PSI for a weighted gauge. Process quart jars and pints for 15 minutes.

STEWED TOMATOES

MAKES APPROXIMATELY 4 QUARTS OR 8 PINTS

PREP: 30 MIN • COOK: 5 MIN • CANNER: 1 HR • PROCESSING: 20 MIN/15 MIN • TOTAL: 1 HR 55 MIN/1 HR 50 MIN

Stewed tomatoes are a common kitchen staple used as a meal starter for many dishes like chili, spaghetti, goulash, and more. When I am pressed for time, I brown 1 pound of Italian sausage or ground beef, season it with 2 teaspoons of my Italian Spice Blend (page 136), and toss in a quart of Stewed Tomatoes. Once it is heated through, I serve it over cooked pasta.

14 to 16 medium to large tomatoes, peeled and chopped (16 cups)

1 cup chopped celery

1 cup chopped yellow onion

½ cup seeded and chopped green bell pepper

1 tablespoon dried parsley flakes

1 tablespoon granulated sugar

1 teaspoon coarse sea salt (optional)

8 tablespoons bottled lemon juice

1. In a large stainless steel stockpot, combine the tomatoes, celery, onion, green bell pepper, parsley flakes, sugar, and salt. Bring to a boil over medium-high heat, stirring often to avoid scorching the tomatoes. Once the mixture is at a boil, reduce the heat to simmer and cover.

2. Simmer for about 10 minutes or until the onions and peppers begin to soften. Stir every few minutes.

3. Add the lemon juice to hot jars: 2 tablespoons in every quart and 1 tablespoon in every pint. Using a slotted spoon, fill jars with stewed tomatoes until 2 inches from jar rim. After each jar is filled with tomatoes, ladle juice over the tomatoes, leaving 1 inch of headspace. Remove any air bubbles and adjust headspace as necessary to maintain 1 inch of headspace.

4. Wipe the rim of each jar with a warm wet washcloth dipped in distilled white vinegar. Place a lid and ring on each jar and hand tighten.

5. Place jars in the pressure canner, lock the pressure canner lid, and bring to a boil on high heat. Let the canner vent for 10 minutes. Close the vent and heat to achieve 10 PSI for both weighted and dial gauge. Process quart jars for 20 minutes and pint jars for 15 minutes.

Try Instead: Add okra for a fun twist on traditional Stewed Tomatoes. This will increase your yield by 1 quart or 2 pints. It takes 35 pods to total approximately 2 cups chopped okra. Soak pods in distilled white vinegar for 30 minutes, rinse, and pat dry. This prevents okra from getting slimy. Remove their stems and cut into 1-inch pieces. Add the okra to the recipe with the tomatoes. Process quart jars for 35 minutes and pint jars for 30 minutes at 10 PSI in a weighted gauge, 11 PSI in a dial gauge.

BASIL DICED TOMATOES

MAKES APPROXIMATELY 4 QUARTS OR 8 PINTS

PREP: 15 MIN • COOK: 5 MIN • CANNER: 1 HR • PROCESSING: 20 MIN/15 MIN • TOTAL: 1 HR 40 MIN/1 HR 35 MIN

This recipe is different from my Stewed Tomatoes (page 46) as its flavor is a bit lighter and not as heavy on the peppers. It works very well when recipes require standard diced tomatoes. A jar of Basil Diced Tomatoes is the perfect addition to soups and stews, or just open a jar and add them to chicken thighs for an easy braised or baked meal. For utmost simplicity, heat up a jar and toss with angel-hair pasta.

32 Roma tomatoes, diced (16 cups)

1 large yellow bell pepper, chopped (1 cup)

1 large sweet onion, chopped (1½ cups)

¼ cup chopped fresh basil

2 tablespoons minced garlic

2 tablespoons coarse sea salt (optional)

1 tablespoon sugar

1 teaspoon ground black pepper

8 tablespoons bottled lemon juice

1. In a large stainless steel stockpot, combine the tomatoes, bell pepper, onion, basil, garlic, salt (if using), sugar, and black pepper. Bring to a boil on medium-high heat, stirring often. Allow to gently boil for 5 minutes, stirring to avoid scorching.

2. Add the lemon juice to hot jars: 2 tablespoons for quarts and 1 tablespoon for pints. Using a slotted spoon, fill the jars with the tomato mixture, leaving a generous 1 inch of head-space. Ladle the remaining liquid over the tomato mixture, being sure to maintain the headspace. Remove any air bubbles and adjust the headspace as necessary.

3. Wipe the rim of each jar with a warm wet washcloth dipped in distilled white vinegar. Place a lid and ring on each jar and hand tighten.

4. Place jars in the pressure canner, lock the pressure canner lid, and bring to a boil on high heat. Let the canner vent for 10 minutes. Close the vent and continue heating to achieve 11 PSI for a dial gauge and 10 PSI for a weighted gauge. Process quart jars for 20 minutes and pint jars for 15 minutes.

Prep Tip: Leave smaller basil leaves whole—they look gorgeous peeking through the jar. Coarsely chop larger basil leaves quickly by piling them on top of each other and slicing them two to three times; that way, every jar will have basil flavor and color.

BLOODY MARY MIX

MAKES APPROXIMATELY 5 QUARTS OR 10 PINTS
PREP: 25 MIN • COOK: 40 MIN • CANNER: 1 HR • PROCESSING: 25 MIN • TOTAL: 2 HR 30 MIN

Most of us enjoy pickling a variety of vegetables to snack on or plunk into a hearty Bloody Mary, but what about replacing store-bought Bloody Mary Mix with your own home creation? This hearty mix covers all the flavor bases by using fresh vegetables, a variety of spices, and a touch of heat. If a jalapeño doesn't provide enough heat for your liking, feel free to add a hot pepper of your choosing. You can also use this delicious mix as a base for pork and beef stews.

40 medium canning tomatoes, cored and quartered

1½ cups chopped bell peppers

1½ cups peeled and diced carrots

1 cup diced celery

1 cup diced yellow onion

1 medium jalapeño pepper, diced

6 garlic cloves, minced

¼ cup fresh parsley leaves, coarsely chopped

2 bay leaves

½ cup bottled lemon juice

¼ cup brown sugar

2 tablespoons horseradish (optional)

1½ tablespoons coarse sea salt (optional)

1 tablespoon Worcestershire sauce

2 teaspoons ground black pepper

1 teaspoon Tabasco sauce

1. In a large stainless steel stockpot, add the tomatoes, bell peppers, carrots, celery, onion, jalapeño, garlic, parsley, and bay leaves. Bring to a slow boil over medium heat to avoid scorching. Stir regularly until juices escape the vegetables. Once the mixture is at a boil, reduce the heat and simmer for 30 to 40 minutes or until carrots break apart easily with a fork. Remove and discard the bay leaves.

2. Purée the mixture in a blender or food processor working in batches, or use an immersion/stick blender to purée directly in the stockpot. After all the Bloody Mary Mix is puréed, press the mixture in batches through a straining sieve, chinois, or food mill to remove seeds and pulp. Capture all the liquid in a clean stockpot.

3. Add the lemon juice, brown sugar, horseradish (if using), salt (if using), Worcestershire sauce, black pepper, and Tabasco sauce to the Bloody Mary Mix. Bring the mix to a boil over medium-high heat, stirring regularly. Let boil 5 minutes then remove from the heat.

4. Ladle the Bloody Mary Mix into jars, leaving 1 inch of headspace.

5. Wipe the rim of each jar with a warm wet washcloth dipped in distilled white vinegar. Place a lid and ring on each jar and hand tighten.

6. Place jars in the pressure canner, lock the pressure canner lid, and bring to a boil on high heat. Let the canner vent for 10 minutes. Close the vent and continue heating to achieve 11 PSI for a dial gauge and 10 PSI for a weighted gauge. Process quarts and pints for 25 minutes.

TOMATO CHUTNEY

MAKES APPROXIMATELY 8 PINTS OR 16 HALF-PINTS
PREP: 30 MIN • COOK: 1 HR • CANNER: 50 MIN • PROCESSING: 10 MIN • TOTAL: 2 HR 30 MIN

Say good-bye to traditional ketchup and hello to Tomato Chutney—you will never look at condiments the same after making this amazing chutney! Full of flavor with a slight kick of ginger and red pepper, this chutney can be used anywhere ketchup is typically enjoyed. Need a good meal idea? Slather a half-pint on your homemade meatloaf and bake as usual.

5 pounds or 10 large tomatoes, peeled and chopped (10 cups)

3 cups lightly packed brown sugar

2½ cups red wine vinegar

2 cups apple cider vinegar

2 cups raisins

2 large red bell peppers, seeded and chopped (1½ cups)

1 large yellow onion, chopped (1½ cups)

1 head garlic, peeled and coarsely chopped

3 tablespoons mustard seeds

2 tablespoons chopped fresh ginger

2 teaspoons coarse sea salt

2 teaspoons ground black pepper

2 teaspoons red pepper flakes

Zest and juice of 1 lime

1. Place the tomatoes, brown sugar, red wine and cider vinegars, raisins, bell peppers, onion, garlic, mustard seeds, ginger, salt, black pepper, red pepper flakes, lime juice and zest into a large stockpot and bring to a slow boil over medium-high heat. Once at a full boil, reduce the heat and simmer for 1 hour with the lid off, stirring frequently as the chutney begins to thicken.

2. Ladle the hot chutney into jars leaving ½ inch of headspace. Remove any air bubbles and add more chutney if necessary to maintain the headspace.

3. Wipe the rim of each jar with a warm wet washcloth dipped in distilled white vinegar. Place a lid and ring on each jar and hand tighten.

4. Place jars in the pressure canner, lock the pressure canner lid, and bring to a boil on high heat. Let the canner vent for 10 minutes. Close the vent and continue heating to achieve 6 PSI for a dial gauge and 5 PSI for a weighted gauge. Process pints and half-pints for 10 minutes.

Ingredient Tip: Prefer more heat to your chutney? Increase the red pepper flakes to 2 tablespoons. Want a warm, fall flavor? Skip the red pepper flakes and add 2 teaspoons ground cinnamon and 1 teaspoon ground cloves.

ROASTED TOMATILLO CHUTNEY

MAKES APPROXIMATELY 4 PINTS OR 8 HALF-PINTS

PREP: 20 MIN • COOK: 40 MIN • CANNER: 1 HR • PROCESSING: 10 MIN • TOTAL: 2 HR 10 MIN

A staple in Mexican cuisine, the tomatillo has a tart flavor and is used to make salsa verde. This versatile fruit from the nightshade plant family also has a sweet side when roasted. Use this delicious chutney alongside pork or chicken dishes, use 3 tablespoons when making couscous or rice, or serve on a cheese plate with cracked pepper water crackers.

32 tomatillos

8 to 10 garlic cloves, peeled and left whole

2 tablespoons olive oil

2 cups raisins

1 medium onion, finely chopped

½ cup lightly packed brown sugar

⅓ cup apple cider vinegar

2 tablespoons grated fresh ginger

1 tablespoon mustard seeds

1 teaspoon ground allspice

¼ teaspoon ground cloves

½ teaspoon red pepper flakes

1. Preheat the oven to 400°F.

2. Line a cookie sheet, or two, with foil. Remove the outer husks of the tomatillos and rinse well in a colander in the sink. Cut the tomatillos in half and place flesh-side down on the foil. Once all the tomatillos are lined up tight on the cookie sheet, space the peeled garlic cloves evenly throughout the tomatillos. Drizzle the tomatillos with the olive oil.

3. Roast in the oven for 25 minutes or until the tomatillo tops start to brown.

4. While the tomatillos are roasting, combine the raisins, onion, brown sugar, vinegar, ginger, mustard seeds, allspice, cloves, and red pepper flakes in a stainless steel stockpot. Bring to a boil over medium heat, stirring to blend seasonings. Reduce the heat and simmer for 5 minutes, or until the onion is translucent.

5. Remove the roasted tomatillos and garlic from the oven, being careful not to spill the juices. Allow to cool for 5 minutes so they are safer to handle.

6. Place the roasted tomatillos and garlic and their juices in a food processor and pulse on high until everything is puréed but not liquefied. Add the mixture to the stockpot and mix well. Bring to a boil over medium-high heat, and simmer for 10 minutes to reduce some of the liquid.

7. Ladle the hot chutney into warm jars, leaving ½ inch of headspace. Remove any air bubbles and adjust headspace as necessary.

8. Wipe the rim of each jar with a warm wet washcloth dipped in distilled white vinegar. Place a lid and ring on each jar and hand tighten.

9. Place jars in the pressure canner, lock the pressure canner lid, and bring to a boil on high heat. Let the canner vent for 10 minutes. Close the vent and continue heating to achieve 6 PSI for a dial gauge and 5 PSI for a weighted gauge. Process pints and half-pints for 10 minutes.

Ingredient Tip: Like most nightshade plants, tomatillos store well for up to 2 weeks if you do not refrigerate them and keep the exterior husk on the fruit. I keep them on my countertop out of direct sunlight alongside my tomatoes.

CANDIED JALAPEÑOS

MAKES APPROXIMATELY 8 PINTS OR 16 HALF-PINTS

PREP: 45 MIN • COOK: 15 MIN • CANNER: 50 MIN • PROCESSING: 10 MIN • TOTAL: 2 HR

Also hailed as Cowboy Candy, this will soon become your newest favorite home-canned vegetable! The sweet, spicy tang goes beautifully with cream cheese or straight out of the jar. The longer the jars sit, the sweeter the jalapeños become. Don't feel like slicing into rings? Chop them small into relish-size bits and use them on burgers and brats or to jazz up egg salad sandwiches or deviled eggs.

4 pounds fresh jalapeño peppers

8 cups sugar

3 cups apple cider vinegar

½ cup mustard seeds

¼ cup garlic powder

1 teaspoon turmeric

1 teaspoon celery seed

1 teaspoon cayenne pepper

1. Slice off the stem end of the jalapeños and discard. Shake out excess seeds and discard. Slice the jalapeños into uniform ⅛- or ¼-inch rounds. Set aside.

2. In a large stainless steel stockpot, combine the sugar, apple cider vinegar, mustard seeds, garlic powder, turmeric, celery seed, and cayenne pepper. Bring to a boil over medium-high heat, stirring until the sugar is dissolved. Once the mixture is at a boil, reduce the heat and simmer for 5 minutes.

3. Add the jalapeño slices, mix well, and simmer for 5 minutes.

4. Using a slotted spoon, fill hot jars with the hot peppers, leaving 1 inch of headspace.

5. Bring the cooking liquid remaining in the stockpot to a full rolling boil for 5 minutes, then immediately remove from the heat.

6. Using a canning funnel, ladle the hot liquid over the jalapeños. Remove any air bubbles and adjust the headspace as necessary to maintain 1 inch of headspace.

7. Wipe the rim of each jar with a warm wet washcloth dipped in distilled white vinegar. Place a lid and ring on each jar and hand tighten.

8. Place jars in the pressure canner, lock the pressure canner lid, and bring to a boil on high heat. Let the canner vent for 10 minutes. Close the vent and continue heating to achieve 6 PSI for a dial gauge and 5 PSI for a weighted gauge. Process pints and half-pints for 10 minutes.

Recipe Tip: There will likely be leftover liquid. Do NOT discard. Fill hot jars with the remaining liquid, leaving 1 inch of headspace. Place a lid and ring on each jar and hand tighten. Process alongside jars of Candied Jalapeños for the above specified time and PSI. The delicious liquid makes an excellent marinade for meat.

Ingredient Tip: If you grow your own jalapeños, be sure to allow some to turn orange and red on the vine to give your Candied Jalapeños a gorgeous array of green, orange, and red colors. Or can red peppers separately for festive holiday gift-giving.

CARAWAY AND GINGER CARROTS

MAKES APPROXIMATELY 6 QUARTS OR 12 PINTS

PREP: 30 MIN • COOK: 10 MIN • CANNER: 1 HR. • PROCESSING: 30 MIN/25 MIN TOTAL: 2 HR 10 MIN/2 HR 5 MIN

Fall is harvest time for your long-awaited root crops! A colorful and healthy favorite in my home is the carrot. Exposing carrots to heat increases their beta-carotene. Turn a boring side dish into something fantastic with the simple addition of caraway and ginger. These delicious carrots make a wonderful side dish to complement any dinner and can be used as the base for carrot soup.

10 pounds carrots, peeled and cut into ¼-inch rounds

2 tablespoons minced fresh ginger

2 tablespoons caraway seeds

1. Fill a large stockpot half full of water and bring to a boil over high heat, approximately 8 to 10 minutes. Once the water is at a boil, reduce the heat and simmer. Place a lid on the stockpot.

2. Wash, peel, and wash the carrots a second time. In my home, we like round, inch-thick pieces, however cut according to your preference so long as they are uniform in size. Have a stockpot of boiling water ready on the stove while chopping.

3. Add ginger and caraway seeds to each jar: 1 teaspoon ginger and 1 teaspoon caraway seeds to quart jars and ½ teaspoon minced ginger and ½ teaspoon caraway seeds to pint jars. Raw pack the carrots tightly into warm jars, leaving 1 inch of headspace. Ladle boiling water over the carrots.

4. Remove any excess air bubbles and adjust the water level as needed to keep 1 inch of headspace.

5. Wipe the rim of each jar with a warm wet washcloth dipped in distilled white vinegar. Place a lid and ring on each jar and hand tighten.

6. Place jars in the pressure canner, lock the pressure canner lid, and bring to a boil on high heat. Let the canner vent for 10 minutes. Close the vent and continue heating to achieve 11 PSI for a dial gauge and 10 PSI for a weighted gauge. Process quart jars for 30 minutes and pint jars for 25 minutes.

Ingredient Tip: While ginger provides a delicious flavor, feel free to mix it up and use turmeric root. It will give the carrots an earthy flavor that pairs well with caraway seed and also gives each jar a vibrant yellow color that comes from using turmeric.

CREAM-STYLE CORN

MAKES APPROXIMATELY 9 PINTS

PREP: 30 MIN • COOK: 10 MIN • CANNER: 1 HR • PROCESSING: 1 HR 25 MIN • TOTAL: 3 HR 5 MIN

There are so many fun uses for Cream-Style Corn: Mix a pint with an 8-ounce brick of softened cream cheese and 1 cup shredded pepper Jack cheese for a fun party dip. Use Cream-Style Corn in soups for a creamy texture without the dairy. Use in frittatas, casseroles, and cornbread. You'll wonder why you didn't add this versatile vegetable to your pantry shelf sooner.

36 ears of corn

1. Fill a large stockpot half full of water and bring to a boil over high heat.

2. Husk the corn and remove the silk. Wash the ears. Blanch the corn in boiling water for 5 minutes. Set aside to cool.

3. Drain the water used to blanch the corn; rinse the stockpot and refill halfway with fresh water. Bring to a boil over high heat.

4. After the corn has cooled to the touch, cut the end tip off each ear and discard. Using a sharp knife or corn cutter, cut kernels off the cob, being sure not to dig into the cob. Catch the kernels in a measuring cup. Measure 2 cups kernels then place into a second stockpot. Add 1 cup boiling water for every 2 cups kernels. Continue until all the corn kernels are cut from the cobs. Place this stockpot on low heat.

5. After all kernels are free from the cob, scrape the knife across the cob to extract the pulp and milk into the corn kernels. Be sure to extract all the way around the cob. Discard the cobs when each has been milked.

6. Bring the corn to a boil over medium-high heat, stirring often. Reduce the heat and boil gently for 5 minutes.

7. Ladle the hot creamed corn into hot pint jars, leaving 1 inch of headspace.

8. Wipe the rim of each jar with a warm washcloth dipped in distilled white vinegar. Place a lid and ring on each jar and hand tighten.

9. Place jars in the pressure canner, lock the pressure canner lid, and bring to a boil on high heat. Let the canner vent for 10 minutes. Close the vent and continue heating to achieve 11 PSI for a dial gauge and 10 PSI for a weighted gauge. Process pints for 1 hour 25 minutes.

Use Tip: Here is one recipe in particular where every main ingredient is home-canned: Quick Potato Corn Chowder. Dice a medium onion and sauté in 1 tablespoon olive oil until translucent. Add 1 quart Chicken Stock (page 98), 1 quart drained potatoes, and 1 pint Cream-Style Corn. Bring to a boil, then reduce the heat to a simmer for 8 to 10 minutes. Whisk ½ cup milk with ⅓ cup ClearJel® in a bowl and add to the soup. Return to a boil for 2 minutes or until the soup thickens. Add salt and pepper to taste. Serve hot.

BEETS

MAKES APPROXIMATELY 4 QUARTS OR 8 PINTS

PREP: 5 MIN • COOK: 30 MIN • CANNER: 1 HR • PROCESSING: 35 MIN/30 MIN • TOTAL: 2 HR 10 MIN/2 HR 5 MIN

There are many benefits to home canning beets. Use them as a side dish to accompany any meal, slice them for salads and sandwich toppers or use when making Borscht (page 108). For those new to pressure canning, beets in water is another great place to start.

12 pounds red beets, greens intact

1. You will need two stockpots: one to boil the beets and one to boil fresh water to hot pack the jars. Fill one stockpot half full with water. Bring to a boil on high heat. Once the water is at a boil, turn down to a simmer.

2. Leave the roots on the beets, but cut off the greens, leaving 2 or 3 inches of stems on each beet. Thoroughly wash the beets and place them inside the second stainless steel stockpot, being sure to place the largest beets at the bottom. Add enough water to cover the beets by 2 inches. Bring to a boil and cook for 30 minutes, or until the beets are tender.

3. Using a slotted spoon or tongs, remove the beets from boiling water and place them directly into a bowl of cold water resting in the sink. Keep cool tap water running over the beets to cool them quickly. One at a time, hold a beet in both hands under the cool stream and use your thumbs to gently rub and massage the beet. The skin will slip right off.

4. Using a paring knife, remove the roots and stems from the skinned beets. Cut the beets into similar-size pieces: quarter larger ones and cut smaller ones in half or leave them whole.

5. Pack each jar with beets, leaving 1 inch of headspace. Using your funnel, ladle the boiling water over the beets, being sure to maintain 1 inch of headspace. Remove any air bubbles and readjust the headspace if necessary.

6. Wipe the rim of each jar with a warm washcloth dipped in distilled white vinegar. Place a lid and ring on each jar and hand tighten.

7. Place jars in the pressure canner, lock the pressure canner lid, and bring to a boil on high heat. Let the canner vent for 10 minutes. Close the vent and continue heating to achieve 11 PSI for a dial gauge and 10 PSI for a weighted gauge. Process quart jars for 35 minutes and pint jars for 30 minutes.

Prep Tip: It is important to cut vegetables to uniform size. This allows the required temperature during processing to adequately penetrate the foods. If foods are a variety of sizes, it will take longer to process the larger pieces while the smaller ones over-process and might turn to mush.

Variation Tip: Before filling the jars, add 3 whole cloves to each jar and pack as specified. This gives your beets a luscious hint of cloves that is perfect for relish trays and salads. Just be sure to label your lids before storage.

PUMPKIN AND WINTER SQUASH

MAKES APPROXIMATELY 7 QUARTS OR 14 PINTS
PREP: 30 MIN • CANNER: 1 HR • PROCESSING: 1 HR 30 MIN/55 MIN • TOTAL: 3 HR/2 HR 25 MIN

Fall is the season for pumpkins, squash and gourds—and all things harvest fun! Although these vegetables last for months in dry storage, preserving their freshness in a jar guarantees you can enjoy them well into spring and summer. Having home-canned pumpkin on hand is a great alternative to store-bought!

When selecting from the many squash varieties (acorn, butternut, Hubbard), be sure to choose those with hard rinds, free from damage and mold spots. Pie pumpkins are the best for preserving as their pulp has less water, is less stringy, and has a better flavor compared to traditional carving pumpkins.

Note: It takes about 2½ pounds pumpkin/squash for every 1-quart jar. If canning in pints, 2½ pounds will yield approximately two pint jars.

18 pounds pie pumpkins or squash

1. You will need two stockpots. One to boil the pumpkin/squash and one to boil fresh water to hot pack the jars. Fill your second stockpot half full with water. Bring to a boil on high heat. Once the water is at a boil, turn down to a simmer.

2. Wash the exterior of your pumpkin and/or squash to remove any dirt or debris. Cut the pie pumpkins or squash in half and remove all of the seeds using a large spoon. Using a peeler, carefully remove the rind. Cut the flesh into 1-inch cubes.

3. Put the cubed pumpkin or squash in a second stainless steel stockpot and add enough of the boiling water to cover. Bring to a boil over medium-high heat and boil hard for 2 minutes. Do not over-boil or let the pumpkin or squash get soft.

4. Drain the pumpkin or squash cubes in a large colander in the sink. Using a ladle and funnel, pack the hot cubes into hot jars, being sure to leave a generous 1 inch of headspace.

5. Ladle fresh boiling water over the cubes, being sure to maintain the headspace. Remove any air bubbles and readjust the headspace if necessary.

6. Wipe the rim of each jar with a warm washcloth dipped in distilled white vinegar. Place a lid and ring on each jar and hand tighten.

7. Place jars in the pressure canner, lock the pressure canner lid, and bring to a boil on high heat. Let the canner vent for 10 minutes. Close the vent and continue heating to achieve 11 PSI for a dial gauge and 10 PSI for a weighted gauge. Process quart jars for 1 hour 30 minutes and pint jars for 55 minutes.

Prep Tip: Because the interior flesh of pumpkin and squash is so dense, especially when mashed or puréed, it is not recommended this vegetable be home-canned in such a dense state. To ensure proper heat transfer, it is best to cube pumpkin and squash. When using the home-canned pumpkin and squash, drain and then mash or purée to use in pies, breads, and more!

PEPPERED BACON GREEN BEANS

MAKES APPROXIMATELY 9 QUARTS OR 18 PINTS

PREP: 30 MIN • COOK: 5 MIN • PROCESSING: 25 MIN/20 MIN • TOTAL: 1 HR/55 MIN

This recipe makes a delicious side dish for any meal. It is also a great starter for that holiday favorite, green bean casserole. The peppered bacon gives each jar a bit of flavorful protein, transforming a boring side dish into something quite delightful. Get creative with the style and flavor of bacon, modifying this recipe to suit your flavor palate.

2 pounds thick-cut black pepper bacon

10 pounds green beans, trimmed and rinsed

1. Using kitchen scissors, cut the raw bacon into 1-inch wide chunks. In a large skillet on medium-high heat, fry the bacon until the bacon fat is translucent and the meat is cooked through, about 8 to 10 minutes. Cool the bacon in paper towel to remove excess grease. When the bacon has cooled, crumble into small pieces. Set the bacon aside in a clean bowl.

2. Discard any damaged or rusty green beans and remove stems but leave the end tips. Cut the beans into 2-inch lengths. Place the prepped beans in a stockpot, cover with water, and bring to a boil over medium heat. Allow to boil for 5 minutes, stirring a few times to evenly distribute heat.

3. Using hot, clean jars, add 2 tablespoons crumbled black pepper bacon to each quart jar and 1 tablespoon to each pint jar. Using a slotted spoon, fill your jars with green beans, being sure to leave 1 inch of headspace. Ladle the hot bean cooking liquid over the beans, maintaining the 1 inch of headspace. Remove any air bubbles and readjust the headspace if necessary.

4. Wipe the rim of each jar with a warm washcloth dipped in distilled white vinegar. Place a lid and ring on each jar and hand tighten.

5. Place jars in the pressure canner, lock the pressure canner lid, and bring to a boil on high heat. Let the canner vent for 10 minutes. Close the vent and continue heating to achieve 11 PSI for a dial gauge and 10 PSI for a weighted gauge. Process quart jars for 25 minutes and pint jars for 20 minutes.

Substitution Tip: If you are on a low-sodium diet or do not eat pork, feel free to skip the bacon; however, you can still flavor your green beans with fresh cracked black pepper or any other dried herb or spice of your liking. Simply add ⅛ teaspoon to each pint or ¼ teaspoon to each quart.

MIXED VEGETABLES

MAKES APPROXIMATELY 7 QUARTS OR 14 PINTS

PREP: 1 HR • COOK: 5 MIN • CANNER: 1 HR • PROCESSING: 1 HR 30 MIN/1 HR 15 MIN
TOTAL: 3 HR 35 MIN/3 HR 20 MIN

While this garden variety makes a yummy side dish, it is also a great starter for vegetable soup. Simply add a jar of your home-canned Vegetable Broth (page 105) and your favorite seasonings and a meal is born. If you already have a use in mind, preseason your Mixed Vegetables, choosing a yummy spice blend from page 39.

2½ pounds (about 18 medium) carrots, peeled and chopped (6 cups)

12 ears sweet corn, kernels sliced from the cobs (6 cups)

2½ pounds green beans, cut into 1-inch pieces (6 cups)

6 cups shelled peas (from 6 pounds pods)

4 large tomatoes, diced (4 cups)

4 large zucchini, diced (4 cups)

7 teaspoons coarse sea salt (optional)

1. Add carrots, corn, green beans, peas, tomatoes, and zucchini to a large stainless steel stockpot and add enough water to cover. Bring to a boil over medium-high heat, mixing well to keep vegetables on the bottom from scorching.

2. Boil for 5 minutes, then remove from the heat. Ladle the hot vegetables into jars, leaving 1 inch of headspace. Remove any air bubbles and readjust the headspace if necessary.

3. Wipe the rim of each jar with a warm washcloth dipped in distilled white vinegar. Place a lid and ring on each jar and hand tighten. If using salt, add 1 teaspoon to each quart jar or ½ teaspoon to each pint jar.

4. Place jars in the pressure canner, lock the pressure canner lid, and bring to a boil on high heat. Let the canner vent for 10 minutes. Close the vent and continue heating to achieve 11 PSI for a dial gauge and 10 PSI for a weighted gauge. Process quart jars for 1 hour 30 minutes and pint jars for 1 hour 15 minutes.

Ingredient Tip: Feel free to use frozen carrots, corn, green beans and peas when making this recipe. No need to thaw, simply add the frozen vegetables to the stockpot with fresh tomatoes and zucchini and bring to a boil. It may take a bit longer to come to a boil, but they will work just fine—a perfect solution if you happen to be making this recipe off-season.

GARLIC AND BACON BRUSSELS SPROUTS

MAKES APPROXIMATELY 7 QUARTS OR 14 PINTS

PREP: 20 MIN • COOK: 8 MIN • CANNER: 1 HR • PROCESSING: 1 HR 30 MIN/1 HR 15 MIN

TOTAL: 2 HR 58 MIN/2 HR 43 MIN

In my family, everything tastes better with bacon, including not-so-favored vegetables like Brussels sprouts! This side dish is sure to please even the pickiest of eaters. While the pressure canner tenderizes the Brussels sprouts, the broth, bacon, and garlic tone down the sprouts' pungent flavor.

1 pound sliced bacon

7 pounds Brussels sprouts, ends trimmed and exterior leaves removed

18 cups Chicken Broth (page 104)

Cloves from 1 head garlic, peeled and coarsely chopped

Coarse sea salt and ground black pepper

1. Using kitchen scissors, cut the bacon into 2-inch-long strips and fry in a skillet until the fat is translucent, about 5 to 8 minutes. Remove from the skillet and place on a plate lined with paper towel to absorb excess grease. Crumble the bacon into smaller bits.

2. Remove the ends and pull away the exterior leaves from the Brussels sprouts and rinse in a colander. Shake off any excess water. Set like-size whole sprouts in groups. Keep the smaller sprouts whole and cut the larger in half lengthwise. All Brussels sprouts or pieces should be no larger than 2 inches in diameter.

3. In a stainless steel stockpot, bring the Chicken Broth to a boil. Reduce the heat and simmer for 2 minutes, then turn off the burner.

4. Add 2 tablespoons bacon and 2 teaspoons chopped garlic to each warm quart jar or 1 tablespoon bacon and 1 teaspoon garlic to each warm pint jar. Add a dash or two of salt and pepper per jar to taste.

5. Raw pack the Brussels sprouts into warm jars, leaving a generous inch of headspace. Maneuver sprouts to tightly pack but avoid over-packing jars.

6. Ladle the hot broth over the Brussels sprouts, leaving 1 inch of headspace. Gently tap the jar on the cutting board to release trapped air. Add additional broth if necessary to maintain 1 inch of headspace.

7. Wipe the rim of each jar with a warm washcloth dipped in distilled white vinegar. Place a lid and ring on each jar and hand tighten.

8. Place jars in the pressure canner, lock the pressure canner lid, and bring to a boil on high heat. Let the canner vent for 10 minutes. Close the vent and continue heating to achieve 11 PSI for a dial gauge and 10 PSI for a weighted gauge. Process quart jars for 1 hour 30 minutes and pint jars for 1 hour 15 minutes.

Ingredient Tip: If you prefer a bit of zing to your Brussels sprouts, feel free to add ½ tablespoon balsamic vinegar to each quart jar or ¾ teaspoon to each pint jar prior to processing. This subtle addition gives the sprouts a little something extra when eating.

SOUTHERN COLLARD GREENS

MAKES APPROXIMATELY 4 QUARTS OR 8 PINTS

PREP: 20 MIN • COOK: 10 MIN • CANNER: 1 HR • PROCESSING: 1 HR 30 MIN/1 HR 15 MIN • TOTAL: 3 HR/2 HR 45 MIN

These are my favorite greens of all time! I will often wind up with a quart less for my pantry because I keep one in the kitchen to enjoy the very next day. Serve these delicious mixed greens alongside fried chicken or breaded pork chops. Be sure to whip up additional sides such as cornbread, black-eyed peas, and creamy mac 'n' cheese for a traditional Southern meal.

12 cups water

2 smoked ham hocks

1 teaspoon coarse sea salt

½ teaspoon ground black pepper

2 teaspoons garlic powder

1 teaspoon red pepper flakes

½ pound bacon

½ cup finely chopped yellow onion

14 pounds collard greens, untrimmed

4 pounds turnip greens, untrimmed

1. In a stainless steel stockpot, combine the water, ham hocks, salt, pepper, garlic powder, and red pepper flakes. Bring to a boil over medium-high heat. Once the mixture is at a boil, reduce the heat to low and simmer while cooking the bacon and prepping the greens.

2. Slice the bacon into 1-inch-long strips, then place in a skillet on medium heat. Add the onion and mix well. Cook the mixture for 5 to 8 minutes or until onions are translucent. Scrape everything into the stockpot and continue to simmer.

3. Wash the greens thoroughly. Remove the stem from the leaf by holding the base of the stem in one hand and stripping the leaf with the other, or use a paring knife to cut out the stem, if that's easier.

4. Once all the stems are removed, stack 8 to 10 leaves on top of each other, roll them up, and cut into ½-inch-thick slices to create ribbons.

5. Remove any remaining meat from the ham hocks. Return the meat to the cooking liquid in the stockpot and discard the hock. Add the cut greens to the stockpot and mix well. Remove from the heat.

6. Using tongs, hot pack the greens into jars, leaving 1 inch of headspace. Using a slotted spoon, be sure to evenly disperse any remaining bits of meat and onion into the jars, tamping them down to maintain the required headspace. Ladle enough of the hot ham hock liquid over the greens to cover completely and maintain 1 inch of headspace.

7. Wipe the rim of each jar with a warm washcloth dipped in distilled white vinegar. Place a lid and ring on each jar and hand tighten.

8. Place jars in the pressure canner, lock the pressure canner lid, and bring to a boil on high heat. Let the canner vent for 10 minutes. Close the vent and continue heating to achieve 11 PSI for a dial gauge and 10 PSI for a weighted gauge. Process quart jars for 1 hour 30 minutes and pint jars for 1 hour 15 minutes.

Ingredient Tip: If ham hocks aren't readily available, feel free to replace the water with 3 quarts of Chicken Stock (page 98). Also, if you prefer a bit more heat to your greens, feel free to double the red pepper flakes.

CHAPTER FIVE

BEANS AND LEGUMES

BEANS ARE A HEALTHY, versatile, and affordable food. They are high in fiber, antioxidants, and proteins as well as B vitamins and minerals like iron, magnesium, potassium, copper, and zinc. The beauty of using a pressure canner is the processing time and temperature rehydrate the dried beans so there is no need to presoak them unless they are going to be cooked with acidic ingredients like tomatoes. This chapter describes how to safely preserve dried beans and gives delicious recipes for a variety of meals and meal starters.

Preparing Beans for Canning

After picking your favorite dried bean, follow these simple steps to have home-canned beans at the ready:

1. Start by rinsing your dried beans in a colander in the sink. Using both hands, be sure to sort through the beans and remove any disfigured or shriveled beans and any rocks or debris that may have made their way into the bag. Next, fill a small stockpot halfway with cool water and submerge the beans. Remove and discard any that float to the top as they likely have imperfections. Stir the beans with both hands in a vigorous motion to remove dirt and debris. After a couple minutes, dump the beans back into a colander and rinse again, being sure to inspect for rocks.

2. Place the required amount of clean, dried beans in jars according to the Basic Dried Bean and Legume Processing Chart (see next page).

3. Cover the dried beans with hot water, leaving 1 inch of headspace. Gently tamp each jar on a cutting board to remove any trapped air pockets and add additional water if necessary to maintain the 1 inch of headspace.

4. Wipe the rim of each jar with a warm washcloth dipped in distilled white vinegar. Place a lid and ring on each jar and hand tighten.

5. Place jars in the pressure canner, lock the pressure canner lid, and bring to a boil on high heat. Let the canner vent for 10 minutes. Close the vent and heat to achieve 10 PSI. Process pint jars for 1 hour 15 minutes and quart jars for 1 hour 30 minutes.

Basic Dried Bean and Legume Processing

Having home-canned beans on your pantry shelf is such a blessing when crunched for time. You don't need to presoak beans when pressure canning, which is another time saver. Like pressure cooking, when canning you expose each jar of beans in water to a high heat (240–250°F) for a specified length of time which makes presoaking dried beans optional. Pressure canning a tested ratio of cleaned, dried beans with soft water in each jar simultaneously softens the exterior of the bean and cooks them for consumption. Do note, however, this method is specific to just dried beans in water, not the other recipes. We have to presoak beans in various recipes because they are exposed to acidic ingredients which prevent beans from softening.

Use this handy chart to determine how much of a particular bean you will need so you may yield your desired amount (see next page). Because dried beans all process for the same time and PSI, you may place a variety of different types in the same canner at the same time. For taller canners, you may double-stack your pints, so take advantage of the canner space by using a second flat rack.

WHAT DO I DO IF I HAVE HARD WATER?

———— ❉ ————

Dried beans soften best in soft water, meaning the water is free from minerals like calcium and magnesium. Soft water is typically treated water where the only ion is salt. For those of us with well water, we struggle to soften our beans, even when soaking overnight. If you have hard water and do not have an in-home water softener, use distilled water or create soft water using the following ratio:

3 tablespoons salt to every 1 gallon water (16 cups) for every 1 pound beans (16 ounces)

BASIC DRIED BEAN AND LEGUME PROCESSING CHART

DRIED INGREDIENT	DRIED QUANTITY PER PINT JAR	DRIED QUANTITY PER QUART JAR
Black Beans	¾ cup	1½ cups
Kidney Beans	½ cup	1 cup
Cannellini Beans	½ cup	1 cup
Pinto Beans	½ cup	1 cup
Navy Beans	¾ cup	1½ cups
Red Beans	½ cup	1 cup
Great Northern Beans	½ cup	1 cup
Black Eyed Peas	½ cup	1 cup
Garbanzo Beans (Chickpeas)	¾ cup	1½ cups
Lima Beans	½ cup	1 cup
Lentils	¼ cup	½ cup
Split Peas	⅓ cup	⅔ cup

FIVE-BEAN MEDLEY

MAKES APPROXIMATELY 8 QUARTS OR 16 PINTS

PREP: 15 MIN • COOK: 0 MIN • CANNER: 1 HR • PROCESSING: 1 HR 30 MIN/1 HR 15 MIN

TOTAL: 1 HR 45 MIN/1 HR 30 MIN

I love adding these mixed beans to soups and stews and often make them a focal point in meal creation. Having a variety of flavors and colors makes a hearty and flavorful refried bean recipe to use in Mexican dishes like burritos. Because the pressure canner will cook and soften the beans, there is no need to presoak or precook.

12 cups hot water

3 cups dried pinto beans (16 ounces)

2½ cups dried kidney beans (16 ounces)

2¼ cups dried black beans (16 ounces)

2¼ cups dried split peas (16 ounces)

2½ cups dried great northern beans (16 ounces)

7 teaspoons coarse sea salt (optional)

1. Add the water to the stockpot and bring to a boil on high heat.

2. Thoroughly rinse and clean the dried beans, discarding any disfigured or shriveled beans and any rocks or debris.

3. If using, add 1 teaspoon salt per quart jar or ½ teaspoon salt per pint jar before filling with dried beans.

4. Using a ladle and funnel, fill each quart jar with 1½ cups clean dried beans and each pint jar with ¾ cup. Next, ladle the hot water over the beans, leaving 1 inch of headspace. Remove air with an air bubble remover tool and adjust the headspace with additional water as necessary to maintain the 1 inch of headspace.

5. Wipe the rim of each jar with a warm washcloth dipped in distilled white vinegar. Place a lid and ring on each jar and hand tighten.

6. Place jars in the pressure canner, lock the pressure canner lid, and bring to a boil on high heat. Let the canner vent for 10 minutes. Close the vent and heat to achieve 10 PSI. Process quart jars for 1 hour 30 minutes and pint jars for 1 hour 15 minutes.

BUTTERNUT SQUASH AND CHICKPEA HASH

MAKES APPROXIMATELY 6 QUARTS OR 12 PINTS
PREP: 15 MIN • COOK: 40 MIN • CANNER: 1 HR • PROCESSING: 1 HR 30 MIN/1 HR 15 MIN
TOTAL: 3 HR 25 MIN/3 HR 10 MIN

Gain your protein from garbanzo beans, also known as chickpeas, with this colorful hash. The amazing blend of flavors and vegetables takes an ordinary crop from average to extraordinary. Get a healthy dose of lycopene from the tomatoes and a hefty helping of potassium and magnesium from the squash and zucchini.

3 cups dried chickpeas (16 ounces)

2 tablespoons olive oil

1 large yellow onion, chopped (1½ cups)

2 teaspoons coarse sea salt

¼ teaspoon ground black pepper

12 Roma tomatoes, diced (6 cups)

4 cups water

2 large zucchini, halved lengthwise and cut into 1-inch chunks (3 cups)

1 large butternut squash, peeled and cut into ½-inch chunks (approx. 2½ pounds; 6 cups chunks)

1 tablespoon ground ginger

1 tablespoon ground coriander

1. Thoroughly rinse and clean the chickpeas, discarding any disfigured or shriveled beans and any rocks or debris.

2. In a large pot, add the dried chickpeas and add enough water to cover. Bring to a boil over medium-high heat. Boil for 5 minutes, then reduce the heat to low and simmer with the lid on. Simmer for 15 minutes, then remove from the heat, keeping the lid on.

3. In a second large stockpot, heat the olive oil over medium heat. Add the onion, salt, and pepper. Cook the onion for 5 minutes, stirring frequently. Add the tomatoes and mix well. Cook for 5 minutes to release the juices from the tomatoes, stirring often to avoid scorching the tomatoes. Add the water, zucchini, squash, ginger, and coriander and mix well. Cook for an additional 5 minutes.

4. Drain the chickpeas in a colander in the sink. Add the chickpeas to the stockpot and mix well. Bring to a boil. Boil hard for 5 minutes, stirring often.

5. Ladle the hot hash mixture into hot jars, leaving a generous 1 inch of headspace. Remove any air bubbles and add additional mixture if necessary to maintain the headspace.

6. Wipe the rim of each jar with a warm washcloth dipped in distilled white vinegar. Place a lid and ring on each jar and hand tighten.

7. Place jars in the pressure canner, lock the pressure canner lid, and bring to a boil on high heat. Let the canner vent for 10 minutes. Close the vent and continue heating to achieve 11 PSI for a dial gauge and 10 PSI for a weighted gauge. Process quart jars for 1 hour 30 minutes and pint jars for 1 hour 15 minutes.

Serving Tip: Heat and serve alongside any protein, including eggs, or spread it on crostini topped with fresh cilantro and Parmesan cheese. This hash is also an excellent starter for a vegetable casserole.

HOMESTYLE BAKED BEANS

MAKES 5 PINTS

PREP: 45 MIN • COOK: 25 MIN • CANNER: 1 HR • PROCESSING: 1 HR 15 MIN • TOTAL: 3 HR 25 MIN

Need a quick side for a potluck or sporting event? Pop a few jars of these in your slow cooker and heat through on warm. Homestyle Baked Beans are a total crowd pleaser and the perfect side dish. After canning these once, I never purchased store-bought baked beans again.

2½ cups dried navy or great northern beans (16 ounces)

12 to 14 ounces smoked, uncured bacon, thick cut

1 large sweet onion, diced (1½ cups)

6 garlic cloves, minced

1½ cups Chicken Stock (page 98)

¾ cup packed dark brown sugar

¾ cup tomato paste (6 ounces)

½ cup blackstrap molasses

¼ cup apple cider vinegar

¼ cup ketchup

2 tablespoons Worcestershire sauce

2 tablespoons Dijon mustard

1 teaspoon coarse sea salt

½ teaspoon cayenne pepper

½ teaspoon ground black pepper

1. Thoroughly rinse and clean the dried beans, discarding any disfigured or shriveled beans and any rocks or debris.

2. In a large pot, combine the dried beans with enough water to cover by 2 inches. Bring to a boil over medium-high heat. Boil for 5 minutes, then reduce the heat to low and simmer with a lid on for 30 minutes. Turn off the heat and keep the lid on.

3. Using kitchen scissors, cut the bacon into 1-inch-long pieces and place in a deep skillet. Using medium-high heat, cook the bacon until lightly browned but not crisp, about 8 minutes. Remove the bacon pieces using a slotted spoon and set aside in a bowl. Be sure to reserve as much bacon grease in the skillet as possible.

4. Add the onion and garlic to the skillet and cook until the onion is translucent, about 5 to 8 minutes.

5. In a large bowl, whisk together the Chicken Stock, dark brown sugar, tomato paste, molasses, vinegar, ketchup, Worcestershire sauce, Dijon mustard, salt, cayenne pepper, and black pepper. Whisk until well blended.

6. Drain the beans in a colander in the sink, shaking off any excess liquid. Add the beans to the onions and garlic in the skillet. Add the crumbled bacon and mix well. Heat through on medium-high heat, stirring often, for about 5 minutes.

7. Add the sauce to the skillet, mixing well to coat every bean, and bring to a boil, stirring frequently. Boil for 2 minutes, stirring, then remove from the heat.

8. Ladle the hot beans into pint jars, leaving a generous 1 inch of headspace. Using your air bubble remover tool, tamp down to remove air pockets, and evenly distribute any remaining sauce among the five pint jars, maintaining the headspace.

9. Wipe the rim of each jar with a warm washcloth dipped in distilled white vinegar. Place a lid and ring on each jar and hand tighten.

10. Place jars in the pressure canner, lock the pressure canner lid, and bring to a boil on high heat. Let the canner vent for 10 minutes. Close the vent and heat to achieve 10 PSI. Process pint jars for 1 hour 15 minutes.

Recipe Tip: While it is tempting to double, even triple, this recipe, the best flavor is achieved when it is created in a single batch. I suggest prepping individual batches simultaneously to maximize your time, therefore increasing your yield. A single batch requires 2½ cups dried beans that yields 5½ cups hydrated beans. Use this math to hydrate multiple batches of beans together to save stove-top space. Then, you can create individual batches of sauce and individual skillets of the bacon, onion, and garlic mixture.

PORK AND BLACK BEANS

MAKES APPROXIMATELY 5 QUARTS OR 10 PINTS

PREP: 10 MIN • COOK: 25 MIN • CANNER: 1 HR • PROCESSING: 1 HR 30 MIN/1 HR 15 MIN

TOTAL: 3 HR 5 MIN/2 HR 50 MIN

This is often my go-to jar when I need a quick lunch. Packed with protein, this authentic Mexican-flavored dish is best served hot and topped with fresh cilantro and a dollop of sour cream.

2¼ cups dried black beans (16 ounces)

4 tablespoons olive oil, divided

1½ pounds boneless pork shoulder, surface fat trimmed, cut into 1-inch cubes

1 teaspoon coarse sea salt

½ teaspoon ground black pepper

2 medium white onions, coarsely chopped

2 sprigs fresh epazote, coarsely chopped, or 2 teaspoons dried epazote

4 cups Chicken Broth (page 104)

2 cups water

4 large tomatoes, peeled and diced, with juice (4 cups)

2 serrano peppers, finely chopped

8 garlic cloves, minced

1 tablespoon chili powder

2 teaspoons chopped fresh oregano

2 teaspoons chopped fresh basil

2 teaspoons ground cumin

1. Thoroughly rinse and clean the black beans, discarding any disfigured or shriveled beans and any rocks or debris. Set aside.

2. In a thick-bottomed stockpot, heat 2 tablespoons olive oil on medium-high. Working in batches, place the pork cubes in the oil and lightly brown all sides, about 1 minute each side, seasoning each batch with a dash of salt and pepper. Add 1 additional tablespoon of oil while browning each batch. Do not cook the pork through. Place the browned pork batches in a bowl and set aside.

3. Add the onions and epazote to the drippings in the stockpot. Sauté until the onions are translucent, about 5 to 8 minutes, then add the broth and 2 cups water. Bring to a boil.

4. Once the water is at a boil, add the cleaned black beans to the stockpot. Return to a boil and cook for 5 minutes, stirring often. Add the browned pork, tomatoes, serrano peppers, garlic, chili powder, oregano, basil, cumin, salt, and pepper to the stockpot and mix well. Return to a boil for 5 minutes, stirring often to avoid scorching.

5. Ladle the pork and beans into hot jars, leaving 1 inch of headspace. Be sure to give each jar a good ratio of beans and meat. Remove any air bubbles and add additional mixture or liquid if necessary, to maintain the 1 inch of headspace.

6. Wipe the rim of each jar with a warm washcloth dipped in distilled white vinegar. Place a lid and ring on each jar and hand tighten.

7. Place jars in the pressure canner, lock the pressure canner lid, and bring to a boil on high heat. Let the canner vent for 10 minutes. Close the vent and continue heating to achieve 11 PSI for a dial gauge and 10 PSI for a weighted gauge. Process quart jars for 1 hour 30 minutes and pint jars for 1 hour 15 minutes.

Ingredient Tip: Epazote is a pungent herb often used in Mexican cuisine. Its flavor has notes of oregano, citrus, mint, and anise. Bunches of it can be purchased in some Mexican grocery stores or farmers' markets. Grow epazote in your herb garden to ensure you have this aromatic herb readily available for any meal.

STEWED GARBANZO BEANS

MAKES APPROXIMATELY 5 PINTS

PREP: 15 MIN • COOK: 15 MIN • CANNER: 1 HR • PROCESSING: 1 HR 30 MIN/1 HR 15 MIN • TOTAL: 3 HR/2 HR 45 MIN

Looking for a meatless meal? Use these hearty beans in a variety of ways—as a meal starter, side dish, or main course. Garbanzo beans, also known as chickpeas, are a very versatile legume and are a mainstay in Mediterranean cuisine. Try Stewed Garbanzo Beans over couscous and topped with fresh parsley leaves. Add a splash of lime juice for fun.

3 cups dried chickpeas (16 ounces)

2 tablespoons olive oil

1 large leek, green leaves removed, cut in half lengthwise and cut into ¼-inch pieces

½ cup finely diced white onion

2 garlic cloves, minced

1 tablespoon grated fresh ginger

4 cups Roasted Vegetable Stock (page 100)

8 large Roma tomatoes, diced (4 cups)

1 teaspoon dried parsley

1 teaspoon coarse sea salt

¼ teaspoon ground black pepper

1. Thoroughly rinse and clean the chickpeas, discarding any disfigured or shriveled beans and any rocks or debris.

2. In a large pot, add the chickpeas and enough water to cover. Bring to a boil over medium-high heat. Boil for 5 minutes, then reduce the heat to low and simmer with the lid on.

3. In a second large stockpot, heat the oil over medium-high heat. Add the leek, onion, garlic, and ginger and cook for about 5 to 8 minutes, or until the onion is translucent. Add the Roasted Vegetable Stock to the pot and bring to a boil.

4. Remove the chickpeas from the heat and drain in a colander in the sink. Add the chickpeas to the vegetable stock mixture and return to a boil. Add the tomatoes, parsley, salt, and pepper, mix well, and return to a boil.

5. Reduce the heat and simmer for 10 minutes, stirring frequently.

6. Ladle the hot bean mixture into hot jars, leaving 1 inch of headspace. Remove any air bubbles and add additional mixture if necessary to maintain 1 inch of headspace.

7. Wipe the rim of each jar with a warm washcloth dipped in distilled white vinegar. Place a lid and ring on each jar and hand tighten.

8. Place jars in the pressure canner, lock the pressure canner lid, and bring to a boil on high heat. Let the canner vent for 10 minutes. Close the vent and continue heating to achieve 11 PSI for a dial gauge and 10 PSI for a weighted gauge. Process quart jars for 1 hour 30 minutes and pint jars for 1 hour 15 minutes.

Ingredient Tip: Do you have a particular curry you prefer? Whether it be red, green, or yellow curry, Stewed Garbanzo Beans is a perfect recipe to create fun flavors based on how you plan to serve your beans. Start with 1 teaspoon for milder curry powders and ½ teaspoon or less for hotter varieties.

VEGAN GUMBO

MAKES APPROXIMATELY 8 QUARTS OR 16 PINTS

PREP: 20 MIN • COOK: 20 MIN • CANNER: 1 HR • PROCESSING: 1 HR 30 MIN/1 HR 15 MIN

TOTAL: 3 HR 10 MIN/2 HR 55 MIN

Gumbo is a stew that got its start in Louisiana during the 18th century. While there are many adaptations, this meatless version is sure to please with its hearty, filling, and savory style. Packed with vegetables and proteins, Vegan Gumbo proudly boasts okra and a touch of heat from cayenne pepper. Serve this hearty gumbo with brown rice.

2 cups dried lentils

1 cup dried pinto beans

2 tablespoons olive oil

1 medium onion, diced (1 cup)

6 garlic cloves, coarsely chopped

2 pounds baby button mushrooms

12 cups Roasted Vegetable Stock (page 100)

2 bay leaves

2 celery stalks, chopped (1 cup)

1 small green bell pepper, seeded and chopped (½ cup)

35 okra pods, trimmed and cut into 1-inch pieces (2 cups)

3 large tomatoes, diced (3 cups)

¼ cup chopped fresh parsley

1 teaspoon dried thyme

1 teaspoon cayenne pepper

½ teaspoon ground black pepper

1 teaspoon coarse sea salt

1. Thoroughly rinse and clean the dried lentils and beans, discarding any disfigured or shriveled beans and any rocks or debris. Set aside.

2. In a large stockpot, combine the oil, onion, garlic, and mushrooms. On medium-high heat, cook the mixture until the onions are translucent, about 5 to 8 minutes.

3. Add the Roasted Vegetable Stock, bay leaves, lentils, dried beans, celery, bell pepper, okra, tomatoes, parsley, thyme, cayenne, black pepper and salt. Bring to a boil, mixing well. Reduce the heat and simmer for 15 minutes, stirring frequently. Remove and discard the bay leaves.

4. Ladle the hot gumbo into hot jars, leaving 1 inch of headspace. Be sure to obtain a good ratio of mushrooms, beans, and vegetables in each jar. Remove any air bubbles and add additional gumbo if necessary to maintain the 1 inch of headspace.

5. Wipe the rim of each jar with a warm washcloth dipped in distilled white vinegar. Place a lid and ring on each jar and hand tighten.

6. Place jars in the pressure canner, lock the pressure canner lid, and bring to a boil on high heat. Let the canner vent for 10 minutes. Close the vent and continue heating to achieve 11 PSI for a dial gauge and 10 PSI for a weighted gauge. Process quart jars for 1 hour 30 minutes and pint jars for 1 hour 15 minutes.

Ingredient Tip: For a more traditional gumbo, replace the mushrooms with 4 cups sliced andouille sausage, about ½-inch thick, and gently brown the sausage with the onions, garlic, and oil.

PUMPKIN WITH WHITE BEANS AND BACON

MAKES APPROXIMATELY 6 QUARTS OR 12 PINTS

PREP: 15 MIN • COOK: 20 MIN • CANNER: 1 HR • PROCESSING: 1 HR 30 MIN/1 HR 15 MIN

TOTAL: 3 HR 5 MIN/2 HR 50 MIN

This popular but simple meal is the perfect combination of pumpkin, beans, and bacon providing sustenance on a cold day. The red wine vinegar provides the recipe with a gentle tang of flavor, while the pie pumpkin provides sweet warmth.

2½ cups dried navy, cannellini, or great northern beans (16 ounces)

12 slices bacon

2 small pie pumpkins, peeled, seeded and cut into 1-inch pieces (about 1½ pounds each)

2 tablespoons dried oregano

1 teaspoon coarse sea salt (optional)

½ teaspoon ground black pepper

6 cups Chicken Broth (page 104)

4 cups water

3 tablespoons red wine vinegar (optional)

1. Thoroughly rinse and clean the dried beans, discarding any disfigured or shriveled beans and any rocks or debris. Set aside.

2. Cut the bacon into 2-inch-long pieces using kitchen scissors and place into a large stockpot. On medium heat, cook the bacon for about 5 minutes or until the pieces are slightly crisp. Place the bacon into a bowl, leaving the drippings in the stockpot.

3. Remove the stem from each pie pumpkin, like you would a jack-o'-lantern. Slicing downward from the opening, cut the pie pumpkin lengthwise into long quarters. Remove the seeds and stringy fibers. Working in batches, place the quarters in the microwave, flesh-side down, and microwave on high for 5 minutes. When cool to touch, use a paring knife to easily peel the skin from the pumpkin.

4. Cut the pumpkin into 1-inch chunks and add to the stockpot. Add the oregano, salt, and pepper and mix well. Lightly brown the pumpkin pieces, about 6 to 8 minutes, and toss often to fully coat all the pieces with bacon drippings.

5. Add the broth, crumbled bacon, and dried beans to the stockpot, and stir. Bring to a boil over medium-high heat. Once the mixture is at a boil, reduce the heat and simmer for 5 minutes. Add the water and red wine vinegar and return to a boil. Boil for 2 minutes, then remove from the heat.

6. Using a slotted spoon, fill the jars three-quarters full of pumpkin mixture. Be sure to obtain a good ratio of pumpkins, beans, and bacon in each jar. Ladle the hot pumpkin broth over the mixture, being sure to leave 1 inch of headspace. Tamp the mixture down using an air bubble remover tool and add additional liquid if necessary to maintain the 1 inch of headspace.

7. Wipe the rim of each jar with a warm washcloth dipped in distilled white vinegar. Place a lid and ring on each jar and hand tighten.

8. Place jars in the pressure canner, lock the pressure canner lid, and bring to a boil on high heat. Let the canner vent for 10 minutes. Close the vent and continue heating to achieve 11 PSI for a dial gauge and 10 PSI for a weighted gauge. Process quart jars for 1 hour 30 minutes and pint jars for 1 hour 15 minutes.

Ingredient Tip: Pie pumpkins not easily accessible? Not to worry. Substitute one large or two medium butternut squash. Peel and cut the squash into 1-inch chunks and add to the recipe as you would the pie pumpkins.

WHITE BEAN AND PORTOBELLO POT ROAST

MAKES APPROXIMATELY 8 QUARTS OR 16 PINTS
PREP: 25 MIN • COOK: 25 MIN • CANNER: 1 HR • PROCESSING: 1 HR 30 MIN/1 HR 15 MIN
TOTAL: 3 HR 20 MIN/3 HR 5 MIN

Enjoy this hearty pot roast bursting with flavor compliments of the meaty portobello mushrooms. High in iron, potassium, and vitamin D, the recipe ingredients blend splendidly using fresh rosemary and thyme, and a bit of buttery white wine.

2½ cups dried navy or great northern beans (16 ounces)

8 large portobello mushrooms, sliced lengthwise

3 cups white wine, preferably a chardonnay, divided

1 large onion, diced (2 cups)

12 cups Vegetable Broth (page 105)

8 large carrots, peeled and diced (4 cups)

4 garlic cloves, coarsely chopped

2 sprigs fresh rosemary

1 teaspoon rubbed sage

6 sprigs fresh thyme, leaves stripped from sprig

12 medium red skin potatoes, chopped into 1½-inch cubes (6 cups)

1 tablespoon anchovy-free Worcestershire sauce

2 teaspoons coarse sea salt

1 teaspoon ground black pepper

1. Thoroughly rinse and clean the dried beans, discarding any disfigured or shriveled beans and any rocks or debris. Set aside.

2. In a large stockpot, combine the mushroom slices, 1½ cups wine, and the onion. On medium-high heat, allow the mushrooms to soften and the onions to caramelize, about 8 to 10 minutes.

3. Add the broth, carrots, garlic, rosemary, sage, and thyme leaves. On medium-high heat, bring to a boil, stirring often. Reduce the heat and simmer for 10 minutes.

4. Add the potatoes, dried beans, Worcestershire sauce, the remaining 1½ cups wine, salt, and pepper to the stockpot, mixing well. Return to a boil on medium-high heat, and boil hard for 5 minutes, mixing well to avoid scorching. Remove from the heat. Also remove and discard the rosemary sprigs.

5. Using a slotted spoon, fill jars three-quarters full of the roast mixture. Be sure to obtain a good ratio of mushrooms, beans, and vegetables in each jar. After jars are filled three-quarters full, ladle the hot cooking liquid over the mixture, being sure to leave a generous 1 inch of headspace. Tamp the mixture down using an air bubble remover tool and add additional cooking liquid if necessary to maintain the headspace.

6. Wipe the rim of each jar with a warm washcloth dipped in distilled white vinegar. Place a lid and ring on each jar and hand tighten.

7. Place jars in the pressure canner, lock the pressure canner lid, and bring to a boil on high heat. Let the canner vent for 10 minutes. Close the vent and continue heating to achieve 11 PSI for a dial gauge and 10 PSI for a weighted gauge. Process quart jars for 1 hour 30 minutes and pint jars for 1 hour 15 minutes.

Ingredient Tip: If you are not a vegan and wish to deepen the flavor, replace the Vegetable Broth with Beef Broth (page 103) and the white wine with a robust red wine. This slight modification will not only deepen the flavor but will also deepen the color of the roast mixture to a darker, richer brown.

ROASTED TOMATILLO CHICKPEAS

MAKES APPROXIMATELY 5 PINTS

PREP: 20 MIN • COOK: 50 MIN • CANNER: 1 HR • PROCESSING: 1 HR 30 MIN/1 HR 15 MIN

TOTAL: 3 HR 40 MIN/3 HR 25 MIN

This has officially become one of my favorites! The warmth from the roasted garlic and curry blends beautifully with the tangy tart flavor of the tomatillos. And the chickpeas . . . the most tender, meaty beans thanks to the use of a pressure canner. Honestly, I love eating this right out of the jar! Serve with warm crostini or water crackers or as a side dish with any meal.

3 cups dried chickpeas

20 tomatillos

8 to 10 whole garlic cloves, peeled

3 to 5 tablespoons olive oil, divided

1 medium sweet onion, diced (1 cup)

4 garlic cloves, minced

1 teaspoon paprika

1 teaspoon ground coriander

½ teaspoon ground cumin

1 teaspoon yellow curry powder

1 teaspoon coarse sea salt

4 cups Chicken Stock (page 98)

1. Preheat the oven to 400°F.

2. Thoroughly rinse and clean the dried chickpeas, discarding any disfigured or shriveled beans and any rocks or debris. Place the dried chickpeas in a stockpot and cover with 2 inches of water. Bring to a boil. Let boil for 5 minutes then cover and remove from the heat.

3. Line a cookie sheet, or two, with foil. Remove the outer husks of the tomatillos and rinse well in a colander in the sink. Cut the tomatillos in half and place flesh-side down onto foil. Once all the tomatillos are lined up tight on the cookie sheet, space the peeled garlic cloves evenly throughout the tomatillos. Drizzle the tomatillos with olive oil. Roast in the oven for 25 minutes or until the tomatillo tops start to brown.

4. While the tomatillos are roasting, in a second stockpot, add 1 tablespoon oil, the onion, and minced garlic. Sauté for 5 minutes or until the onions become translucent.

5. Drain the chickpeas and shake off excess water. Add the rehydrated chickpeas to the onions and pan sear, mixing and stirring to avoid burning, about 5 minutes. Stir in the paprika, coriander, cumin, curry, salt, and pepper. Sear and stir an additional 2 minutes. Remove from the heat.

6. Working in batches, puree the roasted tomatillos, garlic, and tomatillo juice in a food processor.

7. Add the pureed roasted tomatillos to the chickpea mixture. Mix well. Add the stock and return to a boil over medium-high heat, stirring often. Cook 2 additional minutes, then remove from the heat.

8. Ladle the hot chickpea mixture into hot pints leaving a generous 1 inch of headspace. Remove any air bubbles and add additional mixture if necessary, keeping the 1¼ inches of headspace.

9. Wipe the rim of each jar with a warm washcloth dipped in distilled white vinegar. Place a lid and ring on each jar and hand tighten.

10. Place jars in the pressure canner, lock the pressure canner lid, and bring to a boil on high heat. Let the canner vent for 10 minutes. Close the vent and continue heating to achieve 11 PSI for a dial gauge and 10 PSI for a weighted gauge. Process quart jars for 1 hour 30 minutes and pint jars for 1 hour 15 minutes.

Ingredient Tip: This is the perfect recipe to explore additional flavors. Want to add some heat? Add ¼ teaspoon (or more) of red pepper flakes. If you prefer a spicier curry, swap out red curry for yellow. Spice and warm tones work well with the tartness of the tomatillo so feel free to explore.

RIBOLLITA

MAKES 7 QUARTS OR 14 PINTS
PREP: 25 MIN • COOK: 15 MIN • CANNER: 1 HR • PROCESSING: 1 HR 30 MIN/1 HR 15 MIN
TOTAL: 3 HR 10 MIN/2 HR 55 MIN

This hearty meal from Tuscany is loaded with vegetables and beans and flavored with fresh herbs. Known for being a versatile dish, upon serving, it can be thickened with bread and made into porridge, crafted into a pancake and sautéed in a skillet or it can be thinned using Chicken Stock (page 98), turning it into a fine soup.

2 cups dried cannellini or navy beans

3 tablespoons virgin olive oil

1 medium red onion, diced (1 cup)

1 large leek, white and light green parts only, diced (1½ cups)

6 garlic cloves, coarsely chopped

10 cups water

4 large carrots, peeled and diced (2 cups)

1 large butternut squash, peeled, seeded, and cut into 1½-inch dice (6 cups)

1 large turnip, peeled and cut into 1-inch dice (1½ cups)

1 celery stalk, diced (½ cup)

1 bouquet garni (3 sprigs each of parsley, oregano, thyme, and rosemary tied together with kitchen twine)

3 bay leaves

1 teaspoon coarse sea salt

½ teaspoon ground black pepper

1 large bunch kale, stemmed and coarsely chopped

1. Thoroughly rinse and clean the dried beans, discarding any disfigured or shriveled beans and any rocks or debris. Set aside.

2. In a thick-bottomed stockpot, combine the oil, onion, leek, and garlic. Mix well and sauté over medium-high heat until the onion is translucent, about 5 to 8 minutes.

3. Add the water, carrots, squash, turnip, celery, bouquet garni, and bay leaves. Bring to a boil stirring often. Boil for 2 minutes.

4. Add the dried beans, salt, and pepper and return to a boil. Boil for 5 minutes then add the chopped kale leaves. Mix well. Boil for 1 additional minute then remove from heat. Remove and discard the bouquet garni and bay leaves.

5. Ladle hot Ribollita into hot jars leaving 1 inch of headspace. Be sure to obtain a good ratio of beans and vegetables in each jar. Remove any air bubbles and add additional mixture if necessary, to maintain the 1 inch of headspace.

6. Wipe the rim of each jar with a warm washcloth dipped in distilled white vinegar. Place a lid and ring on each jar and hand tighten.

7. Place jars in the pressure canner, lock the pressure canner lid, and bring to a boil on high heat. Let the canner vent for 10 minutes. Close the vent and continue heating to achieve 11 PSI for a dial gauge and 10 PSI for a weighted gauge. Process quart jars for 1 hour 30 minutes and pint jars for 1 hour 15 minutes.

Serving Tip: If you want a soup-like consistency, add 1 to 2 cups Chicken Stock (page 98) to a quart-size jar of Ribollita when you heat it; just be sure to stir and taste as you go to obtain the consistency you desire without losing flavor. If you prefer to thicken it like porridge, add 3 or 4 slices of fresh or stale crusty bread, cut into 1-inch cubes, and simmer for 15 minutes or until the bread breaks down and thickens the Ribollita. Regardless of how you prefer to enjoy your home-canned Ribollita, top each hot bowl with shaved Parmesan or Romano cheese, then serve.

CAJUN BLACK-EYED PEAS

MAKES 5 QUARTS OR 10 PINTS
PREP: 20 MIN • COOK: 20 MIN • CANNER: 1 HR • PROCESSING: 1 HR 30 MIN/1 HR 15 MIN
TOTAL: 3 HR 10 MIN/2 HR 55 MIN

Spicy and fun, enjoy this recipe as a main dish or a hearty side. Leeks, andouille sausage, salt pork, and apple cider vinegar give this recipe a robust and authentic Southern flavor, while adorable black-eyed peas grace every jar. Serve with a dash or two of hot sauce alongside cream-style cornbread.

2½ cups dried black-eyed peas (16 ounces)

3 tablespoons olive oil

1 large leek, white and light green parts only, diced (1½ cups)

1 large yellow onion, chopped (1½ cups)

2 celery stalks, diced (1 cup)

6 garlic cloves, minced or sliced thin

1 pound andouille sausage, cut into ¼-inch-thick slices

½ pound salt pork or slab bacon, cut into ½-inch lardons

8 cups Chicken Stock (page 98)

4 cups water

½ cup apple cider vinegar

2 bay leaves

1 medium green bell pepper, finely chopped (1 cup)

1 jalapeño pepper, minced

2 teaspoons coarse sea salt (optional)

½ teaspoon red pepper flakes

½ teaspoon ground black pepper

1 large bunch kale, stemmed and coarsely chopped

1. Thoroughly rinse and clean the dried peas, discarding any disfigured or shriveled beans and any rocks or debris. Set aside.

2. In a large stockpot, combine the oil, leek, onion, celery, and garlic. Mix well and sauté over medium-high heat until the onions are translucent, about 5 to 8 minutes. Add the andouille sausage and salt pork or bacon and cook for an additional 5 to 8 minutes, or until the sausage is lightly browned.

3. Add the stock, water, vinegar, and bay leaves to the stockpot and bring to a boil, stirring often. Add the black-eyed peas, bell pepper, jalapeño, salt, red pepper flakes, and black pepper to the stockpot and return to a boil for 2 minutes, then add the chopped kale leaves. Mix well. Boil for 1 additional minute then remove from the heat.

4. Ladle the hot mixture into hot jars leaving a generous 1 inch of headspace. Be sure to obtain a good ratio of beans, meat, and vegetables in each jar. Remove any air bubbles and add additional mixture if necessary, keeping the 1¼ inches of headspace.

5. Wipe the rim of each jar with a warm washcloth dipped in distilled white vinegar. Place a lid and ring on each jar and hand tighten.

6. Place jars in the pressure canner, lock the pressure canner lid, and bring to a boil on high heat. Let the canner vent for 10 minutes. Close the vent and continue heating to achieve 11 PSI for a dial gauge and 10 PSI for a weighted gauge. Process quart jars for 1 hour 30 minutes and pint jars for 1 hour 15 minutes.

Ingredient Tip: If you are on a low-sodium diet, you may omit the salt pork or slab bacon and increase the andouille sausage by ½ pound. Also, if you are not using your own home-canned Chicken Stock (page 98), feel free to use store-bought low-sodium chicken stock to further reduce the sodium in this recipe.

WHITE BEAN RAGOUT

MAKES APPROXIMATELY 6 QUARTS OR 12 PINTS

PREP: 1 HR 10 MIN • COOK: 15 MIN • CANNER: 1 HR • PROCESSING: 1 HR 30 MIN/1 HR 15 MIN

TOTAL: 3 HR 55 MIN/3 HR 40 MIN

Pronounced *ra-GOO*, the word is a derivative of the French verb *ragoûter*, meaning "to stimulate the appetite." Ragout is a thick and rich French-style stew often made with meat or fish and vegetables, or even just vegetables. White Bean Ragout replaces meat or fish with a legume so you still have the benefits of protein. Eat ragout on its own, or with a starch like couscous or pasta, or on a crusty slice of bread.

2½ cups dried cannellini beans

4 medium white onions, chopped (2 cups)

6 garlic cloves, minced

¼ cup olive oil

1 teaspoon coarse sea salt

½ teaspoon ground black pepper

8 cups Chicken Broth (page 104) or Vegetable Broth (page 105)

3 pints cherry tomatoes, halved

1 tablespoon balsamic vinegar

¼ cup chopped fresh basil

1. Thoroughly rinse and clean the dried beans, discarding any disfigured or shriveled beans and any rocks or debris. Add the cleaned dried beans to a stockpot and cover with 2 inches of water. Bring to a boil over medium-high heat, then reduce the heat, cover and simmer on low for 1 hour. Set aside 1 cup bean cooking liquid. Drain the beans in a colander in the sink.

2. In a stainless steel stockpot, combine the onions, garlic, oil, salt, and pepper. Cook over medium-high heat until the onions are translucent, about 8 to 10 minutes. Add the broth and bring to a boil.

3. Add the drained beans, reserved bean cooking liquid, cherry tomato halves, vinegar, and fresh basil to the stockpot and mix well. Return to a boil, then reduce the heat and simmer for 5 minutes.

4. Ladle hot ragout into hot jars, leaving 1 inch of headspace. Be sure to obtain a good ratio of tomatoes, beans, onions, and liquid in each jar. Remove any air bubbles and add additional liquid if necessary, to maintain the 1 inch of headspace.

5. Wipe the rim of each jar with a warm wash-cloth dipped in distilled white vinegar. Place a lid and ring on each jar and hand tighten.

6. Place jars in the pressure canner, lock the pressure canner lid, and bring to a boil on high heat. Let the canner vent for 10 minutes. Close the vent and continue heating to achieve 11 PSI for a dial gauge and 10 PSI for a weighted gauge. Process quart jars for 1 hour 30 minutes and pint jars for 1 hour 15 minutes.

Serving Recipe Tip: Serve a quart of White Bean Ragout alongside Pan-Seared Sea Bass: Preheat the oven to 400° F. Brush 4 sea bass fillets with olive oil and season with salt and pepper. Using an oven-friendly sauté pan, heat 1 tablespoon olive oil over high heat. Sauté the sea bass, skin-side down, for 2 minutes. Transfer the sauté pan to the oven and bake until done, about 5 to 6 minutes. Do not turn the fish to ensure a crispy skin.

LENTIL SAUSAGE CASSEROLE

MAKES APPROXIMATELY 4 QUARTS OR 8 PINTS

PREP: 15 MIN • COOK: 10 MIN • CANNER: 1 HR • PROCESSING: 1 HR 30 MIN/1 HR 15 MIN

TOTAL: 4 HR 10 MIN/3 HR 55 MIN

Lentils and sausage in a jar is the perfect combination to create a casserole-like consistency. While the lentils naturally swell and thicken, the bacon, sausage, and vegetables create a hearty filling. Want to try a quick version of cassoulet? Pour a quart or two in a cast iron skillet, cover with 4 cups buttery breadcrumbs, top with fresh parsley and chives, and bake at 375°F for 30 minutes.

2 cups dried green lentils

3 tablespoons olive oil

1 pound thick cut bacon, cut into 2-inch-thick strips

12 ounces good-quality kielbasa sausage, cut on a diagonal into ½-inch-thick slices

1 cup finely diced onion

4 large garlic cloves, minced

1 teaspoon coarse sea salt

½ teaspoon ground black pepper

12 cups Beef Broth (page 103)

3 large carrots, peeled and cut into 1-inch dice (1½ cups)

2 celery stalks, diced (1 cup)

2 teaspoons chopped fresh sage

2 teaspoons chopped fresh thyme

½ teaspoon cayenne pepper

1 bay leaf

4 cups chopped fresh spinach

1. Place ¼ cup dried green lentils into each quart and 1½ tablespoons into each pint.

2. In a stockpot, combine the oil, bacon, kielbasa, onion, garlic, salt, and pepper. Cook over medium-heat for 8 to 10 minutes or until the onions are translucent, the bacon is slightly crisp, and the sausage is lightly browned.

3. Add the Beef Broth, carrots, celery, sage, thyme, cayenne, and bay leaf. Bring to a boil, mixing well. Reduce the heat and simmer for 5 minutes. Add the chopped spinach, mix well, then remove from the heat. Remove and discard the bay leaf.

4. Using a slotted spoon, fill each jar half full of the sausage-and-vegetable mixture, doing your best to balance out the ratio of sausage and vegetables in each jar. Once evenly distributed, ladle enough hot broth into each jar to cover the solids, leaving 1 inch of headspace. Remove any air bubbles and add additional broth if necessary to maintain the 1 inch of headspace.

5. Wipe the rim of each jar with a warm washcloth dipped in distilled white vinegar. Place a lid and ring on each jar and hand tighten.

6. Place jars in the pressure canner, lock the pressure canner lid, and bring to a boil on high heat. Let the canner vent for 10 minutes. Close the vent and continue heating to achieve 11 PSI for a dial gauge and 10 PSI for a weighted gauge. Process quart jars for 1 hour 30 minutes and pint jars for 1 hour 15 minutes.

Ingredient Tip: While spinach works wonderfully in this recipe, feel free to explore options by replacing spinach with kale, Swiss chard, or turnip greens. With larger greens like these, be sure to remove the stems and large veins before you chop them and add to the pot.

CHICKEN WITH RED BEANS AND RUM

MAKES APPROXIMATELY 4 QUARTS OR 8 PINTS

PREP: 1 HR 15 MIN • COOK: 25 MIN • CANNER: 1 HR • PROCESSING: 1 HR 30 MIN/1 HR 15 MIN

TOTAL: 4 HR 10 MIN/3 HR 55 MIN

A hearty protein-packed meal or side awaits in every jar. Deep, rich flavors and gorgeous colors are just a couple of its many features. I am proud to say my friend Jeff discovered this little gem when he and I were recipe testing together. The secret is the amber rum, not spiced and not clear. After you discover this dish, I am sure you will find more fun ways to incorporate rum in your cooking.

3 cups dried red beans (16 ounces)

3 tablespoons extra-virgin olive oil

10 boneless, skinless chicken thighs, cut in ½-inch cubes (6 cups)

2 dashes coarse sea salt

2 dashes ground black pepper

4 celery stalks, chopped (2 cups)

1 large red bell pepper, cut into ½-inch dice (1 cup)

1 medium onion, finely diced (½ cup)

1 apple, peeled, cored, and finely diced

3 garlic cloves, minced

1 tablespoon dried sage

1 tablespoon dried thyme

1 tablespoon dried parsley

1 teaspoon coarse sea salt

⅛ teaspoon cayenne pepper

8 cups Chicken Stock (page 98)

1 cup amber rum, not spiced

2 bay leaves

1. Thoroughly rinse and clean the dried beans, discarding any disfigured or shriveled beans and any rocks or debris. Add the cleaned dried beans to a stockpot and enough water to cover by 2 inches. Bring to a boil over medium-high heat, then reduce the heat, cover, and simmer on low for 1 hour. Set aside 1 cup bean cooking liquid. Drain the beans in a colander in the sink.

2. In a thick-bottomed stockpot, heat the oil over medium-high heat. Add the chicken thighs, season with a dash sea salt and pepper, and cook for 5 minutes, or until the chicken is cooked through. Remove the chicken to a bowl and set aside.

3. Add the celery, bell pepper, onion, apple, garlic, sage, thyme, parsley, sea salt, and cayenne to the stockpot. Mix well and cook for 5 to 8 minutes, or until the onion is translucent.

4. Add the Chicken Stock, reserved bean cooking liquid, rum, and bay leaves and mix well. Bring to a boil, then reduce the heat and simmer for 10 minutes. Add the chicken and any drippings from the bowl to the stockpot and simmer for an additional 2 minutes, stirring often. Add the drained red beans and cook for an additional 3 minutes. Remove from the heat. Remove the bay leaves and discard.

5. Using a slotted spoon, fill each jar three-quarters full of chicken-bean mixture. Once evenly distributed, ladle enough hot broth into each jar to cover the chicken-bean mixture, leaving 1 inch of headspace. Remove any air bubbles and add additional broth if necessary to maintain the 1 inch of headspace.

6. Wipe the rim of each jar with a warm washcloth dipped in distilled white vinegar. Place a lid and ring on each jar and hand tighten.

7. Place jars in the pressure canner, lock the pressure canner lid, and bring to a boil on high heat. Let the canner vent for 10 minutes. Close the vent and continue heating to achieve 11 PSI for a dial gauge and 10 PSI for a weighted gauge. Process quart jars for 1 hour 30 minutes and pint jars for 1 hour 15 minutes.

Serving Tip: This dish purposely runs a bit thin, so you may have a variety of options when it comes to serving. Keep it thin and serve it with noodles, couscous, or rice. Prefer a thicker version on garlic mashed potatoes? While heating on the stove top, whisk 1 to 2 teaspoons ClearJel® into a pint and 1 to 1½ tablespoons into a quart. Upon cooling, this dish will thicken.

CHAPTER SIX

STOCKS, BROTHS, SOUPS, AND STEWS

SOUPS AND STEWS ARE some of my favorite recipes to pressure can. They can be made in bulk, they're full of vegetables and protein and lots of nutrients, and they can be reheated whenever you need a quick meal. Home-canned stocks and broths are much lower in salt and more healthful than most store-bought brands. Keep a few quarts on hand, and you can make your own favorite soups and stews whenever the urge strikes—or you can try some of mine, like Enchilada Chicken Soup (page 107), Irish Stout Beef Stew (page 122), Sausage and Bean Soup (page 116), and Sun-Dried Tomato Soup (page 125).

The Difference Between Stock and Broth

Broths and stocks are mainstays in our kitchens, as they are the foundation for so many recipes, especially soups and stews. Understanding their differences and similarities will help you decide which is best to use in a particular recipe, and when it makes more sense to buy instead of make from scratch. While the terms *stock* and *broth* are often used interchangeably, within the culinary world there is a distinct difference.

STOCK

Stock is the key player in many classic cuisines and is the base on which almost every sauce and stew is created. Stocks are rich in flavor and are used to enhance the natural juices of beef, chicken, pork, and fish dishes. The depth and flavor profile of a stock is achieved by using roasted bones, mirepoix (onions, carrots, and celery), aromatic vegetables, and seasonings like garlic and fresh herbs. What sets stock apart from broth is the roasting and lengthy simmering of bones. It is the bone marrow and collagen that give stock its distinct flavor and a gel-like consistency. This body and depth infuses every recipe that uses stock. And, for the record, "bone broth" is actually stock.

BROTH

Broth has a broader use than stock does in the home kitchen; you will find it called for in many side dishes like rice, couscous, mashed potatoes, stuffings, as well as thinner soups. Broth can also replace water in many savory recipes. Although you do use meat and bones to create broth, they are not roasted; they are just added raw to the stockpot and simmered with fresh herbs, mirepoix, and water.

WHICH SHOULD I USE?

There is no wrong use of either stock or broth. However, your choice may come down to cost, time, and availability. For this chapter, I created a variety of soups and stew recipes you may preserve to enjoy at a later date. You will notice when I want a thicker stew or soup base, or I use a seared meat, the recipe calls for stock. When I want to add flavor to a dish that uses beans or a starch as a thickener, the recipe calls for broth.

If any recipe calls for stock and you only have broth on hand, use it. The recipe will still taste delicious! Where you can noticeably tell a difference in flavor is when you use plain water instead of a stock or broth. The depth and body of the overall recipe depends on the use of stock or broth, unless, of course, the ingredients make their own broth while they cook. In that case, just adding water makes sense.

Saving Scraps

We are all familiar with the saying, *waste not, want not*, however not every kitchen scrap should be used when making broth or stock. While we are told there are many benefits to using the scraps from meal preparation, we are not always told what to save or how. This section gives you the basics so you may save more and spend less when making broths and stocks.

Regardless of what is saved, be sure EVERYTHING is properly cleaned prior to slicing, cutting, peeling and trimming. No one wants grit or dirt in their food.

VEGETABLE AND HERB SCRAPS

In a gallon freezer bag, feel free to save the following:

- Onion and scallion ends and peels
- Leek and fennel tops and ends
- Carrot ends, greens and skin peels
- Celery ends

- Beet greens
- Wilted parsley, basil, and oregano

Flatten the freezer bag prior to placing in the freezer. This allows you to stack your bags during storage and gives you more freezer space.

MEAT BONES AND CARCASSES

When cleaning a whole chicken, collect the neck bones in a separate freezer bag. After roasting a whole chicken or any bone-in meat like ham, beef, or lamb, wrap the bones or carcass in freezer paper, place inside a large freezer bag and store in the freezer.

Here are the various types of bones used to make stock:

- Ribs with some meat
- Shank
- Oxtail
- Knuckle bones
- Neck bones
- Marrowbones like femur bones

If you purchase stock bones from the butcher, be sure to have him cut larger bones into usable sizes. A good butcher is a great guide.

SHELLFISH AND FISH

Store shrimp, crab, and lobster shells in a freezer bag to use when making Shellfish Stock (page 102). When storing fish parts for Fish Stock (page 95), save the fish heads, spines, ribs, and tails of mild, nonoily, white-fleshed fish. Snapper, tilefish, halibut, and cod are common fish options. If you use parts from an oily fish like salmon, bluefish, or steelhead trout, please know the Fish Stock will have a strong fishy flavor, which is fine if that is what you want to achieve.

WHAT NOT TO SAVE FOR BROTH AND STOCK

Do not save any guts or organs from the meat or fish. Drain excess blood when cleaning a fresh kill. See page 147 for information about preparing wild game for cooking and preserving.

Do not save potato scraps, beet roots, broccoli, cabbage, asparagus, or kale. The pungent nature of cabbage and asparagus will give an overpowering flavor to the entire recipe, while the broccoli and kale will make your broth bitter. Potato scraps will overpower the broth with starch, and beets will alter the broth's overall color and possibly change the flavor, making it sweeter.

Vital Steps for Making Stock

Because we are using bones from lamb, beef, chicken, pork, veal, and fish to create various stocks in this chapter, you first must follow these vital steps to ensure the bones have been properly prepared to yield the best results.

1. **Roasting and Sweating.** While it sounds like a workout, this crucial step holds all the cards with respect to flavor. Roast bones of chicken, lamb, beef, veal, and pork as well as shellfish shells in an oven until deeply browned but not burnt. Fish heads and bones are gently cooked in a covered pot (a process known as sweating) prior to simmering as follows: Make a thin layer of mirepoix and herbs in a pot, add the fish heads and bones, pour in some dry white wine, and then cover the pot with a lid. Cook gently over medium heat in a covered pot until the flesh clinging to the bones becomes opaque before adding water to simmer.

2. **Time.** With the exception of Fish Stock, do not rush the simmering process. Many chefs leave their stocks to simmer on low overnight for 8 to 12 hours before straining. While my stock recipes state to simmer for 6 hours, feel free to simmer for several hours longer.

3. **Do Not Disturb.** The key to making the best stock is to rarely if ever interrupt the stock while it is simmering on the stove top. Removing foam and debris at the surface is acceptable, however with the exception of a few initial and concluding stirs, leave your stock uninterrupted. Doing so allows us to extract as many nutrients and important collagen from the bones as possible.

4. **The Strain.** Some chefs go to the extreme, straining their stock upwards of 40 times to obtain the "perfect" stock free of any debris. To me, that level of straining is a real strain on my patience, and, while I give kudos to them, I am content with minute debris. At minimum, strain your stock at least once prior to filling your jars, however, you may restrain and strain again as many times as your heart desires.

FISH STOCK

MAKES APPROXIMATELY 8 PINTS

PREP: 10 MIN • COOK: 1 HR • CANNER: 1 HR • PROCESSING: 1 HR 10 MIN • TOTAL: 3 HR 20 MIN

Use this stock to create the perfect base for clam chowder or seafood stew. It's a wonderful addition to seafood risotto and shrimp and fish étouffée—essentially any dish calling for seafood.

¼ cup olive oil

4 medium onions, diced (2 cups)

6 garlic cloves, smashed

8 celery stalks, chopped (4 cups)

8 large carrots, peeled and finely diced (4 cups)

1 bunch fresh thyme

½ bunch fresh parsley

8 pounds fish bones, heads, fins, ribs, and tails

1 cup dry white wine

16 cups boiling water

2 bay leaves

1 tablespoon whole peppercorns

1. In a 12- or 16-quart stockpot, add the oil, onions, garlic, celery, carrots, thyme, and parsley. On medium-high heat, sauté until the onions are translucent, about 5 to 8 minutes. Cover the bottom of the stockpot evenly with the mixture.

2. Cover the onion mixture in the stockpot with the fish parts. Pour in the wine, cover the pot with a lid and let the fish bones sweat for 20 minutes.

3. Add the boiling water, bay leaves, and peppercorns and return to a boil using high heat. Reduce the heat and simmer, uncovered, for 30 minutes.

4. Throughout the simmering process, skim off foam and discard. Do not disturb the stock.

5. Using a slotted spoon, remove the fish parts, vegetables, and herbs from the stockpot and discard. Pour the stock through a fine-mesh chinois strainer or sieve, capturing the strained stock in a large, clean stockpot.

6. Line a strainer with dampened cheesecloth, and strain again, slowly, capturing the strained stock in a large, clean pot.

7. Ladle the hot strained stock into hot jars, leaving 1 inch of headspace.

8. Wipe the rim of each jar with a warm washcloth dipped in distilled white vinegar. Place a lid and ring on each jar and hand tighten.

9. Place jars in the pressure canner, lock the pressure canner lid, and bring to a boil on high heat. Let the canner vent for 10 minutes. Close the vent and continue heating to achieve 11 PSI for a dial gauge and 10 PSI for a weighted gauge. Process pints for 1 hour 10 minutes.

BEEF BONE STOCK

MAKES APPROXIMATELY 7 QUARTS OR 14 PINTS

PREP: 10 MIN • COOK: 6 HR 35 MIN • CANNER: 1 HR • PROCESSING: 25 MIN/20 MIN

TOTAL: 8 HR 10 MIN/8 HR 5 MIN

This nutrient-packed stock is a staple in my pantry. I use this stock as a base for many hearty dishes like Beef Stew (page 110), open-face beef sandwiches, gravies, and more. Because of its nutrient content, heating a small bowl of bone stock helps settle a sour stomach and gives sustenance when ill.

2 bone-in beef short ribs (1½ pounds)

2 beef shanks or 3 oxtails (3 pounds)

4 beef knuckles or femur marrowbones (2½ pounds)

2 to 3 neck bones (2 pounds)

1 teaspoon coarse sea salt

½ teaspoon fresh cracked black pepper

4 tablespoons extra-virgin olive oil, divided

¾ cup tomato paste (6 ounces)

5 carrots, peeled and coarsely chopped

4 celery stalks, coarsely chopped

3 yellow onions, peeled and quartered

2 heads garlic, excess exterior skins removed, tops chopped off to expose the cloves

2 bay leaves

1 bunch fresh flat-leaf parsley

½ bunch fresh thyme

4 sprigs oregano

1 tablespoon whole black peppercorns

4 gallons cold water (64 cups)

1. Preheat the oven to 450°F.

2. Place the beef short ribs, shanks or oxtails, knuckles or marrowbones, and neck bones in a large roasting pan. Sprinkle the bones with salt and black pepper. Drizzle with 2 tablespoons olive oil. Flip the bones over in the pan. Using a butter knife, coat the beef bones evenly with tomato paste. Drizzle the remaining olive oil over the coated bones. Roast the bones for 30 minutes or until they are deep brown but not scorched or burned.

3. In a 16- to 20-quart stockpot, add the roasted bones and all the drippings from the roasting pan. Use ¼ cup warm water and a metal spatula to remove any baked-on drippings and scrape into the stockpot. Add the carrots, celery, onions, garlic heads, bay leaves, parsley, thyme, oregano, and peppercorns. Mix well to distribute flavors throughout the pot.

4. Cover contents of the stockpot with the cold water. Starting on medium heat, bring the stock to a boil. Increase the heat to medium-high and gently boil for 5 minutes. Reduce the heat and simmer, undisturbed and uncovered, for 6 hours. (You may simmer stock for upwards of 12 hours, but please be sure to not leave your stove unattended during simmering.)

5. Throughout the simmering process, skim off foam and discard. Do not disturb the stock.

6. Using a slotted spoon, remove the bones, meat, vegetables, and herbs from the stockpot. The meat may be used to make soup or stew, but discard the bones, vegetables, and herbs. Strain the stock through a fine-mesh chinois strainer or sieve, capturing the strained stock in a large, clean stockpot.

7. Ladle the hot, strained stock into hot jars, leaving 1 inch of headspace.

8. Wipe the rim of each jar with a warm washcloth dipped in distilled white vinegar. Place a lid and ring on each jar and hand tighten.

9. Place jars in the pressure canner, lock the pressure canner lid, and bring to a boil on high heat. Let the canner vent for 10 minutes. Close the vent and continue heating to achieve 11 PSI for a dial gauge and 10 PSI for a weighted gauge. Process quart jars for 25 minutes and pint jars for 20 minutes.

Ingredient Tip: Bone "broth" stock is not just for beef bones. Substitute pork, lamb, or veal bones using the same weights and types. Be sure to label your jar lids with the appropriate type of bone broth as they will likely look the same after processing.

CHICKEN STOCK

MAKES APPROXIMATELY 7 QUARTS OR 14 PINTS
PREP: 10 MIN • COOK: 6 HR 35 MIN • CANNER: 1 HR • PROCESSING: 25 MIN/20 MIN
TOTAL: 8 HR 10 MIN/8 HR 5 MIN

I use this stock, another kitchen staple, to enhance the flavor of poultry dishes and as a base for soups. The natural sediment you see in each jar is a testament to this stock's hearty nature.

4 to 6 pounds chicken carcass, including 1 to 2 necks, if available

4 yellow onions, peeled and halved, divided

2 heads garlic, excess exterior skins removed, tops chopped off to expose the cloves, divided

1 bunch fresh thyme, divided

½ lemon

2 teaspoons coarse sea salt, divided (optional)

2 tablespoons olive oil

5 carrots, peeled and coarsely chopped

4 celery stalks, coarsely chopped

2 bay leaves

1 bunch fresh flat-leaf parsley

4 sprigs oregano

1 tablespoon black peppercorns

4 gallons cold water (64 cups)

1. Preheat the oven to 400°F.

2. Place the chicken carcass in the center of a large roasting pan. Place 4 onion halves, 1 head of garlic, and half the fresh thyme inside the carcass. Squeeze the juice from the lemon over the carcass and place the lemon inside the carcass with the onions and thyme. Sprinkle the carcass with half the sea salt and drizzle the olive oil over the carcass. Roast the carcass in the oven for 30 minutes or until the carcass has browned.

3. In a 16- to 20-quart stockpot, combine the roasted carcass, the contents from its interior, and all the drippings from the roasting pan. Use ¼ cup warm water and a metal spatula to remove any baked-on drippings and scrape into the stockpot. Add the remaining onions and garlic head, with the carrots, celery, bay leaves, parsley, oregano, and peppercorns.

4. Cover the contents of the stockpot with the cold water. Starting on medium heat, bring the stock to a boil. Increase to medium-high heat and gently boil for 5 minutes. Reduce the heat and simmer, undisturbed and uncovered, for 6 hours. (Please be sure to not leave your stove unattended during simmering.)

5. Throughout the simmering process, skim off foam and discard. Do not disturb the stock.

6. Using a slotted spoon, remove the carcass, vegetables, and herbs from the stockpot and discard. Pour the stock through a fine-mesh chinois strainer or sieve, capturing the strained stock in a large, clean stockpot.

7. Ladle the hot strained stock into hot jars, leaving 1 inch of headspace.

8. Wipe the rim of each jar with a warm wash-cloth dipped in distilled white vinegar. Place a lid and ring on each jar and hand tighten.

9. Place jars in the pressure canner, lock the pressure canner lid, and bring to a boil on high heat. Let the canner vent for 10 min-utes. Close the vent and continue heating to achieve 11 PSI for a dial gauge and 10 PSI for a weighted gauge. Process quart jars for 25 min-utes and pint jars for 20 minutes.

Ingredient Tip: While Chicken Stock is the most prevalently used stock, feel free to substitute a turkey carcass, especially if you have one frozen after a holiday meal.

ROASTED VEGETABLE STOCK

MAKES APPROXIMATELY 5 QUARTS OR 10 PINTS
PREP: 10 MIN • COOK: 2 HR 35 MIN • CANNER: 1 HR • PROCESSING: 25 MIN/20 MIN
TOTAL: 4 HR 10 MIN/3 HR 55 MIN

The flavor from the roasted vegetables sets this stock apart from standard vegetable broth. The roasted vegetables add a beautiful flavor to meals, soups, stews, and sides.

3 large yellow onions, quartered

5 carrots, peeled and coarsely chopped

4 celery stalks, coarsely chopped

2 heads garlic, excess exterior skins removed, tops chopped off to expose the cloves

8 large white mushrooms, halved (optional)

6 medium tomatoes, halved

1 teaspoon coarse sea salt (optional)

¼ cup olive oil

3 cups dry white wine

18 cups water

½ bunch parsley

4 sprigs oregano

2 bay leaves

1 tablespoon whole peppercorns

1. Preheat the oven to 400°F.

2. In a deep roasting pan, add the onions, carrots, celery, garlic heads, mushrooms (if using), and tomatoes. Sprinkle with salt (if using) and drizzle with olive oil, tossing to coat well. Roast in the oven for 30 minutes or until the vegetables are browned but not burned.

3. In a 12- to 16-quart stockpot, combine the roasted vegetables and all the drippings from the roasting pan. Use ¼ cup warm water and a metal spatula to remove any baked-on drippings and scrape into the stockpot. Add the wine and bring to a boil on medium-high heat.

4. Add the water, parsley, oregano, bay leaves, and peppercorns, and return to a boil. Boil gently for 5 minutes, then reduce the heat and simmer, undisturbed and uncovered, for 2 hours. Please be sure to not leave your stove unattended during simmering.

5. Throughout the simmering process, skim off foam and discard. Do not disturb the stock.

6. Using a slotted spoon, remove the vegetables and herbs from the stockpot and discard. Pour the stock through a fine-mesh chinois strainer or sieve, capturing the strained stock in a large, clean stockpot.

7. Ladle the hot strained stock into hot jars, leaving 1 inch of headspace.

8. Wipe the rim of each jar with a warm washcloth dipped in distilled white vinegar. Place a lid and ring on each jar and hand tighten.

9. Place jars in the pressure canner, lock the pressure canner lid, and bring to a boil on high heat. Let the canner vent for 10 minutes. Close the vent and continue heating to achieve 11 PSI for a dial gauge and 10 PSI for a weighted gauge. Process quart jars for 25 minutes and pint jars for 20 minutes.

Ingredient Tip: The beauty of vegetable stock is you may control the types of vegetables used as they are what dictate the overall flavor. If you wanted to roast squash and beets with the above ingredients, then add 6 whole cloves to the stockpot when simmering; the color and flavor of the Roasted Vegetable Stock will take on a deeper color and flavor. Just be sure the adaptations do not drastically alter the finished product in which the stock is being used, unless that is the intention.

SHELLFISH STOCK

MAKES APPROXIMATELY 8 PINTS

PREP: 10 MIN • COOK: 1 HR 5 MIN • CANNER: 1 HR • PROCESSING: 1 HR 10 MIN • TOTAL: 3 HR 25 MIN

Use this delicious stock to make seafood gumbos, mussels, and seafood stew. It's an excellent way to reuse shells from a scrumptious shrimp and crab dinner so they may create a flavorful base for any seafood meal.

6 cups shrimp, lobster and crab shells

3 tablespoons olive oil

16 cups boiling water

4 medium onions, diced (2 cups)

8 celery stalks, finely chopped (4 cups)

8 large carrots, finely diced (4 cups)

6 garlic cloves, smashed

1 bunch fresh thyme

½ bunch fresh parsley

½ cup dry white wine

3 tablespoons tomato paste

2 bay leaves

1 tablespoon whole peppercorns

1. Preheat the oven to 400°F.

2. In a roasting pan or rimmed cookie sheet, add the seafood shells and drizzle with the oil. Roast in the oven for 10 minutes.

3. In a 12-quart stockpot add the roasted shells and cover with the boiling water. On medium-high heat, bring to a gentle boil, then reduce the heat and simmer for 20 minutes.

4. Add the onions, celery, carrots, garlic, thyme, parsley, wine, tomato paste, bay leaves, and peppercorns and return to a gentle boil for 5 minutes, then reduce the heat and simmer, undisturbed and uncovered, for 30 minutes. (Please be sure to not leave your stove unattended during simmering.)

5. Throughout the simmering process, skim off foam and discard. Do not disturb the stock.

6. Using a slotted spoon, remove the shells, vegetables, and herbs from the stockpot and discard. Pour the stock through a fine-mesh chinois strainer or sieve, capturing the strained stock in a large, clean stockpot.

7. Line a strainer with dampened cheesecloth and strain again, slowly, capturing the strained stock in a large, clean pot.

8. Ladle the hot strained stock into hot jars, leaving 1 inch of headspace.

9. Wipe the rim of each jar with a warm washcloth dipped in distilled white vinegar. Place a lid and ring on each jar and hand tighten.

10. Place jars in the pressure canner, lock the pressure canner lid, and bring to a boil on high heat. Let the canner vent for 10 minutes. Close the vent and continue heating to achieve 11 PSI for a dial gauge and 10 PSI for a weighted gauge. Process pints for 1 hour 10 minutes.

BEEF BROTH

MAKES APPROXIMATELY 7 QUARTS OR 14 PINTS
PREP: 10 MIN • COOK: 1 HR 5 MIN • CANNER: 1 HR • PROCESSING: 25 MIN/20 MIN
TOTAL: 2 HR 40 MIN/2 HR 25 MIN

Having Beef Broth on hand is perfect when making side dishes, lentil soup, or even a quick stove-top French onion soup. Use Beef Broth to replace water in any beef recipe to enhance the beef flavor.

2 bone-in beef short ribs (1½ pounds)

4 femur bones, cut (2 pounds)

5 carrots, peeled and coarsely chopped

4 celery stalks, coarsely chopped

3 yellow onions, quartered

2 heads garlic, excess exterior skins removed, tops chopped off to expose the cloves

2 bay leaves

1 bunch fresh flat-leaf parsley

½ bunch fresh thyme

4 sprigs oregano

1 tablespoon black peppercorns

4 gallons cold water (64 cups)

1. In a 16- to 20-quart stockpot, combine the beef bones, carrots, celery, onions, garlic heads, bay leaves, parsley, thyme, oregano, and peppercorns. Mix well to distribute flavors throughout the pot.

2. Cover the contents of the stockpot with the cold water. Starting on medium heat, bring to a boil. Increase to medium-high heat and gently boil for 5 minutes. Reduce the heat and simmer, undisturbed and uncovered, for 1 hour.

3. Throughout the simmering process, skim off foam and discard. Do not disturb the stock.

4. Using a slotted spoon, remove the bones, meat, vegetables, and herbs from the stockpot. The meat may be used to make soup or stew, but discard the bones, vegetables, and herbs. Pour the broth through a fine-mesh chinois strainer or sieve, capturing the strained broth in a large, clean stockpot.

5. Ladle the hot strained broth into hot jars, leaving 1 inch of headspace.

6. Wipe the rim of each jar with a warm washcloth dipped in distilled white vinegar. Place a lid and ring on each jar and hand tighten.

7. Place jars in the pressure canner, lock the pressure canner lid, and bring to a boil on high heat. Let the canner vent for 10 minutes. Close the vent and continue heating to achieve 11 PSI for a dial gauge and 10 PSI for a weighted gauge. Process quart jars for 25 minutes and pint jars for 20 minutes.

Ingredient Tip: Substitute pork, lamb, or veal bones using the same weights and types. Be sure to label your jar lids with the appropriate type of broth inside, as they will likely look the same after processing.

CHICKEN BROTH

MAKES APPROXIMATELY 7 QUARTS OR 14 PINTS

PREP: 10 MIN • COOK: 1 HR 5 MIN • CANNER: 1 HR • PROCESSING: 25 MIN/20 MIN

TOTAL: 2 HR 40 MIN/2 HR 25 MIN

Chicken Broth is another staple in my kitchen. I replace water with chicken broth when making rice or risotto, soups, and gravies, and I also keep a jar or two handy in the event I need to make a quick batch of soup.

1 whole chicken cut into pieces, skin on (2 to 4 pounds)

5 carrots, peeled and coarsely chopped

4 celery stalks, coarsely chopped

4 yellow onions, peeled and quartered

2 heads garlic, excess exterior skins removed, tops chopped off to expose the cloves

1 bunch fresh flat-leaf parsley

1 bunch fresh thyme

4 sprigs oregano

1 tablespoon black peppercorns

2 teaspoons coarse sea salt, halved (optional)

2 bay leaves

4 gallons cold water (64 cups)

1. In a 16- to 20-quart stockpot, combine the chicken pieces, carrots, celery, onions, garlic, parsley, thyme, oregano, peppercorns, salt, and bay leaves. Mix well to distribute ingredients.

2. Cover the contents of the stockpot with the cold water. Starting on medium heat, bring to a boil. Increase to medium-high heat and gently boil for 5 minutes. Reduce the heat and simmer, undisturbed and uncovered, for 1 hour.

3. Throughout the simmering process, skim off foam and discard. Do not disturb the stock.

4. Using a slotted spoon, remove the meat, vegetables, and herbs from the stockpot. The meat may be used to make soup or stew, but discard the bones, vegetables, and herbs. Pour the broth through a fine-mesh chinois strainer or sieve, capturing the strained broth in a large, clean stockpot.

5. Ladle the hot strained broth into hot jars, leaving 1 inch of headspace.

6. Wipe the rim of each jar with a warm washcloth dipped in distilled white vinegar. Place a lid and ring on each jar and hand tighten.

7. Place jars in the pressure canner, lock the pressure canner lid, and bring to a boil on high heat. Let the canner vent for 10 minutes. Close the vent and continue heating to achieve 11 PSI for a dial gauge and 10 PSI for a weighted gauge. Process quart jars for 25 minutes and pint jars for 20 minutes.

Ingredient Tip: While chicken is the poultry most prevalently used for this broth, feel free to substitute a whole turkey, pheasant, or two male Cornish game hens. If you are pinched for time, you may also make Chicken Broth using 4 large chicken breasts with rib meat. Keep the skin on regardless of the bird you choose.

VEGETABLE BROTH

MAKES APPROXIMATELY 5 QUARTS OR 10 PINTS
PREP: 10 MIN • COOK: 1 HR 5 MIN • CANNER: 1 HR • PROCESSING: 25 MIN/20 MIN
TOTAL: 2 HR 40 MIN/2 HR 25 MIN

If meat is not in your diet, having Vegetable Broth on hand is key to enhancing your dish's flavor. Replace water with Vegetable Broth when making side dishes and use Vegetable Broth as the base for vegetable soups.

18 cups water

3 cups dry white wine

3 large yellow onions, quartered

6 tomatoes, halved

5 carrots, peeled and coarsely chopped

4 celery stalks, coarsely chopped

2 heads garlic, excess exterior skins removed, tops chopped off to expose the cloves

½ bunch parsley

4 sprigs oregano

2 bay leaves

1 tablespoon whole peppercorns

1 teaspoon coarse sea salt (optional)

1. In a 12- to 16-quart stockpot. combine the water, wine, onions, tomatoes, carrots, celery, garlic, parsley, oregano, bay leaves, peppercorns, and salt (if using). Mix well to evenly distribute ingredients. On medium-high heat, bring to a boil. Boil gently for 5 minutes, then reduce the heat and simmer, undisturbed and uncovered, for 1 hour.

2. Using a slotted spoon, remove the vegetables and herbs from the stockpot and discard. Pour the broth through a fine-mesh chinois strainer or sieve, capturing the strained broth in a large, clean stockpot.

3. Ladle the hot strained broth into hot jars, leaving 1 inch of headspace.

4. Wipe the rim of each jar with a warm washcloth dipped in distilled white vinegar. Place a lid and ring on each jar and hand tighten.

5. Place jars in the pressure canner, lock the pressure canner lid, and bring to a boil on high heat. Let the canner vent for 10 minutes. Close the vent and continue heating to achieve 11 PSI for a dial gauge and 10 PSI for a weighted gauge. Process quart jars for 25 minutes and pint jars for 20 minutes.

CHICKEN SOUP

MAKES APPROXIMATELY 8 QUARTS OR 16 PINTS
PREP: 20 MIN • COOK: 35 MIN • CANNER: 1 HR • PROCESSING: 1 HR 30 MIN/1 HR 15 MIN
TOTAL: 3 HR 25 MIN/3 HR 10 MIN

There's nothing better than having homemade soup gracing your pantry shelf—especially during the cold and flu season. My mom made this very soup for me when I was a kid and it worked like a charm every time. She called it Nature's Penicillin.

32 cups water

1 whole chicken cut in pieces, skin on

3 bay leaves

12 large carrots, peeled and chopped (6 cups)

6 medium Roma tomatoes, diced (3 cups)

4 celery stalks with the leaves, chopped (2 cups)

1½ large onions, diced (2 cups)

5 to 8 garlic cloves, peeled and finely chopped

1 tablespoon dried basil or 2 tablespoons finely chopped fresh basil

1 tablespoon coarse sea salt (optional)

2 teaspoons ground black pepper

1. Combine the water, chicken pieces, and bay leaves in a large stockpot and bring to a boil. Reduce the heat to medium and boil until the chicken is cooked through, approximately 30 minutes. Be sure to stir often to avoid scorching the chicken. Remove the chicken pieces and place on a cutting board to cool. Keep the broth at a simmer.

2. Remove all the skin and bones from the cooled chicken. Using either a knife or your fingers, cut or tear the chicken meat into bite-size pieces and return to the stockpot.

3. Add the carrots, tomatoes, celery, onions, garlic, basil, salt (if using), and pepper to the stockpot. Bring to a boil, and boil for 5 minutes. Remove and discard the bay leaves.

4. Using a slotted spoon, fill each jar three-quarters full with chicken and vegetables. Be sure to obtain a good ratio of chicken and vegetables in each jar. After the jars are filled three-quarters full, ladle the hot chicken broth over the mixture, leaving 1 inch of headspace. Tamp the mixture down using an air bubble remover tool and add additional broth if necessary to maintain the 1 inch of headspace.

5. Wipe the rim of each jar with a warm washcloth dipped in distilled white vinegar. Place a lid and ring on each jar and hand tighten.

6. Place jars in the pressure canner, lock the pressure canner lid, and bring to a boil on high heat. Let the canner vent for 10 minutes. Close the vent and continue heating to achieve 11 PSI for a dial gauge and 10 PSI for a weighted gauge. Process quart jars for 1 hour 30 minutes and pint jars for 1 hour 15 minutes.

Ingredient Tip: There will likely be leftover broth. Do NOT discard. Fill hot jars with remaining broth, leaving 1 inch of headspace. Process alongside jars of soup for the above specified time and PSI. After processing, the broth will be a deep, golden color.

ENCHILADA CHICKEN SOUP

MAKES APPROXIMATELY 9 QUARTS OR 18 PINTS
PREP: 10 MIN • COOK: 25 MIN • CANNER: 1 HR • PROCESSING: 1 HR 30 MIN/1 HR 15 MIN
TOTAL: 3 HR 5 MIN/2 HR 50 MIN

Use this hearty soup alongside any Mexican meal or as a stand-alone dish. Authentic flavors give this soup its traditional flair. To serve, top each bowl with thin tortilla strips, shredded cheese, a dollop of sour cream, and a dash (or two) of hot sauce.

6 chicken thighs, boneless and skinless

4 chicken breasts, boneless and skinless

16 medium Roma tomatoes, diced (8 cups)

6 cups Chicken Stock (page 98)

4 cups corn kernels, fresh or frozen

2½ cups dried black beans, sorted and rinsed (16 ounces)

2 cups water

1 cup canned diced mild green chiles (8 ounces)

3 medium carrots, peeled and chopped (1½ cups)

2 medium yellow onions, diced (1 cup)

6 garlic cloves, minced

2 tablespoons ground chili powder

1 tablespoon ground cumin

1 tablespoon coarse sea salt (optional)

1 teaspoon Spanish paprika

1 teaspoon dried oregano

2 dried whole cayenne peppers

1. In a small stockpot, combine the chicken and cover with 2 inches of water. Boil until cooked through, about 20 minutes. Set the hot chicken on the cutting board to cool. Discard the cooking liquid. Once the chicken has cooled, shred or cut it into bite-size pieces.

2. In a large stockpot, combine the tomatoes, Chicken Stock, corn, black beans, water, chiles, carrots, onions, garlic, chili powder, cumin, salt (if using), paprika, oregano, and dried cayenne peppers. Mix well and bring to a boil on medium-high heat. Reduce the heat and simmer for 5 minutes. Remove and discard the dried cayenne peppers.

3. Using a slotted spoon, fill hot jars three-quarters full with the chicken and vegetables. Next, ladle broth to cover, leaving a generous 1 inch of headspace. Remove any air bubbles and add additional liquid if necessary to maintain the headspace.

4. Wipe the rim of each jar with a warm washcloth dipped in distilled white vinegar. Place a lid and ring on each jar and hand tighten.

5. Place jars in the pressure canner, lock the pressure canner lid, and bring to a boil on high heat. Let the canner vent for 10 minutes. Close the vent and continue heating to achieve 11 PSI for a dial gauge and 10 PSI for a weighted gauge. Process quart jars for 1 hour 30 minutes and pint jars for 1 hour 15 minutes.

Ingredient Tip: Control the heat index of the soup by adding a milder (or hotter) dried pepper. Dried arbol and serrano peppers offer less heat than dried cayenne. Dried chipotle peppers are mild and have great flavor. Dried habanero and ghost peppers are the hottest on the heat index, so adding a fraction to the soup will yield very hot results.

BORSCHT

MAKES APPROXIMATELY 7 QUARTS OR 14 PINTS
PREP: 45 MIN • COOK: 15 MIN • PROCESSING: 1 HR 30 MIN/1 HR 15 MIN • TOTAL: 2 HR 15 MIN/2 HR 30 MIN

This soup is a fun spin on the Russian classic, boasting an earthy, sweet flavor, sure to please beet lovers. The key to achieving a balanced flavor is using cabernet sauvignon—any brand will do. Serve hot and add a touch of sour cream and garnish with a fresh sage leaf.

24 medium red beets (9½ pounds)

3 tablespoons extra-virgin olive oil

½ head red cabbage, thinly sliced

2 medium carrots, peeled and shredded

2 medium Roma tomatoes, diced (1 cup)

1 large sweet onion, chopped (1½ cups)

8 to 10 garlic cloves, peeled and chopped

8 cups Beef Bone Stock (page 96)

2 cups cabernet sauvignon

1 tablespoon raw sugar (optional)

1 tablespoon coarse sea salt (optional)

1 teaspoon ground black pepper

1. Beet Prep: Leave the roots on the beets and cut away the greens, leaving at least 2 inches of stem attached. Thoroughly wash the beets and place inside a stainless steel stockpot, with the largest beets on the bottom. Add enough water to cover the beets by 2 inches. Bring to a boil and cook for 30 minutes or until the largest beet is tender.

2. Using a slotted spoon or tongs, remove the beets from the boiling water and transfer them directly to a bowl of cold water resting in the sink. Keep the tap running to provide a steady stream of cold water to quickly cool the beets. One at a time, hold the beet in both hands under cool running water. Using your thumbs, gently rub and massage the beet, slipping the skin off each beet. Cut the root and stem off each beet with a paring knife. Chop the skinned beets into 2-inch pieces and set aside.

3. In a stainless steel stockpot, heat the olive oil over medium-high heat. Add the cabbage, carrots, tomatoes, onion, and garlic and sauté, until the onions become translucent, about 8 to 10 minutes. Add the Beef Bone Stock and bring to a boil. Stir in the chopped beets and boil for an additional 2 minutes. Remove from the heat.

4. Working in batches, place the beet mixture in a food processor and pulse until it is a fine puréed texture. Place the puréed mixture in a clean stainless steel stockpot. Add the wine, sugar (if using), salt (if using), and pepper and mix well. On medium heat, while stirring frequently, allow the Borscht to gently heat through, about 5 minutes. Stir constantly to avoid scorching.

5. Ladle the hot soup into hot jars, leaving a generous 1 inch of headspace. Remove any air bubbles and add additional soup if necessary to maintain the headspace.

6. Wipe the rim of each jar with a warm washcloth dipped in distilled white vinegar. Place a lid and ring on each jar and hand tighten.

7. Place jars in the pressure canner, lock the pressure canner lid, and bring to a boil on high heat. Let the canner vent for 10 minutes. Close the vent and continue heating to achieve 11 PSI for a dial gauge and 10 PSI for a weighted gauge. Process quart jars for 1 hour 30 minutes and pint jars for 1 hour 15 minutes.

Ingredient Tip: Each quart is roughly four 8-ounce servings, however depending on the size of the beets you are preparing and the consistency of the soup when you purée it, your yield may vary slightly. To avoid a drastic variance in yield, select like-size beets or count two smaller beets as equal to one larger-size beet.

BEEF STEW

MAKES APPROXIMATELY 7 QUARTS OR 14 PINTS

PREP: 30 MIN • COOK: 15 MIN • CANNER: 1 HR • PROCESSING: 1 HR 30 MIN/1 HR 15 MIN TOTAL: 3 HR 15 MIN/3 HR

We love having this versatile stew in our pantry year-round. I particularly crave it on cool, rainy days when comfort food is in order. Filled with a variety of vegetables, herbs, and beautiful cuts of meat, I enjoy it accompanied with freshly baked bread or served over egg noodles or garlic mashed potatoes.

2 tablespoons extra-virgin olive oil, divided

5 pounds stew beef, cut into bite-size pieces

10 cups potatoes, peeled and cubed

8 cups medium carrots, peeled and chopped

3 cups chopped onions

2 cups chopped celery

6 medium Roma tomatoes, diced (3 cups)

4½ teaspoons coarse sea salt (optional)

1 tablespoon dried parsley

1 tablespoon dried oregano

½ tablespoon celery seeds

1 teaspoon ground coriander

1 teaspoon dried thyme

1 teaspoon dried basil

½ teaspoon ground black pepper

8 cups Beef Broth (page 103)

5 cups water

1. In a thick-bottomed stockpot, heat 1 tablespoon oil and brown the beef in batches until all the beef is lightly browned, about 3 to 5 minutes per batch. Add 1 additional tablespoon of oil while browning each batch. Remove each batch from the stockpot and place in a bowl. Be sure not to fully cook the beef.

2. Return the browned beef to the stockpot and add the potatoes, carrots, onions, celery, tomatoes, salt (if using), parsley, oregano, celery seeds, coriander, thyme, basil, and pepper and mix well. Add the Beef Broth and water and mix well. Bring to a boil over medium-high heat, stirring frequently. Boil for 5 minutes then remove from the heat.

3. Ladle the hot stew into hot jars, leaving 1 inch of headspace. Remove any air bubbles and add additional stew if necessary to maintain the 1 inch of headspace.

4. Wipe the rim of each jar with a warm washcloth dipped in distilled white vinegar. Place a lid and ring on each jar and hand tighten.

5. Place jars in the pressure canner, lock the pressure canner lid, and bring to a boil on high heat. Let the canner vent for 10 minutes. Close the vent and continue heating to achieve 11 PSI for a dial gauge and 10 PSI for a weighted gauge. Process quart jars for 1 hour 30 minutes and pint jars for 1 hour 15 minutes.

Ingredient Tip: Using a pressure canner makes even the toughest cuts of meat tender and flavorful. Beef sold for stew typically comes from chuck or round roasts, cut into 1½-inch pieces. Bottom and eye cuts, also known as round, are typically leaner than a chuck roast, which are cuts from the shoulder, leg, and butt. When cutting into bite-size pieces, cut to a size you would feel comfortable seeing on the end of your fork or spoon.

CHICKEN CHOW MEIN SOUP

MAKES APPROXIMATELY 7 QUARTS OR 14 PINTS
PREP: 15 MIN • COOK: 35 MIN • CANNER: 1 HR • PROCESSING: 1 HR 30 MIN/1 HR 15 MIN
TOTAL: 3 HR 20 MIN/3 HR 5 MIN

This soup embodies all of the wonderful flavors we've come to expect from a traditional chicken chow mein recipe. The simplicity of this soup makes preparation quick and easy, especially if you freeze your own garden vegetables or prefer to shop in the frozen section of the grocery store.

1 whole chicken, cut in pieces, skin on

1 gallon water (16 cups)

3 cups fresh or frozen peas (if frozen, do not thaw)

2 cups fresh or frozen green beans, cut into 1½-inch pieces (if frozen, do not thaw)

4 celery stalks, with leaves, chopped (2 cups)

1 large onion, chopped (2 cups)

½ cup fresh or frozen corn kernels (if frozen, do not thaw)

2 tablespoons minced garlic

4 cups Chicken Stock (page 98) or 3 chicken bouillon cubes

1. Combine the chicken pieces with the water in a large stockpot and bring to a boil. Reduce the heat to medium and continue to boil until the chicken is cooked through, about 30 minutes. Be sure to stir often to avoid scorching the chicken. Remove the chicken pieces and place on a cutting board to cool. Keep the cooking liquid at a simmer.

2. Remove the skin and bones from the cooled chicken. Using a knife or your fingers, cut or tear the chicken into bite-size pieces and return them to the stockpot.

3. Add the peas, green beans, celery, onion, corn, garlic, and stock or bouillon cubes to the stockpot. Bring to a boil for 5 minutes.

4. Using a slotted spoon, fill each jar three-quarters full with chicken and vegetables. Be sure to obtain a good ratio of chicken and vegetables in each jar. After the jars are filled three-quarters full, ladle the hot soup liquid over the chicken and vegetables, being sure to leave 1 inch of headspace. Tamp the mixture down using an air bubble remover tool and add additional soup liquid if necessary to maintain the 1 inch of headspace.

5. Wipe the rim of each jar with a warm washcloth dipped in distilled white vinegar. Place a lid and ring on each jar and hand tighten.

6. Place jars in the pressure canner, lock the pressure canner lid, and bring to a boil on high heat. Let the canner vent for 10 minutes. Close the vent and continue heating to achieve 11 PSI for a dial gauge and 10 PSI for a weighted gauge. Process quart jars for 1 hour 30 minutes and pint jars for 1 hour 15 minutes.

Serving Tip: While we cannot preserve pasta in a jar, it's easy to boil a batch of lo mein noodles while heating up a jar of soup on the stove top. Give this soup a finishing touch by serving it with lo mein noodles and a dash or two of soy sauce.

DRUNKEN PORK STEW

MAKES APPROXIMATELY 4 QUARTS OR 8 PINTS
PREP: 15 MIN • COOK: 25 MIN • CANNER: 1 HR • PROCESSING: 1 HR 30 MIN/1 HR 15 MIN
TOTAL: 3 HR 10 MIN/2 HR 55 MIN

This stew has become one of my favorites for its deep, rich flavor and thick tomato base. Blending tomato juice with red wine elevates the pork, while the delicious blend of herbs and spices enhances its depth. Heat this stew and serve as-is, or thicken it to serve on a bed of orzo, thick pasta noodles, or mashed potatoes.

2 tablespoons olive oil, divided

2 pounds boneless pork shoulder or loin, cut into 1-inch chunks

2 medium onions, diced (1 cup)

4 large carrots, cut into ½-inch rounds (2½ cups)

4 medium Roma tomatoes, diced (2 cups)

5 garlic cloves, minced

1½ tablespoons dried oregano

1 tablespoon brown sugar

1 teaspoon ground nutmeg

½ teaspoon cayenne pepper

3½ cups red wine

3½ cups Tomato Juice (page 45)

2 bay leaves

1. In a thick-bottomed stockpot, heat 1 tablespoon oil and brown the pork in batches, until all the pork is lightly browned, about 3 to 5 minutes per batch. Add 1 additional tablespoon of oil while browning each batch. Remove each batch from the stockpot and place in a bowl. Be sure not to fully cook the meat. Set aside.

2. Add the onions, carrots, tomatoes, garlic, oregano, brown sugar, nutmeg, and cayenne pepper to the pork drippings. Mix well and cook for 5 to 8 minutes, or until the onions are translucent. Add the wine, Tomato Juice, and bay leaves, and bring to a boil. Reduce the heat and simmer for 10 minutes. Add the pork and cook for an additional 2 minutes. Remove the bay leaves and discard.

3. Using a slotted spoon, fill each jar three-quarters full with pork and vegetables. Be sure to obtain a good ratio of pork and vegetables in each jar. Ladle the hot stew liquid over the mixture, being sure to leave 1 inch of headspace. Tamp the mixture down using an air bubble remover tool and add additional stew liquid if necessary to maintain the 1 inch of headspace.

4. Wipe the rim of each jar with a warm washcloth dipped in distilled white vinegar. Place a lid and ring on each jar and hand tighten.

5. Place jars in the pressure canner, lock the pressure canner lid, and bring to a boil on high heat. Let the canner vent for 10 minutes. Close the vent and continue heating to achieve 11 PSI for a dial gauge and 10 PSI for a weighted gauge. Process quart jars for 1 hour 30 minutes and pint jars for 1 hour 15 minutes.

Ingredient Tip: I tell people, cook with what you drink. If you prefer to drink a sweet red wine or a red blend, use it in this stew. If a dry red is more up your alley, by all means, give this stew a drink.

LENTIL SOUP WITH CARROTS AND TOMATOES

MAKES APPROXIMATELY 5 QUARTS OR 10 PINTS

PREP: 10 MIN • COOK: 20 MIN • CANNER: 1 HR • PROCESSING: 1 HR 30 MIN/1 HR 15 MIN • TOTAL: 3 HR/2 HR 45 MIN

My mom has made this for our family our whole lives. She taught me to have fun and explore flavors outside of traditional lentil soups. For this reason, we add Beef Bone Stock (page 96), shredded carrots, diced tomatoes and a variety of earthy seasonings. A cup of Mom's lentil soup makes an amazing first course to any dinner or enjoy a bowl all on its own.

12 cups Beef Bone Stock (page 96)

12 cups water

8 large carrots, peeled and shredded (4 cups)

2 medium sweet onions, chopped (2 cups)

4 medium Roma tomatoes, diced (2 cups)

5 garlic cloves, minced

1 tablespoon paprika

1 tablespoon turmeric

2 teaspoons dried parsley

2 teaspoons coarse sea salt

1 teaspoon ground black pepper

2½ cups dried lentils (16 ounces)

1. In a large stockpot, combine the Beef Bone Stock, water, carrots, onions, tomatoes, garlic, paprika, turmeric, parsley, salt, and pepper. Bring to a boil over medium-high heat. Reduce the heat and simmer for 15 minutes. Add the lentils, mix well, and simmer for an additional 2 minutes.

2. Using a slotted spoon, fill each quart with 4 inches of the lentils and vegetables and each pint jar with 2 inches. Tamp down the solids with the air bubble remover tool before measuring. To measure the height of the lentil mixture in the jar before adding the soup stock, place a ruler on the countertop next to the jar. Once solids are dispersed among jars, ladle the hot soup stock over the solids, being sure to leave 1 inch of headspace.

3. Wipe the rim of each jar with a warm washcloth dipped in distilled white vinegar. Place a lid and ring on each jar and hand tighten.

4. Place jars in the pressure canner, lock the pressure canner lid, and bring to a boil on high heat. Let the canner vent for 10 minutes. Close the vent and continue heating to achieve 11 PSI for a dial gauge and 10 PSI for a weighted gauge. Process quart jars for 1 hour 30 minutes and pint jars for 1 hour 15 minutes.

Recipe Tip: It is very important NOT to deviate from the instructed 2-inch height of solids for pints and 4 inches for quarts. After extensive testing, I have learned the exact space required to properly hydrate the lentils, keep enough soup base, and leave enough liquid in each jar. If you add more than the required amount of lentils to the jar, your soup will become a solid mass.

VEGETABLE STEW

MAKES APPROXIMATELY 7 QUARTS OR 14 PINTS
PREP: 1 HR • COOK: 10 MIN • CANNER: 1 HR • PROCESSING: 1 HR 30 MIN/1 HR 15 MIN
TOTAL: 3 HR 40 MIN/3 HR 25 MIN

With tomatoes as its base, this hearty vegetable-packed stew aims to please. The array of colors, shapes, and flavors makes this stew as gorgeous to look at as it is delicious to eat. Enjoy with a grilled cheese sandwich or simply with saltines.

2½ cups dried cannellini or navy beans (16 ounces)

4 cups water

16 medium tomatoes, cored, peeled, and chopped (8 cups)

8 medium carrots, peeled and cut into ½-inch-thick rounds (4 cups)

5 medium russet potatoes, peeled and cubed (3 cups)

2 cups corn kernels, fresh or frozen (if frozen, do not thaw)

2 cups fresh or frozen green beans, cut into 2-inch pieces (if frozen, do not thaw)

4 medium onions, chopped (2 cups)

4 celery stalks, chopped into ½-inch-thick pieces (1 cup)

2 tablespoons dried parsley

6 garlic cloves, minced

1 bay leaf

2 teaspoons coarse sea salt

1 teaspoon ground black pepper

1. Thoroughly rinse and clean the dried beans, discarding any disfigured or shriveled beans and any rocks or debris. Add the cleaned dried beans to a stockpot with enough water to cover with 2 inches. Bring to a boil over medium-high heat, then reduce the heat, cover, and simmer on low for 1 hour. Drain the beans in a colander in the sink. Set aside.

2. In a second stockpot, combine the water, tomatoes, carrots, potatoes, corn, green beans, onions, celery, parsley, garlic, bay leaf, salt, and pepper. Mix well. Bring to a boil over medium-high heat, stirring often. Boil for 5 minutes, then add the drained beans. Cook for an additional 5 minutes, then remove from the heat. Remove and discard the bay leaf.

3. Ladle the hot stew into hot jars, leaving 1 inch of headspace. Remove any air bubbles and add additional stew if necessary to maintain the 1 inch of headspace.

4. Wipe the rim of each jar with a warm washcloth dipped in distilled white vinegar. Place a lid and ring on each jar and hand tighten.

5. Place jars in the pressure canner, lock the pressure canner lid, and bring to a boil on high heat. Let the canner vent for 10 minutes. Close the vent and continue heating to achieve 11 PSI for a dial gauge and 10 PSI for a weighted gauge. Process quart jars for 1 hour 30 minutes and pint jars for 1 hour 15 minutes.

Ingredient Tip: If you prefer not to add the beans and just keep this a vegetable-only stew, you may do so. Removing the beans will yield 2 fewer pints and 1 fewer quart. Without the beans, the recipe will process for less time; process quart jars for 1 hour 15 minutes and pint jars for 1 hour.

CARROT SOUP

MAKES APPROXIMATELY 7 QUARTS OR 14 PINTS

PREP: 10 MIN • COOK: 1 HR • CANNER: 1 HR • PROCESSING: 1 HR 15 MIN/1 HR • TOTAL: 3 HR 25 MIN/3 HR 10 MIN

Carrots come in a variety of colors, such as orange, purple, white, yellow, and red. While most carrot soups are orange in color, if you happen to grow kaleidoscope carrots, incorporate them into this hearty soup for depth of color and a sweeter flavor.

10 pounds carrots, peeled and cut in half

2 large onions, quartered

5 celery stalks, cut in half

8 cups Chicken Stock (page 98)

4 cups water

8 whole garlic cloves, peeled

2 teaspoons ground thyme

2 teaspoons coarse sea salt

1 teaspoon ground black pepper

1. In a large stockpot, combine the carrots, onions, celery, stock, water, garlic, thyme, salt, and pepper and bring to a boil. Turn and mix the vegetables to cook evenly. Boil for 5 minutes, then reduce the heat and simmer for 1 hour.

2. Once the carrots are soft enough to break easily, purée the soup directly in the stockpot with an immersion blender or, if you prefer to use a food processor or blender, purée the soup in batches.

3. Ladle the hot puréed soup into hot jars, leaving 1 inch of headspace. Remove any trapped air using an air bubble remover tool and add additional soup if necessary to maintain the 1 inch of headspace.

4. Wipe the rim of each jar with a warm washcloth dipped in distilled white vinegar. Place a lid and ring on each jar and hand tighten.

5. Place jars in the pressure canner, lock the pressure canner lid, and bring to a boil on high heat. Let the canner vent for 10 minutes. Close the vent and continue heating to achieve 11 PSI for a dial gauge and 10 PSI for a weighted gauge. Process quart jars for 1 hour 15 minutes and pint jars for 1 hour.

Serving Tip: Often you see this soup finished with the addition of half-and-half or heavy cream, however these additions are merely a choice you can make as you heat up a jar on the stove top. The hearty, rich flavor of this soup is made possible by using Chicken Stock, so you may prefer to heat and eat without adding cream. Feel free to serve with fun garnishes like chopped chives, fresh parsley leaves, crumbled bacon, or Parmesan cheese.

SAUSAGE AND BEAN SOUP

MAKES APPROXIMATELY 7 QUARTS OR 14 PINTS

PREP: 30 MIN • COOK: 15 MIN • CANNER: 1 HR • PROCESSING: 1 HR 30 MIN/1 HR 15 MIN

TOTAL: 3 HR 15 MIN/3 HR

This delicious soup is a one of my family's favorites to enjoy during the cold winter months. It has an array of proteins and fresh vegetables so you can give your family a healthy, filling meal in minutes. Serve the soup with a slice of hot-from-the-oven beer bread or with a handful of oyster crackers.

1½ cups dried pinto beans (8 ounces)

1½ cups dried black beans (8 ounces)

2 tablespoons olive oil

1 large onion, finely diced (1½ cups)

2 celery stalks, chopped into ½-inch-thick pieces (1 cup)

4 garlic cloves, minced

2 pounds bulk Italian sausage, spicy or sweet

8 cups Beef Bone Stock (page 96)

4 cups water

4 medium carrots, peeled and cut into ½-inch-thick rounds (2 cups)

2 bay leaves

½ teaspoon coarse sea salt

¼ teaspoon ground black pepper

1 bunch kale, stems removed, leaves coarsely chopped

1. Thoroughly rinse and clean the dried beans, discarding any disfigured or shriveled beans and any rocks or debris. Add the beans to a stockpot with enough water to cover by 2 inches. Bring to a boil over medium-high heat, then reduce the heat, cover, and simmer on low for 30 minutes. Set aside about 1 cup bean cooking liquid. Drain the beans and set aside.

2. In a second large stockpot, heat the olive oil on medium-high heat. Add the onion, celery, and garlic and sauté until the onions are translucent, about 5 minutes. Add the Italian sausage and cook until done, breaking sausage into smaller, bite-size pieces as it cooks.

3. Add the Beef Bone Stock, water, carrots, bay leaves, salt, and pepper. Bring to a boil. Reduce the heat and simmer for 5 minutes. Add the rehydrated beans, 1 cup reserved bean cooking liquid, and the chopped kale to the stockpot and mix well. Cook for an additional 5 minutes. Remove from the heat.

4. Using a slotted spoon, fill each jar three-quarters full with the sausage and vegetables. Be sure to obtain a good ratio of sausage and vegetables in each jar. Ladle the hot soup liquid over the mixture, being sure to leave 1 inch of headspace. Tamp the mixture down using an air bubble remover tool and add additional soup liquid if necessary to maintain the 1 inch of headspace.

5. Wipe the rim of each jar with a warm wash-cloth dipped in distilled white vinegar. Place a lid and ring on each jar and hand tighten.

6. Place jars in the pressure canner, lock the pressure canner lid, and bring to a boil on high heat. Let the canner vent for 10 min-utes. Close the vent and continue heating to achieve 11 PSI for a dial gauge and 10 PSI for a weighted gauge. Process quart jars for 1 hour 30 minutes and pint jars for 1 hour 15 minutes.

Ingredient Tip: Prefer a different type of bean in your soup? Feel free to replace the pinto and black beans with a bean of your choice. If you prefer a good mix of colors and shapes in your soup, feel free to use a variety of dried beans, as long as the total amount of beans stays 3 cups.

TOMATO SOUP

MAKES APPROXIMATELY 6 QUARTS OR 12 PINTS

PREP: 15 MIN • COOK: 40 MIN • CANNER: 1 HR • PROCESSING: 1 HR 15 MIN/1 HR • TOTAL: 3 HR 10 MIN/2 HR 55 MIN

Having several jars of Tomato Soup in your pantry makes it easy to prepare a quick, delicious lunch. Try adding ¼ cup heavy cream to a quart of soup (or 2 tablespoons to a pint) as it warms on the stove, whisking until it thickens. Garnish with crumbled bacon, strips of fresh basil leaves, grated Romano cheese, or a teaspoon of pesto sauce. The possibilities are endless.

3 tablespoons olive oil

4 medium Spanish onions, chopped (2 cups)

8 garlic cloves, coarsely chopped

8 cups Chicken Broth (page 104)

4 cups water

1 bouquet garni (3 sprigs each of parsley, oregano, and thyme tied together with kitchen twine)

2 bay leaves

4 large carrots, peeled and chopped (2 cups)

2 celery stalks, chopped (1 cup)

24 medium or 12 large tomatoes, cored, peeled, and quartered (12 cups)

¼ teaspoon cayenne pepper

1 teaspoon granulated sugar

2 teaspoons coarse sea salt

1 teaspoon ground black pepper

1. In a large stockpot, heat the olive oil on medium-high heat. Add the onions and garlic and sauté for 5 to 8 minutes or until the onions are translucent. Add the Chicken Broth, water, bouquet garni, and bay leaves. Bring to a boil, cover, reduce the heat, and simmer for 10 minutes.

2. Add the carrots, celery, tomatoes, cayenne, sugar, salt, and pepper to the stockpot and mix well. Replace the lid, increase the heat to medium, and cook for an additional 10 minutes, stirring often. Reduce the heat and simmer for an additional 10 minutes. Remove from the heat.

3. Remove and discard the bay leaves and bouquet garni. Purée the soup directly in the stockpot with an immersion blender or, if you prefer to use a food processor or blender, purée the soup in batches. Return the purée to the stockpot and heat through on medium heat, about 5 minutes, stirring often.

4. Ladle the hot Tomato Soup into hot jars, leaving 1 inch of headspace. Remove any air bubbles and add additional soup if necessary to maintain the 1 inch of headspace.

5. Wipe the rim of each jar with a warm washcloth dipped in distilled white vinegar. Place a lid and ring on each jar and hand tighten.

6. Place jars in the pressure canner, lock the pressure canner lid, and bring to a boil on high heat. Let the canner vent for 10 minutes. Close the vent and continue heating to achieve 11 PSI for a dial gauge and 10 PSI for a weighted gauge. Process quart jars for 1 hour 15 minutes and pint jars for 1 hour.

Ingredient Tip: To create an authentic tomato bisque, replace the Chicken Broth with Shellfish Stock (page 102) when canning.

FRENCH ONION SOUP

MAKES APPROXIMATELY 5 QUARTS OR 10 PINTS

PREP: 15 MIN • COOK: 30 MIN • CANNER: 1 HR • PROCESSING: 1 HR 15 MIN/1 HR • TOTAL: 3 HR/2 HR 45 MIN

Onion soups have been popular since Roman times. Throughout history, onions were seen as peasant food, often eaten by the poor. Funny how as time moved on, this soup was modernized and made popular. Originating in Paris, France, in the 18th century, the modern soup we have all come to enjoy to this day is made from beef broth and caramelized onions.

¼ cup butter (½ stick)

8 large sweet onions, sliced (11 cups)

4 sprigs fresh thyme, leaves stripped from stem

8 garlic cloves, minced

2 teaspoons coarse sea salt (optional)

½ teaspoon ground black pepper

12 cups Beef Bone Stock (page 96)

1½ cups red wine

¼ cup brandy

2 bay leaves

1. In a large stockpot, melt the butter over medium-high heat. Add the onions, fresh thyme, garlic, salt (if using), and pepper and mix well. Reduce the heat to medium and cook until the onions are soft and caramelized, about 25 minutes.

2. Add the Beef Bone Stock, wine, brandy, and bay leaves to the stockpot. Bring to a boil, reduce the heat, and simmer for 5 minutes, stirring often. Remove from the heat.

3. Using tongs or a slotted spoon, evenly distribute hot caramelized onions into hot jars, about 2 cups per quart and 1 cup per pint. Ladle the hot broth over the onions, leaving 1 inch of headspace.

4. Wipe the rim of each jar with a warm washcloth dipped in distilled white vinegar. Place a lid and ring on each jar and hand tighten.

5. Place jars in the pressure canner, lock the pressure canner lid, and bring to a boil on high heat. Let the canner vent for 10 minutes. Close the vent and continue heating to achieve 11 PSI for a dial gauge and 10 PSI for a weighted gauge. Process quart jars for 1 hour 15 minutes and pint jars for 1 hour.

Serving Tip: Preheat the oven to 450°F. Open a quart or two and evenly disperse soup into oven-safe bowls. Place one slice of a baguette or a handful of croutons on top of the soup in each bowl. Cover the bread with a slice of provolone and a slice of Swiss cheese. Place the bowls on a cookie sheet lined with foil and broil in the oven until the cheeses bubble and brown slightly. Serve hot.

LOADED POTATO SOUP

MAKES APPROXIMATELY 5 QUARTS OR 10 PINTS

PREP: 20 MIN • COOK: 35 MIN • CANNER: 1 HR • PROCESSING: 1 HR 30 MIN/1 HR 15 MIN

TOTAL: 3 HR 25 MIN/3 HR 10 MIN

This soup is like having a loaded baked potato in every jar! The bacon gives it flavor while the potatoes naturally thicken the soup to a cream-like consistency. When ready to heat up a jar or two to serve, top each bowl with shredded Cheddar cheese, sliced scallions, and more bacon crumbles.

12 ounces bacon

1 large onion, chopped (1½ cups)

5 garlic cloves, minced

1 celery stalk, finely chopped (½ cup)

6 pounds russet potatoes, peeled and cut into 1-inch chunks (16 cups)

8 cups Chicken Broth (page 104)

2 cups water, divided

1 cup chopped bell pepper

2 tablespoons finely chopped fresh chives

1 teaspoon paprika

1 teaspoon coarse sea salt

½ teaspoon ground black pepper

¼ teaspoon cayenne pepper

⅛ teaspoon rubbed sage

½ cup ClearJel®

1. Using kitchen scissors, cut the bacon into 1-inch pieces and place in a thick-bottomed stockpot. Over medium-high heat, cook the bacon until crisp, about 5 to 8 minutes. Place the cooked bacon in a bowl to cool, leaving the drippings in the stockpot. Once cooled, crumble the bacon.

2. Add the onion, garlic, and celery to the bacon drippings and cook until the onion is translucent, about 5 to 8 minutes. Add the potatoes, broth, 1 cup water, bell pepper, and crumbled bacon to the stockpot and mix well. Bring to a boil. Add the chives, paprika, salt, pepper, cayenne, and sage and mix well. Reduce the heat and simmer for 15 minutes or until the potatoes start to break down. Stir frequently.

3. Whisk the ClearJel® into 1 cup water, and then add to the soup, mixing well. Simmer for an additional 5 minutes.

4. Ladle the hot soup into hot jars, leaving 1 inch of headspace. Remove any air bubbles and add additional soup if necessary to maintain the 1 inch of headspace.

5. Wipe the rim of each jar with a warm washcloth dipped in distilled white vinegar. Place a lid and ring on each jar and hand tighten.

6. Place jars in the pressure canner, lock the pressure canner lid, and bring to a boil on high heat. Let the canner vent for 10 minutes. Close the vent and continue heating to achieve 11 PSI for a dial gauge and 10 PSI for a weighted gauge. Process quart jars for 1 hour 30 minutes and pint jars for 1 hour 15 minutes.

Serving Tip: Add ¼ cup heavy whipping cream when heating a quart and 2 tablespoons when heating a pint jar. Stir and heat until the soup reaches the desired texture. Serve thickened soup inside a bread bowl for a special treat.

MOROCCAN SWEET POTATO SOUP

MAKES APPROXIMATELY 6 QUARTS OR 12 PINTS
PREP: 10 MIN • COOK: 5 MIN • CANNER: 1 HR • PROCESSING 1 HR 15 MIN/1 HR
TOTAL: 2 HR 30 MIN/2 HR 15 MIN

Pressure can this hearty vegetarian soup any time of the year, especially when sweet potatoes are readily available. The natural sweetness of potato and corn kernels blends splendidly with the variety of Moroccan spices. Serve hot and garnish with fresh cilantro.

8 cups sweet potatoes, peeled and cut into ½-inch cubes (7 large)

8 cups Vegetable Broth (page 105)

4 cups water

1 medium sweet onion, diced (1 cup)

4 medium Roma tomatoes, diced (2 cups)

1½ cups fresh or frozen corn kernels (if frozen, do not thaw)

4 garlic cloves, minced

1 tablespoon minced fresh ginger

2 teaspoons ground cumin

2 teaspoons ground coriander

1 teaspoon turmeric

1 teaspoon paprika

1 teaspoon ground cinnamon

1 teaspoon coarse sea salt

½ teaspoon ground black pepper

1. In a large stockpot, combine the sweet potatoes, broth, water, onion, tomatoes, corn, garlic, ginger, cumin, coriander, turmeric, paprika, cinnamon, salt, and pepper. Mix well. Over medium-high heat, bring the soup to a boil. Reduce the heat and simmer for 5 minutes, stirring often.

2. Ladle the hot soup into hot jars, leaving 1 inch of headspace.

3. Wipe the rim of each jar with a warm washcloth dipped in distilled white vinegar. Place a lid and ring on each jar and hand tighten.

4. Place jars in the pressure canner, lock the pressure canner lid, and bring to a boil on high heat. Let the canner vent for 10 minutes. Close the vent and continue heating to achieve 11 PSI for a dial gauge and 10 PSI for a weighted gauge. Process quart jars for 1 hour 15 minutes and pint jars for 1 hour.

Ingredient Tip: Prefer a version with meat? Cook 6 to 8 boneless skinless chicken thighs in the stockpot first, about 8 to 10 minutes. Shred thighs using two forks, then add the soup ingredients. Follow the recipe instructions and process at the required PSI, 1 hour 30 minutes for quarts and 1 hour 15 minutes for pints. Adding chicken will increase the yield by 1 quart or 2 pints.

IRISH STOUT BEEF STEW

MAKES APPROXIMATELY 7 QUARTS OR 14 PINTS

PREP: 15 MIN • COOK: 30 MIN • CANNER: 1 HR • PROCESSING: 1 HR 30 MIN/1 HR 15 MIN

TOTAL: 3 HR 15 MIN/3 HR

By far this is one of the most flavorful stews we have ever enjoyed in our home. The addition of a dark coffee and Guinness beer really gives this stew its dark color and rich flavor. Serve this amazing stew alongside a thick slice of freshly baked beer bread slathered in garlic butter.

4 tablespoons olive oil, divided

5 pounds whole boneless beef chuck roast, cut into 2-inch pieces

Pinch coarse sea salt

Pinch ground black pepper

1 cup espresso or strong brewed coffee

8 cups Beef Bone Stock (page 96)

2 (15-ounce) cans Guinness Draught beer

1 bouquet garni (4 sprigs thyme, 3 sprigs parsley, and 2 sprigs oregano, tied together with kitchen twine)

2 bay leaves

3 large carrots, cut into ½-inch rounds (1½ cups)

1 large parsnip, peeled and diced (1 cup)

4 medium yellow onions, diced (2 cups)

6 garlic cloves, chopped

1 tablespoon Asian fish sauce

1 tablespoon soy sauce

1 tablespoon Worcestershire sauce

28 baby potatoes

1. In a thick-bottomed stockpot, heat 1 tablespoon oil and brown the beef in batches, sprinkling each batch with a pinch of salt and pepper, turning as necessary until the beef is lightly browned on all sides, about 3 to 5 minutes per batch. Add more oil if necessary for each batch. Remove each batch from the stockpot and place in a bowl. Be sure not to fully cook the meat. Return the browned beef to the stockpot.

2. Add the espresso, beef stock, beer, bouquet garni, and bay leaves to the stockpot. On medium-high heat, bring to a boil. Boil for 1 minute, and then reduce the heat and simmer covered for 10 minutes, stirring often.

3. Add the carrots, parsnip, onions, garlic, fish sauce, soy sauce, Worcestershire sauce, and potatoes. Mix well. Bring to a boil and cook for an additional 5 minutes. Remove and discard the bay leaves and bouquet garni.

4. Using a slotted spoon, place 4 potatoes in every quart jar and 2 in every pint jar. Next, using the slotted spoon fill each jar three-quarters full with the meat and vegetable mixture. Ladle the cooking liquid from the stew over the meat and vegetables, leaving 1 inch of headspace. Remove any air bubbles and add additional cooking liquid if necessary to maintain the 1 inch of headspace.

5. Wipe the rim of each jar with a warm wash-cloth dipped in distilled white vinegar. Place a lid and ring on each jar and hand tighten.

6. Place jars in the pressure canner, lock the pressure canner lid, and bring to a boil on high heat. Let the canner vent for 10 minutes. Close the vent and continue heating to achieve 11 PSI for a dial gauge and 10 PSI for a weighted gauge. Process quart jars for 1 hour 30 minutes and pint jars for 1 hour 15 minutes.

Ingredient Tip: If you do not have an espresso machine, not to worry. Fill a coffeepot with 1½ cups water and place 4 heaping scoops of coffee grounds in the filter and brew. If you don't drink coffee, purchase a small jar of instant coffee. Mix 4 heaping spoonsful of instant coffee granules into 1 cup boiling water and add to the stew.

HEARTY HAMBURGER STEW

MAKES APPROXIMATELY 7 QUARTS OR 14 PINTS

PREP: 10 MIN • COOK: 20 MIN • CANNER: 1 HR • PROCESSING: 1 HR 30 MIN/1 HR 15 MIN

TOTAL: 3 HR/2 HR 45 MIN

Simple, easy and filling, this delicious stew can be enjoyed any time of the year. When life is busy, this handy stew gives my family a healthy alternative to fast food—and takes zero prep time because we can simply heat, eat, and go. This hearty stew also partners perfectly with a side of warm cornbread.

2 pounds ground beef

½ teaspoon coarse sea salt

¼ teaspoon pepper

2 medium onions, chopped (1 cup)

6 garlic cloves, minced

4 cups finely diced russet potatoes

4 cups fresh or frozen green beans, cut into 2-inch pieces (if frozen, do not thaw)

2 cups fresh or frozen corn kernels (if frozen, do not thaw)

1 medium red bell pepper, finely diced

12 medium Roma tomatoes, finely diced (6 cups)

4 cups Beef Broth (page 103)

2 tablespoons Worcestershire sauce

1 teaspoon dried oregano

¾ cup tomato paste (6 ounces)

2 teaspoons granulated sugar (optional)

1. In a large stockpot, add the ground beef, salt, and pepper and cook over medium-high heat. Using a wooden spoon, break the meat into small bite-size pieces, turning and mixing until cooked through, about 10 minutes. Drain off the fat and discard. Return the browned meat to the stockpot.

2. Add the onions and garlic and cook for 5 minutes over medium-high heat. Add the potatoes, green beans, corn, bell pepper, and tomatoes. Mix well and cook for 2 minutes. Add the broth, Worcestershire sauce, oregano, and tomato paste. Stir well until the paste is evenly distributed. Add the sugar and mix well, cooking for an additional 3 minutes.

3. Ladle the hot soup into hot jars, leaving 1 inch of headspace.

4. Wipe the rim of each jar with a warm washcloth dipped in distilled white vinegar. Place a lid and ring on each jar and hand tighten.

5. Place jars in the pressure canner, lock the pressure canner lid, and bring to a boil on high heat. Let the canner vent for 10 minutes. Close the vent and continue heating to achieve 11 PSI for a dial gauge and 10 PSI for a weighted gauge. Process quart jars for 1 hour 30 minutes and pint jars for 1 hour 15 minutes.

Ingredient Tip: If you would rather use a leaner meat than ground beef, you may replace the ground beef with equal amounts of ground chicken, turkey, or pork. If you do so, you are also welcome to replace the Beef Broth with an equal amount of Chicken Stock (page 98).

SUN-DRIED TOMATO SOUP

MAKES APPROXIMATELY 5 QUARTS OR 10 PINTS

PREP: 10 MIN • COOK: 15 MIN • CANNER: 1 HR • PROCESSING: 1 HR 15 MIN/1 HR

TOTAL: 2 HR 40 MIN/2 HR 25 MIN

Sun-dried tomatoes, whether store-bought or dehydrated at home, are intensely flavorful and packed with nutrients. Enjoy a bowl of Sun-Dried Tomato Soup alongside a pesto grilled cheese sandwich and a tall glass of cold milk.

1 cup sun-dried tomatoes packed in oil, chopped

4 cups crushed tomatoes and juices

3 garlic cloves, smashed

2 teaspoons granulated sugar

2 cups water

2 medium onions, chopped (1 cup)

½ cup grated carrot

1 celery stalk, chopped (½ cup)

1 medium zucchini, grated (1 cup)

8 cups Chicken Stock (page 98)

1 teaspoon coarse sea salt

½ teaspoon ground black pepper

¼ teaspoon red pepper flakes

¾ cup tomato paste (6 ounces)

2 cups baby spinach

1. In a large thick-bottomed stockpot, combine the sun-dried tomatoes, crushed tomatoes and their juice, garlic, sugar, and 2 cups water. Bring to a boil over medium heat. Cover and reduce the heat to simmer. Simmer for 10 minutes.

2. Add the onions, carrot, celery, zucchini, stock, salt, pepper, and red pepper flakes and bring to a boil. Stir in the tomato paste and mix until well distributed. Add the spinach, mix, and let cook for 5 minutes.

3. Using an immersion blender, blend to achieve the desired consistency. If using a food processer, work in batches, pulsing until reaching the desired consistency. (Personally, I like to leave my soup on the chunky side, while others like it finely puréed.)

4. Ladle the hot soup into hot jars, leaving 1 inch of headspace.

5. Wipe the rim of each jar with a warm washcloth dipped in distilled white vinegar. Place a lid and ring on each jar and hand tighten.

6. Place jars in the pressure canner, lock the pressure canner lid, and bring to a boil on high heat. Let the canner vent for 10 minutes. Close the vent and continue heating to achieve 11 PSI for a dial gauge and 10 PSI for a weighted gauge. Process quart jars for 1 hour 15 minutes and pint jars for 1 hour.

Recipe Tip: Puréeing this soup is just one option to enjoy its deliciousness, as many like to add heavy cream when reheating and then garnish with fresh basil. If you prefer to preserve your soup in its natural state without puréeing it, feel free to do so. A fun option when reheating this is to add 1 cup cooked cheese tortellini and top with grated Parmesan. Puréed or not, you can't go wrong.

ZESTY PORK AND SQUASH STEW

MAKES APPROXIMATELY 6 QUARTS OR 12 PINTS
PREP: 25 MIN • COOK: 30 MIN • CANNER: 1 HR • PROCESSING: 1 HR 30 MIN/1 HR 15 MIN
TOTAL: 3 HR 25 MIN/3 HR 10 MIN

Rehydrated California chili purée is the key ingredient to this flavorful stew. A well-balanced blend of squash and meat, this zesty stew is sure to please. Deep in color and packed full of protein and fiber, this stew can be thickened by simmering with the lid off upon reheating and serving it with garlic mashed potatoes.

8 dried red California chiles, stems removed

4 cups boiling water

3 tablespoons olive oil, divided

3 pounds boneless pork shoulder, cut into 2-inch pieces

1 large red onion, diced (1½ cups)

8 garlic cloves, minced

1 tablespoon ground coriander

1 teaspoon coarse sea salt

½ teaspoon ground black pepper

1 tablespoon oregano

½ teaspoon crushed red pepper flakes

4 cups peeled and diced tomatoes

3 pounds kabocha or acorn squash, peeled, seeded, and cut into 1-inch chunks (5 cups)

2½ pounds butternut squash, peeled, seeded, and cut into 1-inch pieces (5 cups)

8 cups Chicken Stock (page 98)

2 cups water

1. Placed the dried California chilies in a deep bowl and cover with the boiling water. Submerge the chilies with a heavy bowl or cup. Let them sit submerged for 15 minutes to fully rehydrate.

2. In a thick-bottomed stockpot, heat 1 tablespoon oil and brown the pork in batches until all the pork is lightly browned, about 3 to 5 minutes per batch. Add 1 additional tablespoon of oil while browning each batch. Remove each batch from the stockpot and place in a bowl. Be sure not to cook the meat through. Set aside.

3. Strain the chiles, reserving ½ cup soaking liquid. Place the rehydrated chilies in a food processor with the reserved liquid. Pulse on high to make a thick paste. Set aside.

4. Add the onion, garlic, coriander, salt, pepper, oregano, and red pepper flakes to the stockpot with the pork drippings. On medium heat, mix and cook until the onions are translucent, about 5 to 8 minutes. Add the browned pork, tomatoes, squash, stock, and 2 cups water. Bring to a boil. Boil for 5 minutes, then add the chile purée and mix well. Reduce the heat and simmer for 5 minutes.

5. Ladle the hot stew into hot jars, leaving 1 inch of headspace. Remove any air bubbles and add additional stew if necessary to maintain the 1 inch of headspace.

6. Wipe the rim of each jar with a warm washcloth dipped in distilled white vinegar. Place a lid and ring on each jar and hand tighten.

7. Place jars in the pressure canner, lock the pressure canner lid, and bring to a boil on high heat. Let the canner vent for 10 minutes. Close the vent and continue heating to achieve 11 PSI for a dial gauge and 10 PSI for a weighted gauge. Process quart jars for 1 hour 30 minutes and pint jars for 1 hour 15 minutes.

Ingredient Tip: Cut squash in half, removing seeds and stringy fibers. Cut squash into long quarters. Working in batches, place quarters in microwave, flesh-side down, and microwave on high for 5 minutes. When cool to touch, use a paring knife to easily peel the skin off squash.

HAM AND NAVY BEAN SOUP

MAKES APPROXIMATELY 6 QUARTS OR 12 PINTS

PREP: 15 MIN • COOK: 85 MIN • CANNER: 1 HR • PROCESSING: 1 HR 30 MIN/1 HR 15 MIN

TOTAL: 4 HR 10 MIN/3 HR 55 MIN

This is the perfect soup for those leftover meaty ham bones from the holidays. Whether fresh or frozen, your soup will boast amazing flavors derived from the meat and bone marrow. If time is of the essence, feel free to start the soup base in a slow cooker on low for 4 hours before bringing it over to the stove top.

1 large, meaty roasted ham bone

2½ cups dried navy beans (16 ounces)

1 tablespoon olive oil

2 medium white onions, diced (1 cup)

4 garlic cloves, minced

4 cups Vegetable Broth (page 105)

2 bay leaves

4 cups water

2 large carrots, peeled and chopped (1 cup)

2 celery stalks, chopped (1 cup)

1 teaspoon coarse sea salt (optional)

½ teaspoon ground black pepper

1. Remove any excessive fat from the ham bone, and if a glaze was used when roasting, be sure to rinse the ham bone with hot running tap water. Set aside.

2. Thoroughly rinse and clean the dried beans, discarding any disfigured or shriveled beans and any rocks or debris. In a large pot, add the dried beans and enough water to cover by 2 inches. Bring to a boil over medium-high heat. Boil for 5 minutes, then reduce the heat to low and simmer with a lid on for 30 minutes. Turn off the heat and keep the lid on.

3. In a large stockpot, add the oil, onions, and garlic and sauté on medium-high heat until the onions are translucent, about 5 to 8 minutes. Add the broth, ham bone, and bay leaves to the stockpot. Bring to a boil. Boil for 5 minutes, then cover and simmer for 30 minutes or until the meat starts to fall off the bone. Remove the ham bone and let it cool on a cutting board. When it is cool enough to handle, pull or cut the ham meat from the bone and cut any large pieces to bite-size.

4. Drain the beans in a colander, shaking off excess liquid.

5. Add the drained beans, ham, 4 cups water, carrots, celery, salt (if using), and pepper to the stockpot. Bring to a boil over medium-high heat. Reduce the heat and simmer for 5 minutes, stirring well.

6. Ladle the hot soup into hot jars, leaving 1 inch of headspace. Remove any air bubbles and add additional soup if necessary to maintain the 1 inch of headspace.

7. Wipe the rim of each jar with a warm washcloth dipped in distilled white vinegar. Place a lid and ring on each jar and hand tighten.

8. Place jars in the pressure canner, lock the pressure canner lid, and bring to a boil on high heat. Let the canner vent for 10 minutes. Close the vent and continue heating to achieve 11 PSI for a dial gauge and 10 PSI for a weighted gauge. Process quart jars for 1 hour 30 minutes and pint jars for 1 hour 15 minutes.

Serving Tip: Using a pint jar of your home-canned Cream-Style Corn (page 54), bake a cast iron skillet full of yummy cornbread. While the bread bakes, heat a quart or two of Ham and Navy Bean Soup in a saucepan on the stove. When the cornbread is ready to cut and serve, place a 3-inch square in a shallow bowl and ladle the soup over the cornbread. Garnish with fresh parsley and grated Romano cheese.

SPLIT PEA SOUP WITH HAM

MAKES APPROXIMATELY 3 QUARTS OR 6 PINTS

PREP: 15 MIN • COOK: 40 MIN • CANNER: 1 HR • PROCESSING: 1 HR 30 MIN/1 HR 15 MIN

TOTAL: 3 HR 25 MIN/3 HR 10 MIN

Pea soup has been eaten since antiquity, dating as far back as 400 BCE. Remember that old nursery rhyme, *pease porridge hot, pease porridge cold*? It was written in 1765 with split pea soup as its focus. Split peas and salt pork have been common staples in many cultures for centuries, up to the present day. My hearty adaptation is Dutch heritage in a jar.

1 tablespoon olive oil

4 celery stalks, diced (2 cups)

2 medium yellow onions, diced (1 cup)

1 medium leek, white and light green parts only, diced (1 cup)

6 garlic cloves, minced

4 cups Chicken Broth (page 104) or Vegetable Broth (page 105)

2 cups water

3 large carrots, peeled and finely diced (1½ cups)

1 teaspoon rubbed sage

1 teaspoon coarse sea salt

½ teaspoon ground black pepper

1 bay leaf

1 pound dried split peas

2 cups diced smoked ham

1. In a large stockpot, add the oil, celery, onions, leek, and garlic. Sauté on medium-high heat until the onions are translucent, about 5 to 8 minutes. Add the broth, 2 cups water, carrots, sage, salt, pepper, and bay leaf to the stockpot and bring to a boil.

2. Thoroughly wash the peas in a colander in the sink, being sure to remove any damaged peas, debris, or rocks. Add the peas and ham to the stockpot, mix well, and return to a boil. Reduce the heat and simmer for 30 minutes, stirring frequently. Remove the soup from the heat. Remove and discard the bay leaf.

3. Ladle the hot soup into hot jars, leaving a generous 1 inch of headspace. Remove any air bubbles and add additional soup if necessary to maintain the headspace.

4. Wipe the rim of each jar with a warm washcloth dipped in distilled white vinegar. Place a lid and ring on each jar and hand tighten.

5. Place jars in the pressure canner, lock the pressure canner lid, and bring to a boil on high heat. Let the canner vent for 10 minutes. Close the vent and continue heating to achieve 11 PSI for a dial gauge and 10 PSI for a weighted gauge. Process quart jars for 1 hour 30 minutes and pint jars for 1 hour 15 minutes.

Ingredient Tip: A single batch can be doubled to yield more soup in jars. If you plan to double the recipe, please be sure to add an additional 4 cups Chicken Broth or Vegetable Broth and allow the soup to simmer for 45 minutes instead of the 30 minutes required for a single batch.

CHAPTER SEVEN

POULTRY, MEAT, WILD GAME, AND FISH

WHAT I FIND MOST VALUABLE about preserving my own meat is that it helps ensure that we are consuming the best quality meat. You know what you put in each jar. Even more important, you may have even raised, hunted, and caught the meat or fish yourself. This chapter provides useful canning techniques and simple recipes, so you may safely preserve fresh meat, fish, and poultry in a jar. For all you wild game hunters, this chapter goes a step further, sharing safe preparation techniques and delicious recipes to enjoy game meat. Once you know how to pressure can animal proteins, you can take full advantage of meat sales and discounts in your area without having to devote precious freezer space for preserving—just clear off a pantry shelf and enjoy precooked meat all year.

Poultry

Home-canned chicken is the perfect starter for so many quick, healthy recipes you'll wonder why you didn't think of this sooner. Simply heat and add seasonings to create meals like chicken curry soup, tacos, enchiladas and chicken alfredo. Home-canned chicken is even great to take camping. The protein-packed possibilities are endless!

PREPARING POULTRY FOR CANNING

While the chart below gives you the math behind what fits into a jar, make sure to use the following tips when filling a jar:

1. Remove excess fat and skin from breasts and thighs.

2. Keep the bones in legs and thighs if preferred.

3. Add cool water when raw packing or hot broth when hot packing for best results.

4. Precook ground poultry and drain any excess liquid or fat.

5. Ground poultry can be canned loose, in patties, or in links.

POULTRY PROCESSING CHART

TYPE	PREPARATION	QUANTITY	PACK TYPE	AMOUNT PER PINT	AMOUNT PER QUART
Boneless Skinless Breasts	cut into 2-inch pieces	22 to 28	Raw	2 breasts	4 breasts
Boneless Skinless Thighs	cut into 2-inch pieces	40 to 55	Raw	4 thighs	8 thighs
Breast, Bone-In	whole, skin removed	14	Raw	1 breast	2 breasts
Thighs, Bone-In	whole, skin removed	35 to 42	Raw	3 or 4 thighs	5 or 6 thighs
Legs, Bone-In	whole, skin removed	42	Raw	3 legs	6 legs
Ground	cooked, fat drained	14 pounds	Hot	1 pound	2 pounds

6. Always give each jar 1¼ inches of headspace when filling.

7. Always wipe the jar rim and rings with a warm wet washcloth dipped in distilled white vinegar.

8. If you raise chickens, be sure to chill dressed poultry for 6 to 12 hours before canning.

9. Adding water to raw-packed chicken is a preference. Meat without the addition of water will make its own broth in the jar while it cooks during processing; however, it is not enough broth to fully cover all the meat. The old instruction that told us not to add water when raw packing was for fear the meat would overproduce liquid, which would then cause grease to get onto the jar rim and prevent a lid seal from forming. As long as you maintain a 1¼-inch headspace and wipe each jar rim with distilled white vinegar, you have sufficiently eliminated the possibility of the lid not sealing. While it is still acceptable to skip the added water when raw packing, I personally prefer to add water so I have the choice to use, or not, the broth in the jar during meal creation. Plus, when I add water during raw packing, I can be sure the meat is fully covered with enough liquid to prevent oxidization, which discolors and dries out the uncovered meat.

YIELD IN PINTS	YIELD IN QUARTS	PROCESSING TIME FOR QUARTS	PROCESSING TIME FOR PINTS	PSI DIAL GAUGE*	PSI WEIGHTED GAUGE*
7	14	1 hr 30 min	1 hr 15 min	11 PSI	10 PSI
7	14	1 hr 30 min	1 hr 15 min	11 PSI	10 PSI
7	14	1 hr 15 min	1 hr 5 min	11 PSI	10 PSI
7	14	1 hr 15 min	1 hr 5 min	11 PSI	10 PSI
7	14	1 hr 15 min	1 hr 5 min	11 PSI	10 PSI
7	14	1 hr 30 min	1 hr 15 min	11 PSI	10 PSI

* For elevations above 1,000 feet, check the Pressure Canning Altitude Chart on page 6 to safely increase PSI.

HOMEMADE CHICKEN SPICE BLEND RECIPES

Adding dried herbs and spices to your home-canned chicken is a great way to pre-flavor the meat so it is ready to be used in recipe creation. Pressure canning the spices into the chicken infuses the meat fibers with flavor, giving each dish depth. When you pack the chicken into the jars, add any of the spice blends below: Add 1½ tablespoons to every quart jar or 2½ teaspoons to every pint jar.

These blends can be doubled or tripled depending on the amount you choose to set aside or use. Once you've mixed the spice blends together, store them in half-pint jars out of direct sunlight. Be sure to label the lid with the month, year, and spice blend name.

White Chili Seasoning Spice Blend

MAKES ABOUT ¼ CUP

2 teaspoons garlic powder

2 teaspoons onion powder

2 teaspoons dried oregano

2 teaspoons ground cumin

½ teaspoon cayenne pepper

1½ teaspoons coarse sea salt

1 teaspoon ground black pepper

Poultry Seasoning Blend

MAKES ABOUT ⅓ CUP

2 tablespoons chopped fresh thyme

1 tablespoon chopped fresh rosemary

1 tablespoon chopped fresh sage

1 teaspoon dried marjoram

½ teaspoon ground black pepper

½ teaspoon celery seeds

½ teaspoon ground nutmeg

Taco Seasoning Spice Blend

MAKES ABOUT ⅓ CUP

2 tablespoons chili powder

2 teaspoons garlic powder

2 teaspoons onion powder

2 teaspoons dried oregano

2 teaspoons paprika

1 teaspoon ground cumin

1 teaspoon coarse sea salt

1 teaspoon ground black pepper

Italian Spice Blend

MAKES ABOUT ⅓ CUP

4 teaspoons dried basil

1 tablespoon dried oregano

2 teaspoons dried thyme

2 teaspoons dried rosemary

1 teaspoon dried sage

1½ teaspoons garlic powder

½ to 1 teaspoon red pepper flakes (optional)

Asian Spice Blend

MAKES ABOUT ⅓ CUP

2 tablespoons yellow curry powder

2 teaspoons garlic powder

2 teaspoons onion powder

2 teaspoons ground ginger

1½ teaspoons coarse sea salt

1 teaspoon ground black pepper

TURKEY SAUSAGE

MAKES APPROXIMATELY 2 QUARTS OR 4 PINTS

PREP: 10 MIN • COOK: 10 MIN • CANNER: 1 HR • PROCESSING: 1 HR 30 MIN/1 HR 15 MIN

TOTAL: 2 HR 50 MIN/2 HR 35 MIN

Ages ago, my Auntie Diane shared a recipe for this healthier alternative to pork sausage with me. The best part: It tastes just like pork sausage! Preserve Turkey Sausage in patties, links, or simply as ground sausage meat. We love taking a jar of sausage patties camping. Doing so makes breakfast a cinch while enjoying the outdoors because it is lightweight and doesn't require refrigeration.

½ cup warm water

2 teaspoons dried basil

2 teaspoons rubbed sage

2 teaspoons red pepper flakes

1½ teaspoons marjoram

1 teaspoon dried mustard

½ teaspoon ground thyme

½ teaspoon coarse sea salt

½ teaspoon ground black pepper

1 teaspoon garlic powder

1 teaspoon paprika

3 pounds ground turkey

½ cup grapeseed or extra-virgin olive oil

1. In a large bowl combine the water, basil, sage, red pepper flakes, marjoram, mustard, thyme, salt, pepper, garlic powder, and paprika. Add the ground turkey, and, using clean hands, mix all the spices into the meat. Shape the turkey into a large ball and place back in the bowl.

2. Cover the ball of turkey meat with oil and use your hands to evenly distribute oil over the entire surface, lifting and turning the ball to coat evenly. Set the turkey ball back into the bowl. Cover the bowl with plastic wrap and refrigerate overnight or for 12 hours.

3. Shape the sausage into patties or links, or leave the turkey loose. Brown patties or links in a skillet on both sides for about 1 minute on each side. Brown loose sausage in a skillet, about 10 minutes. Whichever method you choose, be sure to drain off any excess grease prior to filling jars.

4. Hot pack the meat into hot jars, leaving 1¼ inches of headspace. Wipe the rim of each jar with a warm washcloth dipped in distilled white vinegar. Place a lid and ring on each jar and hand tighten.

5. Place jars in the pressure canner, lock the pressure canner lid, and bring to a boil on high heat. Let the canner vent for 10 minutes. Close the vent and continue heating to achieve 11 PSI for a dial gauge and 10 PSI for a weighted gauge. Process quart jars for 1 hour 30 minutes and pint jars for 1 hour 15 minutes.

Ingredient Tip: If you are on a low-sodium diet, feel free to omit the salt. If you prefer a bit more heat, feel free to increase the red pepper flakes. Some people love seasoning their sausage with nutmeg; if that is you, then by all means, add some to the mix. Craft this to your flavor liking.

Pork

Home-canned pork is another perfect meat to have at the ready. I will typically can pork butt when it's on sale, so I have fully cooked pork shoulder, or butt, available when I am crunched for time and need to get a pulled pork meal on the table. I will also pressure can ground pork when there is a huge sale, which saves me on freezer space and gives me a healthy alternative to ground beef.

PREPARING PORK FOR CANNING

Use this chart to determine how much pork you need for canning, and use the following tips when filling the jars:

1. Remove excess fat, silver skin and gristle, but keep marbleized fat to prevent drying out.

2. Brown all sides in fat and seasonings prior to filling jars for best results.

PORK PROCESSING CHART

CUT	PREPARATION	QUANTITY	PACK TYPE	AMOUNT PER PINT	AMOUNT PER QUART
Tenderloin	cut into 2-inch pieces	14 pounds	Raw	1 pound	2 pounds
Pork Shoulder	cut into 2-inch pieces, browned	14 pounds	Hot	1 pound	2 pounds
Pork Butt	cut into 2-inch pieces, browned	14 pounds	Hot	1 pound	2 pounds
Boneless Pork Chops	cut into 2-inch pieces, browned	14 pounds	Hot	1 pound	2 pounds
Ground	cooked, fat drained	14 pounds	Hot	1 pound	2 pounds

3. Precook ground pork and drain any excess liquid or fat.

4. Ground pork can be canned loose, in patties, or in links.

5. Always give each jar 1¼ inches of headspace when filling.

6. Always wipe the jar rim and screw thread with a warm washcloth dipped in distilled white vinegar.

HOMEMADE PORK SPICE BLEND RECIPES

While any of the spice blends throughout this chapter can be used interchangeably, the pork spice blends were created to really enhance the pork's flavor. These blends are an excellent way to preseason home-canned pork, but if you make a bit extra, they also are an excellent dry-rub when slow-roasting pork shoulder in the oven or in a smoker. When you pack pork into jars, include your favorite spice blend, adding 2½ teaspoons

YIELD IN PINTS	YIELD IN QUARTS	PROCESSING TIME FOR QUARTS	PROCESSING TIME FOR PINTS	PSI DIAL GAUGE*	PSI WEIGHTED GAUGE*
7	14	1 hr 30 min	1 hr 15 min	11 PSI	10 PSI
7	14	1 hr 30 min	1 hr 15 min	11 PSI	10 PSI
7	14	1 hr 30 min	1 hr 15 min	11 PSI	10 PSI
7	14	1 hr 30 min	1 hr 15 min	11 PSI	10 PSI
7	14	1 hr 30 min	1 hr 15 min	11 PSI	10 PSI

* For elevations above 1,000 feet, check the Pressure Canning Altitude Chart on page 6 to safely increase PSI.

to every pint jar and 1½ tablespoons to every quart jar.

These blends can be doubled or tripled depending on the amount you choose to set aside, or use. Mix the spice blends together and store in half-pint jars out of direct sunlight. Be sure to label the lid with the month, year, and spice blend name.

Smoky Bones Spice Blend

MAKES ABOUT ½ CUP

4 teaspoons coarse sea salt

1 tablespoon dried thyme

1 tablespoon onion powder

1 tablespoon smoked paprika (mild or hot)

1 tablespoon paprika

2 teaspoons garlic powder

2 teaspoons cayenne powder

2 teaspoons dried oregano

1 teaspoon ground black pepper

1 teaspoon dried basil

Caribbean Jerk Spice Blend

MAKES ABOUT ⅓ CUP

1 tablespoon ground allspice

1 tablespoon ground cumin

1 tablespoon coconut sugar (or dark brown sugar)

2 teaspoons sage

2 teaspoons nutmeg

1 teaspoon thyme

1 teaspoon coarse sea salt

½ to 1 teaspoon cayenne pepper

Traditional Grilled Pork Spice Blend

MAKES ABOUT ⅓ CUP

1 tablespoon garlic powder

1 tablespoon dried oregano

1 tablespoon ground cumin

1 tablespoon ground coriander

2 teaspoons dried thyme

2 teaspoons coarse sea salt

BBQ PULLED PORK

MAKES APPROXIMATELY 6 QUARTS OR 12 PINTS

PREP: 20 MIN • COOK: 15 MIN • CANNER: 1 HR • PROCESSING: 1 HR 30 MIN/1 HR 15 MIN

TOTAL: 3 HR 5 MIN/2 HR 50 MIN

Capture the flavor of a day's long-smoked BBQ pulled pork recipe in a jar with this delicious adaptation. This time-saving method allows you to raw pack the meat and add BBQ sauce—however, don't hesitate to pressure can your leftover BBQ Pulled Pork. Pressure canning shredded pork leftovers preserves the flavor longer when in a jar and saves on freezer space.

8 to 10 pounds boneless pork shoulder or butt roast

1 cup packed brown sugar

1 cup ketchup

1 cup blackstrap molasses

¾ cup tomato paste (6 ounces)

¼ cup Dijon mustard

¼ cup apple cider vinegar

¼ cup honey

¼ cup Worcestershire sauce

1 teaspoon red pepper flakes

1 teaspoon coarse sea salt

1 teaspoon ground black pepper

2 tablespoons olive oil

3 medium onions, finely chopped (1½ cups)

8 garlic cloves, minced

1. Clean and prepare the pork by removing excess surface fat, being sure to keep the marbling. Some fat is required to keep the pork from drying out. Cut the pork into 2- to 2½-inch chunks and set aside.

2. To make the BBQ sauce, combine the sugar, ketchup, molasses, tomato paste, mustard, vinegar, honey, Worcestershire sauce, red pepper flakes, salt, and pepper in a large bowl. Whisk together until well blended. Set aside.

3. In a deep skillet or small stockpot, add the olive oil, onions, and garlic. Sauté over medium-high heat until the onions are translucent, about 5 to 8 minutes. Add the pork chunks and toss to coat and cook just long enough to render some of the fat, about 10 minutes.

4. Using a slotted spoon, fill each jar with the pork and onion mixture, leaving 1 inch of headspace. Ladle the BBQ sauce over the pork, maintaining the 1 inch of headspace. Remove any air bubbles and add additional sauce if necessary to maintain the 1 inch of headspace.

5. Wipe the rim of each jar with a warm washcloth dipped in distilled white vinegar. Place a lid and ring on each jar and hand tighten.

6. Place jars in the pressure canner, lock the pressure canner lid, and bring to a boil on high heat. Let the canner vent for 10 minutes. Close the vent and continue heating to achieve 11 PSI for a dial gauge and 10 PSI for a weighted gauge. Process quart jars for 1 hour 30 minutes and pint jars for 1 hour 15 minutes.

Recipe Tip: If you would rather slow-roast the pork shoulder with a dry rub prior to shredding and adding BBQ sauce, feel free to do so, then fill your jars and process as stated in the recipe.

Beef

Having jars of precooked roast beef, stew meat, beef tips, and ground beef saves me loads of time when planning and creating meals. Before canning, I like to preseason beef with salt, pepper, garlic, and onions or one of my favorite spice blends to give the meat a leg up on flavor. For instance, if you season your ground beef with the Taco Seasoning Spice Blend (page 144) before canning, you've got taco night—or an easy-to-pack lunch—ready to go at a moment's notice.

PREPARING BEEF FOR CANNING

While the chart below gives you the math behind what fits into a jar, make sure to use the following tips when filling a jar:

1. Remove excess fat, silver skin and gristle, but keep marbleized fat to prevent drying out.

2. Brown all sides in fat and seasonings prior to filling jars for best results.

3. Precook ground beef and drain any excess liquid or fat.

4. Ground beef can be canned loose or in patties.

BEEF PROCESSING CHART

CUT	PREPARATION	QUANTITY	PACK TYPE	AMOUNT PER PINT	AMOUNT PER QUART
Chuck Steak	cut into 2-inch pieces, browned	14 pounds	Hot	1 pound	2 pounds
Round Roast	cut into 2-inch pieces, browned	14 pounds	Hot	1 pound	2 pounds
Stew Meat/ Beef Tips	cut into 2-inch pieces, browned	14 pounds	Hot	1 pound	2 pounds
Ground	cooked, fat drained	14 pounds	Hot	1 pound	2 pounds

5. Always give each jar 1¼ inches of headspace when filling.

6. Always wipe the jar rims and screw thread with a warm washcloth dipped in distilled white vinegar.

7. Beef sold for stew is typically chuck or round roasts cut into 1½-inch pieces. Bottom and eye cuts, also known as round, are typically leaner than a chuck roast, which includes cuts from the shoulder, leg, and butt. When cutting into bite-size pieces, cut to a size you would feel comfortable seeing on the end of your fork or spoon.

HOMEMADE BEEF SPICE BLENDS

I mainly preseasoned ground beef since I use it so often as a meal starter, however, feel free to season beef tips for use in stew and roasts with traditional pot roast flavors, giving your meat added flavor for its intended use. Have a spice blend of your own you enjoy using? Awesome! When packing beef into jars, add 1½ tablespoons of your favorite spice blend to every quart jar and 2½ teaspoons to every pint.

These blends can be doubled or tripled depending on the amount you choose to set aside, or use. Mix the spice blends together and store in

YIELD IN PINTS	YIELD IN QUARTS	PROCESSING TIME FOR QUARTS	PROCESSING TIME FOR PINTS	PSI DIAL GAUGE*	PSI WEIGHTED GAUGE*
7	14	1 hr 30 min	1 hr 15 min	11 PSI	10 PSI
7	14	1 hr 30 min	1 hr 15 min	11 PSI	10 PSI
7	14	1 hr 30 min	1 hr 15 min	11 PSI	10 PSI
7	14	1 hr 30 min	1 hr 15 min	11 PSI	10 PSI

* For elevations above 1,000 feet, check the Pressure Canning Altitude Chart on page 6 to safely increase PSI.

half-pint jars out of direct sunlight. Be sure to label the lid with the month, year, and spice blend name.

Chili Seasoning Spice Blend

MAKES ABOUT ½ CUP

2 tablespoons chili powder

2 teaspoons garlic powder

2 teaspoons onion powder

2 teaspoons red pepper flakes

2 teaspoons dried oregano

2 teaspoons paprika

2 teaspoons ground cumin

2 teaspoons coriander

1½ teaspoons coarse sea salt

1 teaspoon ground black pepper

Taco Seasoning Spice Blend

MAKES ABOUT ⅓ CUP

2 tablespoons chili powder

2 teaspoons garlic powder

2 teaspoons onion powder

2 teaspoons dried oregano

2 teaspoons paprika

1 teaspoon ground cumin

1 teaspoon coarse sea salt

1 teaspoon ground black pepper

Italian Spice Blend

MAKES ABOUT ¼ CUP

4 teaspoons dried basil

1 tablespoon dried oregano

2 teaspoons dried thyme

2 teaspoons dried rosemary

1½ teaspoons garlic powder

1 teaspoon dried sage

½ teaspoon red pepper flakes (optional)

Roast and Stew Seasoning Blend

MAKES ABOUT ⅓ CUP

1 tablespoon dried parsley

1 tablespoon dried oregano

1½ teaspoons celery seeds

1 teaspoon ground coriander

1 teaspoon dried thyme

1 teaspoon dried basil

4½ teaspoons coarse sea salt

½ teaspoon ground black pepper

TENDER MEAT EVERY TIME

The benefit of pressure canning meat is even the toughest of cuts can be made tender. Think of the times you may have pressure cooked cube steak or corned beef. I bet you could almost cut the meat with a fork. The same concept is true when pressure canning meat, the only difference is the meat is in individual glass jars.

Prepare meat and poultry before canning by removing excess fat or undesirable parts such as excessive skin, gristle, bone, silver skin, etc. When canning poultry and rabbit, you may leave various parts on the bone, for instance; preserving legs and thighs with bones in and skin on retains more flavor and cuts down on processing time. Cut the meat into manageable pieces that fit easily into canning jars.

Invest in widemouthed jars for canning and preserving meat to make filling and emptying the jars much easier, and you gain a touch more space compared to a regular-mouth jar.

BEEF TIPS AND GRAVY

MAKES APPROXIMATELY 6 QUARTS OR 12 PINTS
PREP: 35 MIN • COOK: 10 MIN • CANNING: 1 HR • PROCESSING: 1 HR 30 MIN/1 HR 15 MIN
TOTAL: 3 HR 15 MIN/3 HR

This recipe makes an amazing meal starter. Reheat this seasoned, cooked meat and serve alongside vegetables, on mashed potatoes, or mixed with cooked egg noodles for a quick protein-packed meal.

4 tablespoons extra-virgin olive oil, divided

12 pounds beef stew meat

2 teaspoons coarse sea salt (optional)

1 teaspoon ground black pepper

8 cups hot water, divided

½ cup ClearJel®

12 garlic cloves

1. In a deep skillet on medium-high heat, heat 1 tablespoon olive oil. Working in small batches, add the beef and lightly brown each side, about 3 minutes. Season each batch with a dash of sea salt and black pepper while in the skillet. Add 1 additional tablespoon of oil while browning each batch. Work quickly. Do not fully cook the meat. Set batches aside, leaving the delicious drippings in the skillet.

2. Keeping the skillet on medium-high heat, slowly add 4 cups hot water to the skillet. Whisk in the ClearJel® and slowly add the remaining hot water, continuing to whisk. Bring to a boil for 2 minutes, then remove from the heat. Set the gravy aside.

3. Add 2 whole garlic cloves to each warm quart and 1 to each warm pint. Using a slotted spoon, raw pack the meat into jars, leaving a generous 1 inch of headspace. Ladle the hot gravy mixture over the meat, maintaining the headspace. Remove any air bubbles and add additional sauce if necessary to maintain the headspace.

4. Wipe the rim of each jar with a warm washcloth dipped in distilled white vinegar. Place a lid and ring on each jar and hand tighten.

5. Place jars in the pressure canner, lock the pressure canner lid, and bring to a boil on high heat. Let the canner vent for 10 minutes. Close the vent and continue heating to achieve 11 PSI for a dial gauge and 10 PSI for a weighted gauge. Process quart jars for 1 hour 30 minutes and pint jars for 1 hour 15 minutes.

Ingredient Tip: Feel free to add a half sprig of rosemary or thyme to each jar, or maybe you prefer additional garlic cloves. Get creative and add fresh herbs and spices to each jar before filling with gravy, especially if you have an intended use that requires such flavors.

BEEF PAPRIKASH

MAKES APPROXIMATELY 5 QUARTS OR 10 PINTS
PREP: 15 MIN • COOK: 15 MIN • CANNER: 1 HR • PROCESSING: 1 HR 30 MIN/1 HR 15 MIN
TOTAL: 3 HR/2 HR 45 MIN

This is an adaptation similar to Hungarian Goulash (page 174), with rich-flavored meat but without the vegetables. This way, you have more serving options; once the meat is reheated, throw in any fresh veggies you like and serve on a bed of couscous or rice—or even on a baked potato. This is another perfect opportunity to use tougher cuts of beef, as they will tenderize during pressure canning.

3 tablespoons olive oil

4 cups onions, sliced

6 garlic cloves, minced

8 pounds cubed beef stew meat, cut into 1½-inch pieces

1 tablespoon caraway seeds or 1 teaspoon ground caraway seed

2 teaspoons coarse sea salt

½ teaspoon ground black pepper

6 cups chopped red bell peppers

8 cups Beef Broth (page 103)

⅓ cup sweet paprika

¾ cup tomato paste (6 ounces)

1 tablespoon granulated sugar

1. In a stockpot, heat the olive oil on medium-high heat. Add the onions and garlic, stir, and cook for 5 to 8 minutes or until the onions are translucent. Add the stew meat, caraway seeds (or ground caraway), salt, and pepper. Mix well and add the bell peppers. Toss and cook for 5 minutes or until the peppers have softened.

2. Add the Beef Broth and paprika, mix well, and bring to a boil for 5 minutes, then mix in the tomato paste until fully dispersed. Add the sugar, mix again, and cook for 1 minute. Remove from the heat.

3. Ladle the paprikash into jars, leaving 1 inch of headspace. Be sure to have a good ratio of meat and peppers to sauce. Remove any air bubbles using the air bubble remover tool, and add additional sauce if necessary to maintain the 1 inch of headspace.

4. Wipe the rim of each jar with a warm washcloth dipped in distilled white vinegar. Place a lid and ring on each jar and hand tighten.

5. Place jars in the pressure canner, lock the pressure canner lid, and bring to a boil on high heat. Let the canner vent for 10 minutes. Close the vent and continue heating to achieve 11 PSI for a dial gauge and 10 PSI for a weighted gauge. Process quart jars for 1 hour 30 minutes and pint jars for 1 hour 15 minutes.

Serving Tip: When heating a quart of Beef Paprikash, mix in ¼ cup Greek yogurt and serve with boiled egg noodles or boiled young potatoes. Garnish with fresh chopped dill or parsley.

Wild Game

Hunting is a way of life for many people. Venison, goose, and rabbit feed many families throughout the year, as do caribou, moose, and elk. While freezing is a great way to preserve meat, it provides a limited shelf life. Pressure canning wild game is easy and has many benefits, including tenderizing tough cuts of meat and removing some of the "gamy" flavor.

Only use high-quality, properly dressed and cleaned wild game for canning. It must be kept refrigerated or frozen and then thawed in the refrigerator prior to canning. No matter the recipe, all wild game meat must always process the full standard time, which is 1 hour 15 minutes for pints and 1 hour 30 minutes for quarts.

Large game animals like elk, deer, caribou, and moose are canned as you would beef, while small game animals and birds, like rabbit, duck, squirrel, and pheasant, are canned like poultry. Wild game benefits best from hot packing every recipe with a broth, however there is nothing wrong with raw packing, with or without water.

PREPARING WILD GAME FOR CANNING

Here are a few tips to consider before you begin preserving wild game in your pressure canner:

Choose chilled, high-quality meat from healthy game animals and birds. While inspecting meat, be sure to not use any cuts that contain dark bruising or tumors. Do not simply remove the tumor, discard the entire cut and do not eat or preserve meat from that animal. Remove excess fat from high-quality cuts, then soak for 1 hour in brine containing 1 tablespoon canning salt for every 1 quart of water. After soaking, rinse the meat well. Remove any large bones and undesirables like gristle, silver skin, etc. You may preserve small game and wild birds bone-in without issue.

Prepare cuts as indicated in the recipe. If preparing venison meat, remove every bone. In many areas throughout our country, venison cannot be preserved bone-in due to chronic wasting disease. Because of this disease, venison bones cannot be used to make broth, either. When canning venison, use broth made from beef or pork bones or that is store-bought. Check with your state's Department of Natural Resources or Department of Environmental Conservation to learn if the deer in your area are of concern.

Add tomato juice or tomato paste to the warm broth when raw packing large game meat. The tomato flavor draws out the gamy flavor. This, of course, is a preference, as many have had great success simply raw packing with or without water.

VENISON

Deer meat, or venison, is a wholesome, nourishing food. Venison tends to have a finer texture and is leaner than beef. Venison is higher in moisture, similar in protein content, and lower in calories, cholesterol, and fat than most cuts of grain-fed beef, pork, or lamb. However, like beef, leaner cuts can be tougher. More often than not, venison requires the addition of a fat such as olive oil, bacon grease, or lard to keep it from drying out while cooking.

RABBIT

Rabbit meat is a great source of protein, even more so than beef or chicken. Better yet, it is an easily digestible protein that is almost cholesterol free. Back in the 1940s and 1950s, rabbit meat was a common meat for many families, almost as common as chicken is today. It is the meat that got many through the Great Depression. Although it is not as popular now, there are still many good reasons to consume rabbit. Not only is it an excellent source of iron, containing more than 4 mg a serving, it also provides a wide range of minerals and high levels of phosphorous and potassium.

WILD GAME MEAT PROCESSING CHART

CUT	PREPARATION	QUANTITY	PACK TYPE	AMOUNT PER PINT	AMOUNT PER QUART
Large Game					
Chuck Steak	cut into 2-inch pieces, browned	14 pounds	Hot	1 pound	2 pounds
Round Roast	cut into 2-inch pieces, browned	14 pounds	Hot	1 pound	2 pounds
Stew Meat Tips	cut into 2-inch pieces, browned	14 pounds	Hot	1 pound	2 pounds
Shoulder, Shank & Neck Meat	cut into 2-inch pieces, browned	14 pounds	Hot	1 pound	2 pounds
Ground	cooked, fat drained	14 pounds	Hot	1 pound	2 pounds
Small Game & Birds					
Boneless Skinless Breasts	cut into 2-inch pieces	22 to 28	Raw	2 breasts	4 breasts
Boneless Skinless Thighs	cut into 2-inch pieces	40 to 55	Raw	4 thighs	8 thighs
Breasts, Bone-In	whole, skin removed	14	Raw	1 breast	2 breasts
Thighs, Bone-In	whole, skin removed	35 to 42	Raw	3 or 4 thighs	5 or 6 thighs
Legs, Bone-In	whole, skin removed	42	Raw	3 legs	6 legs
Ground	cooked, fat drained	14 pounds	Hot	1 pound	2 pounds

YIELD IN PINTS	YIELD IN QUARTS	PROCESSING TIME FOR QUARTS	PROCESSING TIME FOR PINTS	PSI DIAL GAUGE*	PSI WEIGHTED GAUGE*
7	14	1 hr 30 min	1 hr 15 min	11 PSI	10 PSI
7	14	1 hr 30 min	1 hr 15 min	11 PSI	10 PSI
7	14	1 hr 30 min	1 hr 15 min	11 PSI	10 PSI
7	14	1 hr 30 min	1 hr 15 min	11 PSI	10 PSI
7	14	1 hr 30 min	1 hr 15 min	11 PSI	10 PSI
7	14	1 hr 30 min	1 hr 15 min	11 PSI	10 PSI
7	14	1 hr 30 min	1 hr 15 min	11 PSI	10 PSI
7	14	1 hr 15 min	1 hr 5 min	11 PSI	10 PSI
7	14	1 hr 15 min	1 hr 5 min	11 PSI	10 PSI
7	14	1 hr 15 min	1 hr 5 min	11 PSI	10 PSI
7	14	1 hr 30 min	1 hr 15 min	11 PSI	10 PSI

* For elevations above 1,000 feet, check the Pressure Canning Altitude Chart on page 6 to safely increase PSI.

VENISON STEAK DIANE

MAKES APPROXIMATELY 4 QUARTS OR 8 PINTS

PREP: 10 MIN • COOK: 15 MIN • CANNER: 1 HR • PROCESSING: 1 HR 30 MIN/1 HR 15 MIN

TOTAL: 2 HR 55 MIN/2 HR 40 MIN

Melt-in-your-mouth venison tenderloin or back-strap medallions are a dream in this delicious recipe. While the onions, Dijon, and Worcestershire sauce give this wild game version a kick, the brandy complements the venison superbly. This is also an opportunity to tenderize tougher cuts of venison like neck meat.

3 tablespoons olive oil, divided

3 to 5 pounds venison backstrap or tenderloin, cut into 2½-inch medallions

1 teaspoon coarse sea salt

½ teaspoon ground black pepper

1 cup brandy

1 cup diced sweet onion

4 garlic cloves, minced

2 shallots, finely chopped

3 tablespoons Worcestershire sauce

2 tablespoons Dijon mustard

4 cups Beef Broth (page 103)

¾ cup tomato paste (6 ounces)

1. In a skillet, starting with 1 tablespoon oil, brown the venison in batches on medium-high heat until all the venison is lightly browned, about 3 to 5 minutes per batch. Season each batch with a dash of sea salt and pepper. Add 1 additional tablespoon of oil while browning each batch. Remove each batch from the stockpot and place in a bowl. Be sure not to fully cook the meat.

2. Add the brandy to the skillet, and on high heat, deglaze being sure to scrape all the bits off the bottom of the pan.

3. In a large stockpot, add the browned venison and the deglazed drippings from the skillet. Add the onion, garlic, shallots, Worcestershire sauce, and Dijon mustard, and mix well. Bring the contents to a boil on medium-high heat for 5 minutes. Whisk together the Beef Broth and tomato paste and add to the stockpot. Return to a boil for an additional 5 minutes, mixing well.

4. Using a slotted spoon, fill each hot jar three-quarters full of venison. Ladle the hot cooking liquid over the mixture, leaving 1 inch of headspace. Remove any air bubbles and add additional liquid if necessary to maintain the 1 inch of headspace.

5. Wipe the rim of each jar with a warm washcloth dipped in distilled white vinegar. Place a lid and ring on each jar and hand tighten.

6. Place jars in the pressure canner, lock the pressure canner lid, and bring to a boil on high heat. Let the canner vent for 10 minutes. Close the vent and continue heating to achieve 11 PSI for a dial gauge and 10 PSI for a weighted gauge. Process quart jars for 1 hour 30 minutes and pint jars for 1 hour 15 minutes.

Serving Tip: When heating a quart on the stove top, be sure to add ¼ cup heavy whipping cream, mix well and finish heating through, about 3 minutes. Do not boil the cream.

VENISON STROGANOFF

MAKES APPROXIMATELY 3 QUARTS OR 6 PINTS
PREP: 15 MIN • COOK: 10 MIN • CANNER: 1 HR • PROCESSING: 1 HR 30 MIN/1 HR 15 MIN
TOTAL: 2 HR 55 MIN/2 HR 40 MIN

This is the perfect dish for tougher cuts of venison like neck meat because the pressure canner tenderizes the meat and the herbs and stock permeate the meat fibers. Like Beef Stroganoff (page 160), the pieces of venison become tender enough to cut with a fork. Instead of serving Venison Stroganoff over egg noodles, change things up and serve it with spaetzle.

2 tablespoons olive oil, divided

5 pounds venison, cut into 2-inch pieces

1 cup red wine

1 pound mushrooms, sliced (4 cups)

1 large onion, thinly sliced (2 cups)

5 garlic cloves, minced

¼ cup Worcestershire sauce

¼ teaspoon ground black pepper

6 cups Beef Bone Stock (page 96)

⅓ cup ClearJel®

1. In a skillet, starting with 1 tablespoon oil, brown venison in batches on medium-high heat until all venison is lightly browned, about 3 to 5 minutes per batch. Add 1 additional tablespoon of oil while browning each batch. Remove each batch from the stockpot and place in a bowl. Be sure not to fully cook the meat.

2. Add the wine to the skillet, and deglaze on high heat, being sure to scrape all the drippings off the bottom of the pan, about 3 minutes.

3. In a large stockpot, add the browned venison and deglazed drippings. Add the mushrooms, onion, garlic, Worcestershire sauce, and pepper. On medium-high heat, bring the contents to a boil for 5 minutes. Whisk together the Beef Bone Stock and ClearJel® and add to the stockpot. Return to a boil for an additional 5 minutes, mixing well.

4. Using a slotted spoon, fill each hot jar three-quarters full of Stroganoff solids. Ladle the hot cooking liquid over the mixture, leaving 1 inch of headspace. Remove any air bubbles and add additional liquid if necessary to maintain the 1 inch of headspace.

5. Wipe the rim of each jar with a warm washcloth dipped in distilled white vinegar. Place a lid and ring on each jar and hand tighten.

6. Place jars in the pressure canner, lock the pressure canner lid, and bring to a boil on high heat. Let the canner vent for 10 minutes. Close the vent and continue heating to achieve 11 PSI for a dial gauge and 10 PSI for a weighted gauge. Process quart jars for 1 hour 30 minutes and pint jars for 1 hour 15 minutes.

Serving Tip: To give your home-canned Stroganoff a creamy texture prior to serving, pour 1 quart stroganoff into a saucepan and heat on medium-high. Next add 1 cup sour cream and ¼ cup softened cream cheese to the saucepan and mix well.

RABBIT (OR PHEASANT) CACCIATORE

MAKES APPROXIMATELY 5 QUARTS OR 10 PINTS
PREP: 20 MIN • COOK: 20 MIN • CANNER: 1 HR • PROCESSING: 1 HR 30 MIN/1 HR 15 MIN
TOTAL: 3 HR 10 MIN/2 HR 55 MIN

Cacciatore means "hunter" in Italian, so having a dish made *alla cacciatora* means the meal is prepared "hunter-style," which traditionally includes onions, herbs, tomatoes, bell peppers, and sometimes wine. Cacciatore is also excellent prepared with pheasant.

3 tablespoons olive oil

8 cups cubed boneless, skinless rabbit, cut into 2-inch pieces

1 tablespoon dried oregano

1 tablespoon dried basil

1 teaspoon dried thyme

1 teaspoon dried rosemary, crushed

1 teaspoon coarse sea salt

½ teaspoon ground black pepper

½ cup red wine

4 cups diced tomatoes with juice

2 cups white mushrooms, trimmed and sliced

3 cups chopped sweet onion

3 cups Tomato Juice (page 45)

1 large red bell pepper, chopped (1½ cups)

1 celery stalk, chopped (½ cup)

6 garlic cloves, minced

¾ cup tomato paste (6 ounces)

1 tablespoon granulated sugar

1. In a thick-bottomed stockpot, add the oil and rabbit. Mix well to coat the rabbit. Cook the rabbit on medium-high heat for 3 minutes, stirring often. Add the oregano, basil, thyme, rosemary, salt, and pepper. Mix well and cook for an additional 3 minutes. Add the red wine, place the lid on the stockpot, and let the mixture cook for 5 more minutes undisturbed.

2. Add the tomatoes, mushrooms, onion, Tomato Juice, bell pepper, celery, and garlic. Mix well and bring to a boil. Boil for 5 minutes. Add the tomato paste and sugar, mixing well to distribute the paste. Boil for an additional 5 minutes. Remove from the heat.

3. Using a slotted spoon, fill each hot jar three-quarters full of rabbit and vegetables. Ladle the hot tomato sauce over the mixture, leaving 1 inch of headspace. Remove any air bubbles and add additional sauce if necessary to maintain the 1 inch of headspace.

4. Wipe the rim of each jar with a warm washcloth dipped in distilled white vinegar. Place a lid and ring on each jar and hand tighten.

5. Place jars in the pressure canner, lock the pressure canner lid, and bring to a boil on high heat. Let the canner vent for 10 minutes. Close the vent and continue heating to achieve 11 PSI for a dial gauge and 10 PSI for a weighted gauge. Process quart jars for 1 hour 30 minutes and pint jars for 1 hour 15 minutes.

Serving Tip: This dish is traditionally served over pasta noodles, and topped with fresh chopped parsley and shaved Parmesan cheese. For a fun kick, use V8® juice, regular or spicy, or your home-canned Bloody Mary Mix (page 48).

GERMAN RABBIT STEW

MAKES APPROXIMATELY 2 QUARTS OR 4 PINTS

PREP: 20 MIN • COOK: 25 MIN • CANNER: 1 HR • PROCESSING: 1 HR 30 MIN/1 HR 15 MIN
TOTAL: 2 HR 30 MIN/2 HR 15 MIN

Often referred to as hasenpfeffer, this traditional German stew is made from either rabbit or hare that is braised with onions, wine, and vinegar. Enjoy this fun adaptation in a lighter broth flavored with lemon and bay leaves. Try serving this wholesome stew with sour cream and capers over boiled young potatoes.

4 tablespoons butter, divided

2 cottontail rabbits, or 1 domestic rabbit, cut into
   2- to 2½-inch pieces

1 teaspoon coarse sea salt

½ teaspoon ground black pepper

2 medium onions, chopped (1 cup)

4 garlic cloves, minced

½ cup dry white wine

4 cups Chicken Stock (page 98)

Zest and juice of one lemon

3 bay leaves

2 sprigs thyme

1. In a deep skillet, melt 2 tablespoons butter on medium-high heat. Working in batches, brown the rabbit meat about 3 minutes on each side, seasoning each batch with a dash of salt and pepper. Add more butter as necessary for additional batches. Once all the pieces are browned, set the meat aside, keeping all the drippings in the pan.

2. Add the onions and garlic to the skillet, cooking until the onions are translucent, about 5 to 8 minutes. Add the wine to the skillet and turn the heat up to high, keeping the onions moving. Return the rabbit to the skillet and add the Chicken Stock, lemon zest and juice, bay leaves, and thyme. Bring to a boil and reduce the heat, cover, and simmer for 5 minutes. Remove the bay leaves and discard.

3. Using a slotted spoon, fill each hot jar three-quarters full of the rabbit mixture. Ladle the hot sauce over the mixture, leaving 1 inch of headspace. Remove any air bubbles and add additional sauce if necessary to maintain the 1 inch of headspace.

4. Wipe the rim of each jar with a warm washcloth dipped in distilled white vinegar. Place a lid and ring on each jar and hand tighten.

5. Place jars in the pressure canner, lock the pressure canner lid, and bring to a boil on high heat. Let the canner vent for 10 minutes. Close the vent and continue heating to achieve 11 PSI for a dial gauge and 10 PSI for a weighted gauge. Process quart jars for 1 hour 30 minutes and pint jars for 1 hour 15 minutes.

Ingredient Tip: When heating a quart jar to serve, bring the stew to a boil, reduce the heat, then stir in ½ cup sour cream and 2 tablespoons capers. Mix well and remove from the heat. Serve with boiled young potatoes or thick egg noodles and garnish with fresh chopped parsley.

Fish

Canning is a popular method for preserving seafood and fish. When canned correctly, seafood is high in quality and safe to eat. Fresh- and saltwater fish can be safely preserved by pressure canning, but the processing time is much longer than the standard processing time for meat.

Freshwater fish like catfish, northern pike, salmon, smelt, and trout are perfect candidates for canning, whereas panfish like perch, bass, and walleye are better suited to freezing or eating fresh. Tuna requires more attention when canning, and shrimp can easily be preserved using brine.

PREPARING FISH FOR CANNING

Freshly caught fish is very perishable and requires special handling. Freshly caught fish must be kept cold and gutted by removing internal organs soon after they are caught, or within 24 hours. Keep cleaned fish on ice or in the refrigerator below 40°F until ready for use. Be sure to pressure can the gutted and cleaned fish within 2 days of being caught. It is safe to pressure can fish that have been frozen—just be sure to fully thaw the fish in the refrigerator prior to packing in jars.

As you do for meats, pressure can fish in widemouthed pint and half-pint jars. For larger fish, remove the bones and fat from skinned fillets and cut fillets into 2- to 3-inch pieces. Smaller fish, like smelt, are canned whole, with their heads and tails removed. You need roughly 1 pound fish to fill 1 widemouthed pint jar.

PRESSURE CANNING FISH, EXCEPT TUNA

1. Bleed and eviscerate fish immediately after catching (never more than 2 hours after they have been caught). Chill the cleaned fish immediately and keep on ice until you are ready to can. If the fish is frozen, thaw it completely in the refrigerator before canning.

2. Remove the head, tail, and fins. Wash the fish carefully in cold water. Split the fish lengthwise and cut into lengths suitable for the size jar you are using. Bones and skin can be removed or left in, with the exception of halibut, which must have the bones and skin removed prior to canning.

3. Cut filleted fish into 2- to 3-inch pieces depending on whether you are packing into widemouthed pint or half-pint jars. Pack the fish tightly into the jars, leaving 1 inch of headspace. If desired, add 1 teaspoon salt to each pint jar and ½ teaspoon salt to each half-pint jar. Do not cover the fish with water.

4. Wipe the rim of each jar with a warm wet washcloth dipped in distilled white vinegar. Place a lid and ring on each jar and hand tighten.

5. Place jars in the pressure canner, lock the pressure canner lid, and bring to a boil on high heat. Let the canner vent for 10 minutes. Close the vent and continue heating to achieve 11 PSI for a dial gauge and 10 PSI for a weighted gauge. Process both pints and half-pints for 1 hour 40 minutes.

6. When home canning salmon, do note that glass-like crystals of magnesium ammonium phosphate sometimes form on the salmon. This is not harmful and is perfectly safe to eat. They will dissolve when heated. There is no way for a home canner to prevent this from happening.

PRESSURE CANNING TUNA

1. Tuna may be precooked and hot packed or left raw and raw packed. Whether raw or hot packing, tuna must be skinned.

2. If raw packing, it is easiest to cut tuna when it is partially frozen. Remove the skin with a sharp knife and scrape the surface lightly to remove blood vessels and discolored flesh.

3. If hot packing, remove the viscera and wash in cold water. Drain all the blood from the tuna and remove the skin with a sharp knife. Place the cleaned tuna belly-down on a baking sheet and bake at 350°F for 1 hour or to an internal temperature of 165°F. Refrigerate the tuna overnight to firm.

4. Separate the tuna into quarters by cutting the meat away from the bones. Pull off and cut out all bones and the fin base, then scrape and cut out all of the very dark flesh as it has a very strong flavor and will make the other meat distasteful.

5. Cut the quartered tuna crosswise into 2- to 4-inch lengths, depending on whether you are packing into widemouthed pint or half-pint jars. Pack the tuna tightly into the jars, leaving 1 inch of headspace. If desired, add 1 teaspoon salt to each pint jar and ½ teaspoon salt to each half-pint jar. Do not cover the tuna with water. If you precooked the tuna, add 1 tablespoon vegetable oil to each pint jar and a ½ tablespoon to each half-pint jar, to maintain a 1-inch headspace.

6. Wipe the rim of each jar with a warm washcloth dipped in distilled white vinegar. Place a lid and ring on each jar and hand tighten.

7. Place jars in the pressure canner, lock the pressure canner lid, and bring to a boil on high heat. Let the canner vent for 10 minutes. Close the vent and continue heating to achieve 11 PSI for a dial gauge and 10 PSI for a weighted gauge. Process both pints and half-pints for 1 hour 40 minutes.

PRESSURE CANNING SHRIMP

1. Remove the heads from shrimp as soon as they are caught. Chill on ice until you are ready to pressure can. When ready to preserve, rinse and drain the shrimp in a colander.

2. In a large stockpot, create a brine by adding ½ cup canning salt and 1 cup distilled white vinegar to every gallon of water. Add the deheaded shrimp and bring to a boil for 8 to 10 minutes. Drain the cooked shrimp in a colander and rinse with cold water for 3 minutes.

3. In a saucepan, create another brine, adding 2 tablespoons canning salt to 1 gallon water. Stir well to dissolve the salt. Bring to a full boil over high heat.

4. Peel the shrimp and pack into jars, leaving 1 inch of headspace. Ladle the hot brine over the shrimp, maintaining the 1-inch headspace. Remove any air bubbles and add additional brine if necessary to maintain the 1-inch headspace.

5. Wipe the rim of each jar with a warm washcloth dipped in distilled white vinegar. Place a lid and ring on each jar and hand tighten.

6. Place jars in the pressure canner, lock the pressure canner lid, and bring to a boil on high heat. Let the canner vent for 10 minutes. Close the vent and continue heating to achieve 11 PSI for a dial gauge and 10 PSI for a weighted gauge. Process both pints and half-pints for 45 minutes.

Preparation Tip: Retain shrimp peels in a plastic freezer bag and freeze immediately after all shrimp have been peeled. Shells may be used to make Shellfish Stock (page 102).

CHAPTER EIGHT

MEALS IN A JAR

IN THIS CHAPTER, YOU'LL FIND delicious meals and meal starters that are pressure canned in mason jars in convenient portions. There are many benefits to preserving meals in a jar, but the biggest one is that, on the busiest days, you know you have a healthy, chemical- and preservative-free meal already made, just waiting in your pantry. Talk about knowing where your food comes from!

You'll notice that there's a lot less overview and basic instruction in this chapter. If you have questions or concerns about processing specific ingredients, refer to chapters 4 through 7, which offer tips and detailed instructions on canning tomatoes and vegetables (see page 37); beans and legumes (see page 63); stocks, broths, soups, and stews (see page 91); and different meats (see page 133).

BEEF BURGUNDY

MAKES APPROXIMATELY 6 TO 8 QUARTS OR 12 TO 16 PINTS
PREP: 30 MIN • COOK: 2 HR 10 MIN • CANNER: 1 HR • PROCESSING: 1 HR 30 MIN/1 HR 15 MIN
TOTAL: 5 HR 10 MIN/4 HR 55 MIN

This dish is truly a delicacy in a jar. The tender beef just melts in your mouth while the wine, bacon, and caramelized onions infuse every bite with amazing flavor. Properly called Boeuf Bourguignon, this dish was once considered a peasant dish yet over time has become a standard in French cuisine. Julia Child made this dish famous in her very first episode of *The French Chef* in 1963. I have adapted the recipe from *Mastering the Art of French Cooking* by Julia Child, Louisette Bertholle, and Simone Beck (Alfred A. Knopf, 1961) by using a pressure canner.

6 to 7 pounds chuck roast

½ cup extra-virgin olive oil

2 pounds thick-cut bacon

10 garlic cloves, mashed

6 medium onions, coarsely chopped (3 cups)

18 shallots, peeled and sliced thin lengthwise

2½ pounds mushrooms, sliced

1 tablespoon coarse sea salt

1½ teaspoons ground black pepper

2 bottles burgundy wine

2 cups Beef Bone Stock (page 96)

1 cup cognac

10 large carrots, peeled and cut in 2-inch strips (5 cups)

1. Trim your roast by removing the excess surface fat and any silver skin. Keep the marbleized fat. Cut into 2-inch strips or bite-size chunks. Essentially, cut the beef into the size you prefer to see on the end of your fork. Pat the beef dry with a paper towel.

2. In a large skillet, add 1 tablespoon oil and heat on medium-high. Working in batches, add the beef to the hot oil to brown on all sides, about 3 to 5 minutes per batch. Turn the beef as necessary to brown evenly on all sides. As each batch is browned, transfer the beef to a large stockpot and let it rest. Add 1 tablespoon oil to the skillet for each additional batch and continue until all the beef is browned.

3. Return the same skillet you used for the beef with renderings to medium heat, add the bacon, and cook, stirring as needed, until the bacon is cooked through but not crisp. Add the garlic, onions, shallots, mushrooms, salt, and pepper and sauté until the onions are translucent, about 8 to 10 minutes. Add the bacon-onion-mushroom mixture to the beef. Mix well.

4. Deglaze the skillet with 1 cup burgundy, being sure to scrape the skillet to loosen and dissolve the browned drippings, about 2 minutes. Add the deglazed bits to the beef mixture in the stockpot. Mix well.

5. Add the remaining burgundy, Beef Bone Stock, and cognac to the beef in the stockpot. Put the stockpot on medium heat and bring to a boil, stirring often. Once a boil is reached, reduce the heat to low and simmer until the wine has reduced for 1 hour. The goal is to reduce the wine and blend the flavors. Add the carrots and simmer for another hour, stirring every 15 minutes.

6. Ladle the hot Beef Burgundy into hot jars, leaving a generous 1 inch of headspace. Remove any air bubbles and add additional mixture if necessary, to maintain the headspace.

7. Wipe the rim of each jar with a warm washcloth dipped in distilled white vinegar. Place a lid and ring on each jar and hand tighten.

8. Place jars in the pressure canner, lock the pressure canner lid, and bring to a boil over high heat. Let the canner vent for 10 minutes. Close the vent and continue heating to achieve 11 PSI for a dial gauge and 10 PSI for a weighted gauge. Process quart jars for 1 hour 30 minutes and pint jars for 1 hour 15 minutes.

Ingredient Tip: There are several big decisions to make while at the market selecting your ingredients. First, your cut of beef should always be nicely marbled. Choose a traditional chuck roast or ask your butcher for a blade roast. The next big decision is the alcohol. Use a young, full-bodied red. I use Malbec red wine for its robust flavors, and I strongly recommend using a good quality cognac for the best results.

BEEF STROGANOFF

MAKES APPROXIMATELY 3 QUARTS OR 6 PINTS
PREP: 15 MIN • COOK: 10 MIN • CANNER: 1 HR • PROCESSING: 1 HR 30 MIN/1 HR 15 MIN
TOTAL: 2 HR 55 MIN/2 HR 40 MIN

Beef Stroganoff, properly known as Beef Stroganov, originates from mid-19th century Russia and was a dish of sautéed pieces of beef served in a sauce with *smetana*, or sour cream. We grew up watching my mom make this dish, slow-cooking tougher cuts of meats. Because the pressure canner tenderizes the meat while processing, feel free to use tough cuts of beef like round steak in this dish.

2 tablespoons olive oil, divided

5 pounds stewing beef, round steak, or sirloin, cut into 2-inch pieces

1 cup red wine

1 pound mushrooms, sliced (4 cups)

1 large onion, thinly sliced (2 cups)

5 garlic cloves, minced

¼ cup Worcestershire sauce

¼ teaspoon ground black pepper

6 cups Beef Bone Stock (page 96)

⅓ cup ClearJel

1. In a skillet, heat 1 tablespoon oil on medium-high heat. Add the beef in batches and cook until the beef is lightly browned on all sides, about 3 to 5 minutes per batch. Add 1 additional tablespoon of oil while browning each batch. Remove each batch from the stockpot and place in a bowl. Be sure not to cook the meat.

2. Add the wine to the skillet, and on high heat, deglaze the pan, being sure to scrape all the drippings from the bottom of the pan.

3. In a large stockpot, combine the browned beef and deglazed drippings. Add the mushrooms, onion, garlic, Worcestershire sauce, and black pepper. On medium-high heat, bring to a boil. Boil for 5 minutes. Whisk together the Beef Bone Stock and ClearJel® and add to the stockpot. Return to a boil for an additional 5 minutes, mixing well.

4. Using a slotted spoon, fill each hot jar three-quarters full of Stroganoff. Ladle the hot cooking liquid over the mixture, leaving 1 inch of headspace. Remove any air bubbles and add additional liquid if necessary to maintain the 1 inch of headspace.

5. Wipe the rim of each jar with a warm washcloth dipped in distilled white vinegar. Place a lid and ring on each jar and hand tighten.

6. Place jars in the pressure canner, lock the pressure canner lid, and bring to a boil on high heat. Let the canner vent for 10 minutes. Close the vent and continue heating to achieve 11 PSI for a dial gauge and 10 PSI for a weighted gauge. Process quart jars for 1 hour 30 minutes and pint jars for 1 hour 15 minutes.

Serving Tip: Give your home-canned Stroganoff a creamy texture prior to serving: Add 1 quart Stroganoff to a saucepan and heat on medium-high. Next add 1 cup sour cream and ¼ cup softened cream cheese and mix well. Pour the mixture over cooked egg noodles and serve.

CHICKEN CACCIATORE

MAKES APPROXIMATELY 7 QUARTS OR 14 PINTS

PREP: 20 MIN • COOK: 20 MIN • CANNER: 1 HR • PROCESSING: 1 HR 30 MIN/1 HR 15 MIN

TOTAL: 3 HR 10 MIN/2 HR 55 MIN

Cacciatore means "hunter" in Italian, so a dish made *alla cacciatora* means the meal is prepared "hunter-style." Cacciatore is popularly made with chicken or rabbit. Enjoy my family's adaptation using both white and dark meat and tomato juice.

3 tablespoons olive oil

8 large breasts boneless, skinless chicken breasts, cut into 2-inch cubes (8 cups)

12 boneless, skinless chicken thighs, cut into 2-inch pieces (6 cups)

1 tablespoon dried oregano

1 tablespoon dried basil

1 teaspoon dried thyme

1 teaspoon dried rosemary, crushed

1 teaspoon coarse sea salt

½ teaspoon ground black pepper

1 cup red wine

4 cups diced tomatoes, with their juice

4 cups Tomato Juice (page 45)

2 cups sliced white mushrooms

3 cups coarsely chopped sweet onion

1 large red bell pepper, chopped (1½ cups)

1 celery stalk, chopped (½ cup)

6 garlic cloves, minced

¾ cup tomato paste (6 ounces)

1 tablespoon granulated sugar

1. In a thick-bottomed stockpot, combine the oil and the chicken breasts and thighs. Mix well to coat the chicken. Cook the chicken on medium-high heat for 3 minutes, stirring often. Add the oregano, basil, thyme, rosemary, salt, and pepper. Mix well and cook for an additional 3 minutes. Add the red wine, cover the stockpot, and let cook for 5 more minutes undisturbed.

2. Add the tomatoes, Tomato Juice, mushrooms, onion, bell pepper, celery, and garlic. Mix well and bring to a boil. Boil for 5 minutes. Add the tomato paste and sugar, mixing well to distribute paste. Boil for an additional 5 minutes. Remove from the heat.

3. Using a slotted spoon, fill each hot jar three-quarters full with the chicken and vegetables. Ladle the hot tomato sauce over the mixture, leaving 1 inch of headspace. Remove any air bubbles and add additional sauce if necessary to maintain the 1 inch of headspace.

4. Wipe the rim of each jar with a warm wash-cloth dipped in distilled white vinegar. Place a lid and ring on each jar and hand tighten.

5. Place jars in the pressure canner, lock the pressure canner lid, and bring to a boil on high heat. Let the canner vent for 10 minutes. Close the vent and continue heating to achieve 11 PSI for a dial gauge and 10 PSI for a weighted gauge. Process quart jars for 1 hour 30 minutes and pint jars for 1 hour 15 minutes.

Serving Tip: This dish is traditionally served over pasta noodles, flat or spaghetti, and topped with fresh chopped parsley and shaved Parmesan cheese. For a fun kick, use V8® juice, regular or spicy, instead of Tomato Juice.

CHICKEN POTPIE FILLING

MAKES APPROXIMATELY 7 QUARTS OR 14 PINTS

PREP: 45 MIN • COOK: 20 MIN • CANNER: 1 HR • PROCESSING: 1 HR 30 MIN/1 HR 15 MIN

TOTAL: 3 HR 35 MIN/3 HR 20 MIN

There are so many uses for this heavenly pie filling that actually making a pie isn't even necessary. This truly is my family's favorite when we are crunched for time and need a quick meal. Simply bake a batch of biscuits, heat the filling, and away you go!

10 boneless, skinless chicken breasts

2 cups chopped celery

2 cups chopped onion

¼ cup unsalted butter

4 cups fresh or frozen chopped carrots (if frozen, do not thaw)

2 cups fresh or frozen peas (if frozen, do not thaw)

2 cups fresh or frozen corn (if frozen, do not thaw)

1 tablespoon coarse sea salt (optional)

2 teaspoons ground black pepper

2 teaspoons celery seeds

2 teaspoons garlic powder

1⅓ cups ClearJel

1. In a small stockpot, cover chicken with 2 inches of water and boil until cooked through, about 20 minutes. Remove chicken from pot and set on cutting board to cool. Measure 10 cups broth, created from boiling the chicken and set aside. Once the chicken has cooled, chop or tear it into bite-size pieces.

2. In a large, thick-bottomed stainless steel stockpot, combine the celery, onion, and butter and cook on medium-heat until the onions are translucent, about 8 to 10 minutes. Add the carrots, peas, corn, chicken, salt (if using), pepper, celery seeds, garlic powder, and 8 cups reserved broth to the onion mixture. Mix well using a long-handled spoon. Bring to a boil, stirring frequently. Add more broth if necessary (see Ingredient Tip below). Once the mixture is at a boil, stir in the ClearJel®, being sure to mix well until the filling starts to thicken, about 5 to 7 minutes. Remove from the heat.

3. Ladle the hot potpie filling into hot jars leaving a generous 1 inch of headspace. Remove any air bubbles and add additional filling if necessary to maintain the headspace.

4. Wipe the rim of each jar with a warm washcloth dipped in distilled white vinegar. Place a lid and ring on each jar and hand tighten.

5. Place jars in the pressure canner, lock the pressure canner lid, and bring to a boil on high heat. Let the canner vent for 10 minutes. Close the vent and continue heating to achieve 11 PSI for a dial gauge and 10 PSI for a weighted gauge. Process quart jars for 1 hour 30 minutes and pint jars for 1 hour 15 minutes.

Ingredient Tip: There should be about 2 cups hot Chicken Broth waiting in the wings since you measured out 10 cups. This is handy in the event the mixture soaks up more liquid than expected prior to adding the ClearJel®. If your mixture appears dry while heating through, stir in more broth, 1 cup at a time. This will make the texture creamier when you add the ClearJel®.

SLOPPY JOES

MAKES APPROXIMATELY 5 QUARTS OR 10 PINTS
PREP: 5 MIN • COOK: 20 MIN • CANNER: 1 HR • PROCESSING: 1 HR 30 MIN/1 HR 15 MIN
TOTAL: 2 HR 55 MIN/2 HR 40 MIN

A fun all-American classic preserved in a jar for you to heat, eat, and enjoy any time of the year! My kids love having pints of this in the pantry as it makes a great summertime lunch they can safely heat themselves and toss between two burger buns.

6 pounds ground beef

½ teaspoon coarse sea salt (optional)

½ teaspoon ground black pepper

2 cups finely chopped onion

1 cup finely chopped green bell pepper

6 garlic cloves, minced

3 tablespoons Worcestershire sauce

4 cups tomato sauce

1 tablespoon yellow mustard

¼ cup packed brown sugar

¼ cup apple cider vinegar

2 cups Beef Broth (page 103)

1. In a large stockpot, add the ground beef, salt (if using), and pepper. Cook the beef through on medium-high heat, about 10 minutes. Drain off the fat and return the cooked beef to a clean stockpot.

2. Add the onion, bell pepper, garlic, and Worcestershire sauce to the beef and mix well. On medium-high heat, cook the mixture until the onion is soft, about 5 minutes. Add the tomato sauce, mustard, sugar, vinegar, and Beef Broth, mix well. Bring to a boil and boil hard for 5 minutes, stirring to avoid scorching.

3. Ladle the hot Sloppy Joes into hot jars, leaving 1 inch of headspace. Remove any air bubbles and add additional Sloppy Joes if necessary to maintain the 1 inch of headspace.

4. Wipe the rim of each jar with a warm washcloth dipped in distilled white vinegar. Place a lid and ring on each jar and hand tighten.

5. Place jars in the pressure canner, lock the pressure canner lid, and bring to a boil on high heat. Let the canner vent for 10 minutes. Close the vent and continue heating to achieve 11 PSI for a dial gauge and 10 PSI for a weighted gauge. Process quart jars for 1 hour 30 minutes and pint jars for 1 hour 15 minutes.

Ingredient Tip: Ketchup is typically used when making Sloppy Joes on the stove top. To give this recipe more depth, I omitted the ketchup and used tomato sauce. If you prefer the flavor of ketchup and have it on hand, by all means, feel free to use equal parts sauce and ketchup. In that case, omit the apple cider vinegar to avoid making your sauce too acidic.

MEAT AND BEAN CHILI

MAKES APPROXIMATELY 8 QUARTS OR 16 PINTS
PREP: 1 HR 15 MIN • COOK: 30 MIN • CANNER: 1 HR • PROCESSING: 1 HR 30 MIN/1 HR 15 MIN
TOTAL: 4 HR 15 MIN/4 HR

This chili is a pantry staple in our home. Yes, we enjoy chili all year 'round. Whether it is served on a cold winter night alongside freshly baked bread or used to top hot dogs just off the grill in the summer months, this recipe is sure to please. It is also the perfect addition to any weekend omelet. Simply add 3 tablespoons of chili to the omelet center, fold egg over the top, and serve.

1 cup dried black beans (8 ounces)

1 cup dried kidney beans (8 ounces)

½ cup dried pinto beans (4 ounces)

5 pounds ground beef

2 pounds Italian sausage

1 large onion, finely chopped (2 cups)

1 medium green bell pepper, finely chopped (1 cup)

8 garlic cloves, minced

2 jalapeño peppers, seeded and finely chopped

1 cup chili powder

¼ cup dried parsley

¼ cup ground cumin

4 teaspoons coarse sea salt (optional)

1 teaspoon cumin seeds

1 to 2 teaspoons red pepper flakes

6 to 8 drops Tabasco' sauce

1 teaspoon ground black pepper

24 medium Roma tomatoes, chopped (12 cups)

1. Bean Prep: The acid in tomatoes prevents beans from softening, so for this recipe, the beans must be rehydrated prior to adding to chili. Sort the dried beans, discarding any damaged beans, debris, and rocks. Thoroughly rinse the beans in a colander in the sink to remove any dirt. Place the dried beans in a large stockpot with enough water to cover the beans by 3 inches. Bring to a boil, and then boil for 10 minutes, cover, and let sit for 1 hour.

2. In a thick-bottomed stockpot, cook the ground beef and sausage on medium-high heat for about 10 minutes or until cooked through. Drain off the grease and return to a clean stockpot.

3. Add the onion, bell pepper, garlic, jalapeños, chili powder, parsley, ground cumin, salt (if using), cumin seeds, red pepper flakes, Tabasco®, and pepper to the meat mixture. Stir well and cook on medium-heat until the onion is tender, about 5 minutes.

4. Drain the beans in a colander and add to the meat mixture with the tomatoes. Mix well and bring to a boil on medium-high heat. Reduce the heat and boil gently for 10 to 15 minutes, stirring often.

5. Ladle the hot chili into hot jars leaving a generous 1 inch of headspace. Remove any air bubbles and add additional chili if necessary to maintain the headspace.

6. Wipe the rim of each jar with a warm washcloth dipped in distilled white vinegar. Place a lid and ring on each jar and hand tighten.

7. Place jars in the pressure canner, lock the pressure canner lid, and bring to a boil on high heat. Let the canner vent for 10 minutes. Close the vent and continue heating to achieve 11 PSI for a dial gauge and 10 PSI for a weighted gauge. Process quart jars for 1 hour 30 minutes and pint jars for 1 hour 15 minutes.

Ingredient Tip: If you do not have the 1-hour prep time to rehydrate the beans called for in this recipe, feel free to soak dried beans overnight prior to commencing this recipe. Although dried beans are the most healthy and cost-effective, commercially canned beans are also quite suitable in this recipe. Simply add 2 cans each of black and kidney beans and 1 can of pinto beans.

WHITE CHICKEN CHILI

MAKES APPROXIMATELY 5 QUARTS OR 10 PINTS

PREP: 45 MIN • COOK: 20 MIN • CANNER: 1 HR • PROCESSING: 1 HR 30 MIN/1 HR 15 MIN

TOTAL: 3 HR 35 MIN/3 HR 20 MIN

A fun spin on traditional chili uses white beans, a light broth, and chicken. If you prefer to use pork, feel free to replace the chicken with chunks of pork roast. Serve hot White Chicken Chili garnished with a dollop of sour cream, chopped cilantro, and shredded pepper Jack cheese.

2½ cups dried cannellini, navy or northern beans, (16 ounces)

1 tablespoon olive oil

4 large boneless, skinless chicken breasts, cut in 1-inch pieces (4 cups)

24 boneless, skinless chicken thighs, cut in 1-inch pieces (2 cups)

1 medium onion, chopped (1 cup)

5 garlic cloves, minced

¼ cup ground cumin

1 tablespoon dried oregano

1 teaspoon cayenne pepper

8 cups Chicken Broth (page 104)

2 cups water

1 cup canned diced mild green chiles

1. Thoroughly rinse and clean the dried beans, discarding any disfigured or shriveled beans and any rocks or debris.

2. In a large pot, add the dried beans and enough water to cover by 2 inches. Bring to a boil over medium-high heat. Boil for 5 minutes, then reduce the heat to low and simmer with a lid on for 30 minutes. Turn off the heat and keep the lid on.

3. In a large skillet, combine the oil and chicken pieces and mix to coat the chicken with oil. On medium-high heat, cook the chicken for 10 minutes, mixing well to keep it from sticking to the pan. Add the onion, garlic, cumin, oregano, and cayenne pepper. Mix well and cook for an additional 5 minutes.

4. Drain the beans and add to the chicken with the Chicken Broth, water, and chiles. Mix well and bring the chili to a boil, then reduce the heat and simmer for 5 minutes.

5. Ladle the hot chili into hot jars leaving a generous 1 inch of headspace. Remove any air bubbles and add additional chili if necessary to maintain the headspace.

6. Wipe the rim of each jar with a warm washcloth dipped in distilled white vinegar. Place a lid and ring on each jar and hand tighten.

7. Place jars in the pressure canner, lock the pressure canner lid, and bring to a boil on high heat. Let the canner vent for 10 minutes. Close the vent and continue heating to achieve 11 PSI for a dial gauge and 10 PSI for a weighted gauge. Process quart jars for 1 hour 30 minutes and pint jars for 1 hour 15 minutes.

Serving Tip: If you prefer your White Chicken Chili to have a creamy texture, try this when heating a jar on the stove top prior to serving: Add 1 cup sour cream and ¼ cup cream cheese to 1 quart of chili and heat through, stirring continuously. Serve hot.

CABBAGE ROLL STUFFING

MAKES APPROXIMATELY 4 QUARTS OR 8 PINTS
PREP: 15 MIN • COOK: 25 MIN • CANNER: 1 HR • PROCESSING: 1 HR 30 MIN/1 HR 15 MIN
TOTAL: 3 HR 10 MIN/2 HR 55 MIN

Save time creating a stuffed cabbage roll dinner by having the filling precooked and on your pantry shelf. Simply add cooked rice and soften a head of cabbage in water while your stuffing mix heats in a pan. Add additional diced tomatoes to the baking dish before placing stuffed cabbage rolls in the oven.

2 pounds ground beef

2 pounds ground pork

1 cup chopped onion

6 garlic cloves, minced

1 cup finely chopped carrots

4 cups diced tomatoes

3 cups tomato sauce

1 cup Tomato Juice (page 45)

½ teaspoon red pepper flakes

3 tablespoons finely chopped fresh parsley

1 teaspoon coarse sea salt

½ teaspoon ground black pepper

1. In a thick-bottomed stockpot, cook the ground beef and pork on medium-high heat for about 20 minutes or until cooked through. Drain grease and return to a clean stockpot.

2. Add onion, garlic, carrots, tomatoes, tomato sauce, Tomato Juice, red pepper flakes, parsley, salt, and pepper to meat. Stir well and bring to a boil, then simmer for 5 minutes.

3. Ladle the hot stuffing mixture into hot jars, leaving 1 inch of headspace. Remove any air bubbles and add additional stuffing if necessary to maintain the 1 inch of headspace.

4. Wipe the rim of each jar with a warm washcloth dipped in distilled white vinegar. Place a lid and ring on each jar and hand tighten.

5. Place jars in the pressure canner, lock the pressure canner lid, and bring to a boil on high heat. Let the canner vent for 10 minutes. Close the vent and continue heating to achieve 11 PSI for a dial gauge and 10 PSI for a weighted gauge. Process quart jars for 1 hour 30 minutes and pint jars for 1 hour 15 minutes.

Serving Tip: Who says you've got to stuff cabbage leaves to enjoy this yummy mix? Have fun creating a cabbage roll casserole with a jar or two of stuffing: Layer a baking dish with ½ inch of chopped cabbage. Combine 2 cups tomato sauce with 2 quarts Cabbage Roll Stuffing and heat through. Cook rice as directed to make 3 cups cooked rice, then stir into the stuffing and tomato sauce. Spoon the hot mixture over chopped cabbage and bake at 350°F for 25 minutes or until the sauce is bubbling.

SPAGHETTI MEAT SAUCE

MAKES APPROXIMATELY 7 QUARTS OR 14 PINTS

PREP: 45 MIN • COOK: 25 MIN • CANNER: 1 HR • PROCESSING: 1 HR 10 MIN/1 HR

TOTAL: 3 HR 20 MIN/3 HR 10 MIN

This is my go-to sauce when making a variety of meals that require a red sauce base. My family's favorite is stuffed shells using this sauce as the base and the topper when serving. The benefit of pressure canning is you have the ability to play with the ingredients and still stay safe. Prefer ground turkey rather than beef or pork? No problem, make the switch. Not a fan of mushrooms? No worries, remove them.

30 pounds Roma tomatoes, approximately ½ bushel

1½ pounds bulk Italian sausage

1½ pounds ground beef

1 large onion, chopped (1½ cups)

1 small green bell pepper, seeded and chopped (½ cup)

½ pound white mushrooms, trimmed and sliced

8 garlic cloves, minced

6 tablespoons chopped fresh parsley

¼ cup finely chopped fresh basil

2 tablespoons dried oregano

4 teaspoons coarse sea salt (optional)

1 tablespoon ground black pepper

½ cup packed brown sugar

1. Core the tomatoes and cut into quarters and, working in batches, purée in a food processor. Place the purée in a large thick-bottomed stainless steel stockpot. Bring to a boil over medium heat, stirring frequently to avoid scorching. Once the purée is at a boil, reduce the heat and simmer for 10 minutes, stirring often. Remove from the heat and set aside.

2. In a second stockpot, cook the sausage and ground beef on medium-high heat until cooked through, about 8 to 10 minutes. Drain off any excess fat and return the meat mixture to a clean stockpot. Add the onion, green pepper, mushrooms, garlic, parsley, basil, oregano, salt (if using), and black pepper. Cook on medium-high heat until the onion is translucent and the green pepper is soft, about 10 minutes. Stir often.

3. Add the meat mixture to the puréed tomatoes and mix well. Stir in the brown sugar. Bring to a boil over medium-high heat, stirring often. Reduce the heat and simmer for 5 minutes.

4. Ladle the hot sauce into hot jars, leaving 1 inch of headspace. Remove any air bubbles and add additional sauce if necessary to maintain the 1 inch of headspace.

5. Wipe the rim of each jar with a warm washcloth dipped in distilled white vinegar. Place a lid and ring on each jar and hand tighten.

6. Place jars in the pressure canner, lock the pressure canner lid, and bring to a boil on high heat. Let the canner vent for 10 minutes. Close the vent and continue heating to achieve 11 PSI for a dial gauge and 10 PSI for a weighted gauge. Process quart jars for 1 hour 10 minutes and pint jars for 1 hour.

Ingredient Tip: I have learned it takes approximately 18 average-size Roma tomatoes to make 8 cups puréed tomatoes. If you decide to use traditional canning tomatoes, please be sure to do the following before puréeing: Blanch and remove skins (see page 38); halve each blanched tomato, remove seeds, and place in a colander to drain for 3 hours to remove the excess liquid that may make your spaghetti sauce thin and runny.

GARDEN SPAGHETTI SAUCE

MAKES APPROXIMATELY 7 QUARTS OR 14 PINTS

PREP: 45 MIN • COOK: 10 MIN • CANNER: 1 HR • PROCESSING: 1 HR 10 MIN/1 HR • TOTAL: 3 HR 5 MIN/2 HR 55 MIN

Enjoy this meatless spaghetti sauce throughout the year on any dish requiring a red sauce. This version is best to make and preserve in late summer when the garden is at its height of production. Garden Spaghetti Sauce features a variety of garden vegetables for a gorgeous color and texture.

30 pounds Roma tomatoes (½ bushel)

9 large carrots, peeled and finely chopped (3 cups)

4 large zucchini, shredded (3 cups)

1 large onion, chopped (1½ cups)

½ pound white mushrooms, trimmed and sliced (optional)

2 medium summer squash, shredded (1 cup)

1 medium green bell pepper, seeded and chopped (1 cup)

1 celery stalk, finely chopped (½ cup)

8 garlic cloves, minced

6 tablespoons chopped fresh parsley

¼ cup finely chopped fresh basil

2 tablespoons dried oregano

4 teaspoons coarse sea salt (optional)

1 tablespoon ground black pepper

½ cup packed brown sugar

1. Core the tomatoes and cut into quarters and, working in batches, purée in a food processor. Place the purée in a large thick-bottomed stainless steel stockpot. Bring to a boil over medium heat, stirring frequently to avoid scorching. Once the purée is at a boil, reduce the heat and simmer for 10 minutes, stirring often.

2. Add the carrots, zucchini, onion, mushrooms (if using), summer squash, green pepper, celery, garlic, parsley, basil, oregano, salt (if using), and black pepper. Mix well. Cook on medium heat for 5 minutes, stirring often to avoid scorching. Stir in the brown sugar and simmer for an additional 5 minutes.

3. Ladle the hot sauce into hot jars, leaving 1 inch of headspace. Remove any air bubbles and add additional sauce if necessary to maintain the 1 inch of headspace.

4. Wipe the rim of each jar with a warm washcloth dipped in distilled white vinegar. Place a lid and ring on each jar and hand tighten.

5. Place jars in the pressure canner, lock the pressure canner lid, and bring to a boil on high heat. Let the canner vent for 10 minutes. Close the vent and continue heating to achieve 11 PSI for a dial gauge and 10 PSI for a weighted gauge. Process quart jars for 1 hour 10 minutes and pint jars for 1 hour.

Ingredient Tip: If you would rather purée all of the vegetables, not just the tomatoes, feel free to food process the carrots, zucchini, squash, celery, onions, green peppers, garlic, parsley and basil together with ½ cup water, then add the purée to the tomatoes before bringing to a boil. Do not purée the mushrooms.

TASTY BEEF AND VEGETABLES

MAKES APPROXIMATELY 7 QUARTS OR 14 PINTS
PREP: 15 MIN • COOK: 15 MIN • CANNER: 1 HR • PROCESSING: 1 HR 30 MIN/1 HR 15 MIN
TOTAL: 3 HR/2 HR 45 MIN

Have some fun and get creative with this one! There is nothing stopping you from using ground chicken, turkey, or pork instead of beef. Choose your favorite seasoning blend (I like steak seasoning). Feel free to add less potato or more vegetables or double up on the meat, if you desire more protein. I've given you the guide to fill 7 quarts; now you can make it yours.

4 pounds ground beef, browned and fat drained

3½ quarts Beef Broth (page 103) or hot water with 3 beef bouillon cubes

7 cups fresh or frozen corn kernels, green beans, peas, or carrots, or a mix (if frozen, do not thaw)

4 to 6 cups chopped red-skinned potatoes (1-inch pieces)

1 cup diced red onion

7 tablespoons favorite dried seasoning blend (I like steak seasoning)

1. Use widemouthed jars for this recipe as they give you more space to arrange your layers and it is easier to remove foods from the jar when you are ready to heat and serve.

2. In a skillet on medium-high heat, cook the ground beef for about 15 minutes or until cooked through. Drain the grease and place the browned beef in a clean bowl.

3. In a large pot, heat the Beef Broth (or water with bouillon cubes) to a near boil. Cover and remove from the heat.

4. Place warm canning jars on a cutting board and add the ingredients in layers (see Recipe Tip for filling pint jars), tamping down each layer with an air bubble remover tool: 1 cup beef; 1 cup vegetables; ½ cup potatoes. Top with 2 tablespoons red onion and 1 tablespoon seasoning blend.

5. Ladle warm broth into the jars, leaving 1 inch of headspace. Remove any air bubbles and add additional broth if necessary to maintain the 1 inch of headspace.

6. Wipe the rim of each jar with a warm washcloth dipped in distilled white vinegar. Place a lid and ring on each jar and hand tighten.

7. Place jars in the pressure canner, lock the pressure canner lid, and bring to a boil on high heat. Let the canner vent for 10 minutes. Close the vent and continue heating to achieve 11 PSI for a dial gauge and 10 PSI for a weighted gauge. Process quart jars for 1 hour 30 minutes and pint jars for 1 hour 15 minutes.

Recipe Tip: If you are interested in preserving in pints, simply fill each pint with half the amount called for in quarts, tamping down each ingredient before adding the next. For pint jars, layer in ½ cup beef, ½ cup vegetables, and ¼ cup potatoes. Top with 1 tablespoon red onion and 1½ teaspoons seasoning blend.

CHICKEN CORN CHOWDER

MAKES APPROXIMATELY 7 QUARTS OR 14 PINTS
PREP: 10 MIN • COOK: 40 MIN • CANNER: 1 HR • PROCESSING: 1 HR 30 MIN/1 HR 15 MIN
TOTAL: 3 HR 20 MIN/3 HR 5 MIN

Here is a traditional chowder sure to please. Serve this thick chowder as a main course topped with shredded Cheddar cheese, a dash of paprika, and a handful of oyster crackers. Want to give it a little kick? Mix in a pinch of red pepper flakes or a quick dash of cayenne pepper for the perfect touch of heat.

2 tablespoons unsalted butter

1 cup diced onion

1 cup diced celery

5 garlic cloves, minced

1 teaspoon coarse sea salt (optional)

½ teaspoon ground black pepper

4 large boneless, skinless chicken breasts, cut into 1-inch pieces (4 cups)

4 boneless, skinless, chicken thighs, cut into 1-inch pieces (2 cups)

4 cups diced potatoes (1-inch pieces)

4 cups fresh or frozen corn kernels (if frozen, thaw in a bowl to capture the kernel milk)

1 medium red bell pepper, finely chopped (1 cup)

16 cups Chicken Broth (page 104), divided

⅓ cup ClearJel®

1. In a large stockpot, melt the butter over medium-high heat. Add the onion, celery, garlic, salt (if using), and pepper. Mix well and cook until the onion is translucent, about 5 to 8 minutes. Add the chicken, toss well to coat, and continue to cook for 10 minutes or until the chicken is cooked through.

2. Add the potatoes, corn and corn milk, red bell pepper, and 15 cups Chicken Broth, reserving 1 cup broth to mix with the ClearJel®. Mix well and bring to a boil. Boil for 5 minutes.

3. Whisk the ClearJel® with the reserved 1 cup Chicken Broth and add to the chowder. Mix well and boil for an additional 5 minutes. Remove from the heat.

4. Ladle the hot chowder into hot jars, leaving 1 inch of headspace. Remove any air bubbles and add additional chowder if necessary to maintain the 1 inch of headspace.

5. Wipe the rim of each jar with a warm washcloth dipped in distilled white vinegar. Place a lid and ring on each jar and hand tighten.

6. Place jars in the pressure canner, lock the pressure canner lid, and bring to a boil on high heat. Let the canner vent for 10 minutes. Close the vent and continue heating to achieve 11 PSI for a dial gauge and 10 PSI for a weighted gauge. Process quart jars for 1 hour 30 minutes and pint jars for 1 hour 15 minutes.

Ingredient Tip: ClearJel®, also known as Canning Gel, thickens upon cooling so be sure to work quickly but efficiently when filling jars. ClearJel® is the only approved cornstarch for home canning because it does not impede heat transfer during processing.

CLASSIC GOULASH BASE

MAKES APPROXIMATELY 5 QUARTS OR 10 PINTS
PREP: 10 MIN • COOK: 15 MIN • CANNER: 1 HR • PROCESSING: 1 HR 15 MIN/1 HR
TOTAL: 2 HR 40 MIN/2 HR 25 MIN

Better known as American goulash, this recipe provides a fully cooked goulash base, something my family has dubbed "comfort food in a jar." Goulash is popular in the Midwest, however every region across the nation has made its own mark on the recipe. If you have added specific ingredients to suit your family's liking over the years, feel free to tweak my ingredients to mirror yours.

3 pounds ground beef

4 cups tomato sauce

3 cups Tomato Juice (page 45)

8 medium tomatoes, diced

2 large sweet onions, diced (3 cups)

1 medium green bell pepper, diced (1 cup)

6 garlic cloves, minced

3 tablespoons Worcestershire sauce

1 tablespoon dried oregano

1 tablespoon dried basil

½ teaspoon ground black pepper

1. In a thick-bottomed stockpot, cook the ground beef on medium-high heat for about 10 minutes or until cooked through. Drain the grease and return to a clean stockpot.

2. Add the tomato sauce and juice, diced tomatoes, onions, bell pepper, garlic, Worcestershire sauce, oregano, basil, and pepper to the beef. Stir well and bring to a boil, then reduce the heat and simmer for 5 minutes.

3. Ladle the hot goulash base into hot jars, leaving 1 inch of headspace. Remove any air bubbles and add additional base if necessary to maintain the 1 inch of headspace.

4. Wipe the rim of each jar with a warm washcloth dipped in distilled white vinegar. Place a lid and ring on each jar and hand tighten.

5. Place jars in the pressure canner, lock the pressure canner lid, and bring to a boil on high heat. Let the canner vent for 10 minutes. Close the vent and continue heating to achieve 11 PSI for a dial gauge and 10 PSI for a weighted gauge. Process quart jars for 1 hour 15 minutes and pint jars for 1 hour.

Serving Tip: Because pressure canning pasta has not been thoroughly tested, it is best to cook elbow macaroni noodles in a separate pan as you heat a jar of Classic Goulash Base on the stove top. For every 1 quart of goulash base, boil 1 cup dried macaroni or ½ cup for every pint.

HUNGARIAN GOULASH

MAKES APPROXIMATELY 7 QUARTS OR 14 PINTS
PREP: 20 MIN • COOK: 20 MIN • CANNER: 1 HR • PROCESSING: 1 HR 30 MIN/1 HR 15 MIN
TOTAL: 3 HR 10 MIN/2 HR 55 MIN

The origin of this thick stew-like meal dates back to 9th-century medieval Hungary. This is one of the national dishes of Hungary and a symbol of the country. Other variations include sauerkraut and sour cream while some include smoked pork or veal.

12 to 14 slices bacon, cut into 2-inch pieces (1 pound)

5 pounds well-marbled boneless beef chuck, cut into 1½-inch pieces

1 teaspoon coarse sea salt

½ teaspoon ground black pepper

1 cup dry red wine

3 quarts Beef Bone Stock (page 96)

2 large yellow onions, chopped (2 cups)

½ cup Hungarian sweet paprika

2 teaspoons caraway seeds

¾ cup tomato paste (6 ounces)

4 cups potatoes, cut into 1-inch cubes

1 large green bell pepper, coarsely chopped (2 cups)

1. In a large heavy bottomed stockpot, cook the bacon on medium-high heat until cooked through but not crisp, about 5 to 8 minutes. Remove the bacon and set aside, keeping bacon grease in the stockpot. Working in batches, brown the beef in the bacon grease, browning each side but not cooking through, about 3 to 5 minutes per batch. Season each batch with a pinch of the salt and pepper. Set the beef aside with bacon.

2. Deglaze the stockpot over high heat by adding the wine, scraping up any browned drippings, about 3 minutes. Reduce the heat to medium-high and add the Beef Bone Stock, onions, paprika, and caraway seeds. Bring to a boil.

3. Add the tomato paste and mix well to distribute. Add the bacon and beef, potatoes, and bell pepper and return to a boil. Boil for 5 more minutes, stirring often to avoid scorching.

4. Using a slotted spoon, fill each hot jar three-quarters full with goulash, being sure there is a good ratio of meat and vegetables in each jar. Ladle the hot cooking liquid over the mixture, leaving 1 inch of headspace. Remove any air bubbles and add additional liquid if necessary to maintain the 1 inch of headspace.

5. Wipe the rim of each jar with a warm washcloth dipped in distilled white vinegar. Place a lid and ring on each jar and hand tighten.

6. Place jars in the pressure canner, lock the pressure canner lid, and bring to a boil on high heat. Let the canner vent for 10 minutes. Close the vent and continue heating to achieve 11 PSI for a dial gauge and 10 PSI for a weighted gauge. Process quart jars for 1 hour 30 minutes and pint jars for 1 hour 15 minutes.

Serving Tip: If you prefer a thicker base, feel free to mix 3 tablespoons ClearJel® with ½ cup hot water and add to a quart as you warm it on the stove top.

ASIAN CHICKEN THIGHS

MAKES APPROXIMATELY 5 QUARTS OR 10 PINTS

PREP: 15 MIN • COOK: 0 MIN • CANNER: 1 HR 10 MIN • PROCESSING: 1 HR 30 MIN/1 HR 15 MIN

TOTAL: 2 HR 55 MIN/2 HR 40 MIN

This is one of my family's favorite dishes. I make a side of white rice, steam 4 cups broccoli florets, and heat a quart or two of thighs. Toss all the ingredients together for a truly delicious meal. These seasoned thighs make the perfect starter to stir-fries and various other Asian-inspired dishes.

40 boneless, skinless chicken thighs, excess fat removed

2 bunches scallions, white and green parts, sliced

1 cup honey

1 cup water

¾ cup soy sauce

¾ cup tomato paste (6 ounces)

¼ cup rice vinegar or apple cider vinegar

1 tablespoon sriracha sauce

1 tablespoon onion powder

2 teaspoons garlic powder

3 tablespoon ClearJel

1. Raw pack about 8 thighs per quart jar or 4 thighs per pint, leaving a generous 1 inch of headspace. Add 1 tablespoon chopped scallions to each jar.

2. In a mixing bowl, combine the honey, water, soy sauce, tomato paste, vinegar, sriracha sauce, onion and garlic powders, and ClearJel®. Whisk well until all ingredients are combined into a smooth sauce.

3. Ladle the sauce into jars over the thighs, maintaining the headspace. Remove any air bubbles using the air bubble remover tool and add additional sauce if necessary to maintain the headspace.

4. Wipe the rim of each jar with a warm washcloth dipped in distilled white vinegar. Place a lid and ring on each jar and hand tighten.

5. Because this is raw packed cold, be sure the water in the canner is also cold. Count on an additional 10 minutes for the pressure canner to increase in temperature prior to venting because you start with the canner on medium heat for the first 10 minutes, then turn to high heat.

6. Place the jars in the pressure canner and lock the pressure canner lid. Start on medium heat for 10 minutes, then increase the heat to high and bring to a boil. Let the canner vent for 10 minutes. Close the vent and continue heating to achieve 11 PSI for a dial gauge and 10 PSI for a weighted gauge. Process quart jars for 1 hour 30 minutes and pint jars for 1 hour 15 minutes.

Ingredient Tip: Feel free to use a low-sodium soy sauce if you must watch your sodium intake. You may also use half the required soy and increase the water to dilute the salt. If you cannot have soy sauce at all, replace it with equal parts blackstrap molasses.

SALSA VERDE CHICKEN

MAKES APPROXIMATELY 6 QUARTS OR 12 PINTS
PREP: 15 MIN • COOK: 40 MIN • CANNER: 1 HR • PROCESSING: 1 HR 30 MIN/1 HR 15 MIN
TOTAL: 3 HR 25 MIN/3 HR 10 MIN

This hearty chicken dinner can be used in so many ways. The green sauce is made with fresh tomatillos, however, feel free to use store-bought salsa verde if tomatillos are not in season or you are crunched for time. Heat a jar of Salsa Verde Chicken and serve in tacos, enchiladas, or even use to create a yummy stack of nachos.

20 tomatillos

8 to 10 garlic cloves, peeled

3 to 5 tablespoons olive oil, divided

6 large boneless, skinless chicken breasts, cut into 1-inch pieces (6 cups)

8 boneless, skinless chicken thighs, cut into 1-inch pieces (4 cups)

4 cups Chicken Broth (page 104)

4 cups diced tomatoes

1 large onion, chopped (2 cups)

¼ cup lime juice

1 tablespoon ground cumin

1 tablespoons chili powder

1 tablespoon ground coriander

2 teaspoons coarse sea salt

1. Preheat the oven to 400°F.

2. Line a cookie sheet, or two, with foil. Remove the outer husks of the tomatillos and rinse well in a colander in the sink. Cut the tomatillos in half and place flesh-side down onto foil. Once all the tomatillos are lined up tight on the cookie sheet, space the peeled garlic cloves evenly throughout the tomatillos. Drizzle the tomatillos with 3 tablespoons olive oil. Roast in the oven for 25 minutes or until the tomatillo tops start to brown.

3. Working in batches, purée the roasted tomatillos and garlic with their juices in a food processor. Set aside.

4. In a stockpot, add 2 tablespoons oil and the chicken breasts and thighs. Mix to coat the chicken with oil. On medium-high heat, cook the chicken for 10 minutes, stirring often. Add the broth, tomatoes, onion, lime juice, cumin, chili powder, coriander, and salt. Mix well and bring to a boil. Boil for 1 minute, then add the puréed tomatillos. Mix well. Return to a boil and boil for 5 minutes, stirring often.

5. Ladle the hot chicken salsa verde into hot jars, leaving 1 inch of headspace. Remove any air bubbles and add additional chicken salsa verde if necessary to maintain the 1 inch of headspace.

6. Wipe the rim of each jar with a warm washcloth dipped in distilled white vinegar. Place a lid and ring on each jar and hand tighten.

7. Place jars in the pressure canner, lock the pressure canner lid, and bring to a boil on high heat. Let the canner vent for 10 minutes. Close the vent and continue heating to achieve 11 PSI for a dial gauge and 10 PSI for a weighted gauge. Process quart jars for 1 hour 30 minutes and pint jars for 1 hour 15 minutes.

Ingredient Tip: If you would like to add some heat to the flavor, feel free to add 1 to 2 teaspoons red pepper flakes when boiling chicken mixture. You may also add 2 to 3 dried chile peppers instead of pepper flakes. Just be sure to remove and discard dried chiles before filling jars.

POT ROAST

MAKES APPROXIMATELY 7 QUARTS AND 14 PINTS

PREP: 25 MIN • COOK: 5 MIN • CANNER: 1 HR • PROCESSING: 1 HR 30 MIN/1 HR 15 MIN • TOTAL: 3 HR/2 HR 45 MIN

Each layered jar is a gorgeous display of scrumptious pot roast. The genius of this recipe is that it saves you time in the future whenever roasting something in the oven is not an option at dinnertime. There is no sautéing or precooking as this recipe is raw packed then covered with a robust blend of red wine and Beef Bone Stock. The pressure canner does all the work of roasting and tenderizing meat during processing.

4 cups Beef Bone Stock (page 96)

1 cup red wine

2 tablespoons Worcestershire sauce

2 teaspoons dried thyme

4 garlic cloves, minced

½ teaspoon ground black pepper

7 bay leaves

7 pounds boneless beef chuck, trimmed and cut into 2-inch chunks

2 cups peeled and chopped parsnips (cut into ½-inch pieces)

4 cups peeled and chopped russet potatoes (cut into 1-inch pieces)

2 cups chopped celery (cut into ½-inch pieces)

4 cups peeled and chopped carrots (cut into ½-inch pieces)

2 cups diced tomatoes

1 cup diced red onion

1. Use widemouthed quarts for this recipe as it will give you more space to arrange each food and will be easier to remove foods from the jar when ready to heat and serve.

2. Place the Beef Bone Stock, wine, Worcestershire sauce, thyme, garlic, and pepper in a pan and bring to a boil on medium-high heat. Reduce the heat to low and simmer, uncovered, for 5 minutes. Remove from the heat while raw packing the jars.

3. Be sure the jars are room temperature prior to raw packing. Place the jars on a cutting board and add one bay leaf per jar. Next, add 1½ cups beef chunks to each quart jar, evenly distributing the beef among the jars. Tamp the beef down using an air bubble remover tool. For each quart jar, add the following in layers (see Recipe Tip for filling pint jars), tamping each layer down before adding the next: ¼ cup parsnips, ½ cup potatoes, ¼ cup celery, ½ cup carrots, ¼ cup tomatoes, and 2 tablespoons red onion.

4. Ladle warm broth into the jars to cover the layers, leaving 1 inch of headspace. Remove any air bubbles and add additional broth if necessary to maintain the 1 inch of headspace.

5. Wipe the rim of each jar with a warm washcloth dipped in distilled white vinegar. Place a lid and ring on each jar and hand tighten.

6. Place jars in the pressure canner, lock the pressure canner lid, and bring to a boil on high heat. Let the canner vent for 10 minutes. Close the vent and continue heating to achieve 11 PSI for a dial gauge and 10 PSI for a weighted gauge. Process quart jars for 1 hour 30 minutes and pint jars for 1 hour 15 minutes.

Recipe Tip: If you are interested in preserving in pints, simply fill each pint with half the amount called for in quarts, tamping down each ingredient before adding the next. For pint jars, layer in ¾ cup beef chunks, 2 tablespoons parsnips, ¼ cup potatoes, 2 tablespoons celery, ¼ cup carrots, 2 tablespoons tomatoes, and 1 tablespoon red onion. The headspace remains the same. Pints are perfect personal-size pot roasts you may take with you for lunch or when having a quiet meal at home.

FALL POT ROAST

MAKES APPROXIMATELY 7 QUARTS OR 14 PINTS
PREP: 15 MIN • COOK: 1 HR 5 MIN • CANNER: 1 HR • PROCESSING: 1 HR 30 MIN/1 HR 15 MIN
TOTAL: 3 HR 50 MIN/3 HR 35 MIN

Fall is harvesttime and root crops are in season. Create a yummy seasonal roast, one my kids call Thanksgiving in a Jar. Like that of a traditional Thanksgiving dinner, the various vegetables, turkey and gravy, and dried cranberries warm both body and soul, a mixture of delicious flavor and fond holiday memories.

1 whole turkey or chicken, innards removed (7 to 9 pounds)

16 cups water

3 pounds Brussels sprouts, outer leaves removed and end removed

4 medium sweet potatoes, peeled and cut into 2-inch cubes (6 cups)

4 large carrots, peeled and cut 3 inches thick (4 cups)

1 large onion, coarsely chopped (2 cups)

6 garlic cloves, smashed

¼ cup olive oil

1 teaspoon coarse sea salt

½ teaspoon fresh cracked black pepper

1 cup dried cranberries

1. Preheat the oven to 400°F.

2. In a large stockpot, combine the turkey or chicken and water. Bring to a boil over medium-high heat. Boil for 30 minutes or until the turkey or chicken is cooked through, stirring often. Remove the turkey or chicken from the stockpot and set aside to cool. Reserve the cooking liquid (broth).

3. Place the Brussels sprouts, sweet potatoes, carrots, onion, and garlic in the roasting pan. Drizzle the vegetables with olive oil and sprinkle with coarse salt and cracked pepper. Place in the oven and roast for 15 minutes, mixing once, then roast for an additional 10 minutes. When done, let the pan of vegetables rest on the stove top.

4. Pull the meat from the bones, being sure to freeze the carcass to use for stock or soup in the future. Tear or cut the meat into bite-size pieces and add to the roasting pan, and mix well to distribute flavors. Add 1 cup broth to the roasting pan and return to the oven for 5 minutes. Remove the roasting pan from the oven, mix in the dried cranberries, and set aside. Using a slotted spoon, evenly distribute the turkey or chicken and vegetables among the jars, leaving a generous 1 inch of headspace. Keep a good ratio of turkey or chicken and vegetables in each jar.

THE COMPLETE GUIDE TO PRESSURE CANNING

5. To make the gravy, place the roasting pan on medium-high heat and add 2 cups broth. Deglaze the roasting pan by stirring and scraping to loosen any browned drippings. Bring to a boil. Add an additional 4 cups broth and whisk in ClearJel®. Bring to a boil for 1 minute, and then remove from the heat.

6. Ladle the hot gravy into the jars over the filling, leaving a generous 1 inch of headspace. Remove any air bubbles and add additional gravy if necessary to maintain the headspace.

7. Wipe the rim of each jar with a warm washcloth dipped in distilled white vinegar. Place a lid and ring on each jar and hand tighten.

8. Place jars in the pressure canner, lock the pressure canner lid, and bring to a boil on high heat. Let the canner vent for 10 minutes. Close the vent and continue heating to achieve 11 PSI for a dial gauge and 10 PSI for a weighted gauge. Process quart jars for 1 hour 30 minutes and pint jars for 1 hour 15 minutes.

Ingredient Tip: Not a fan of Brussels sprouts? Not to worry. Simply replace them with 4 cups of a vegetable of your choice, like butternut squash, or increase the amount of sweet potatoes or carrots. Any fall vegetable tastes delicious in this recipe, even beets. Just be sure to use yellow beets, unless you don't mind everything taking on a purple hue.

IRISH JIG IN A JAR

MAKES APPROXIMATELY 7 QUARTS OR 14 PINTS

PREP: 20 MIN • COOK: 5 MIN • CANNER: 1 HR • PROCESSING: 1 HR 30 MIN/1 HR 15 MIN

TOTAL: 2 HR 55 MIN/2 HR 40 MIN

Enjoy St. Patty's day all year 'round with this authentic corned beef and cabbage meal in a jar. Chunks of corned beef, traditional spices, potatoes, carrots, and cabbage cooked to perfection. Simply pop a lid, heat, and eat. If you're worried about the cabbage flavor overpowering the jar, omit the cabbage. You may always steam cabbage while heating a quart to eat.

8 cups Beef Bone Stock (page 96)

2 12-ounce bottles of pale ale'or dry hard cider

¼ cup pickling spice

1 head green cabbage

7 bay leaves

7 garlic cloves, peeled

2 (4-pound) corned beef briskets, excess fat removed, cut into 2-inch pieces

8 to 10 medium red skin potatoes, cut into 2-inch cubes (4 cups)

4 cups chopped carrots (½-inch pieces)

4 cups chopped onions

1. Use widemouthed jars for this recipe, as it will give you more space to arrange each layer, and it is easier to remove foods from the jar when you are ready to heat and serve. (See Recipe Tip if you prefer to make pint jars.)

2. In a stockpot, combine the Beef Bone Stock, ale or hard cider, and pickling spice. Bring to a boil, boil for 1 minute, then reduce the heat and simmer for 5 minutes. Cover with a tight-fitting lid and remove from the heat.

3. Cut the cabbage into 3-inch-thick wedges lengthwise and then cut crosswise into pieces that will fit easily in the jars.

4. Be sure the jars are room temperature prior to raw packing. Place jars on the cutting board and add one bay leaf and one garlic clove to each jar. Next add layers as follows, tamping down each layer before adding the next: 2 cups corned beef pieces, evenly distributing the corned beef between the jars, ½ cup potatoes, ½ cup carrots, and one or two cabbage wedges on top of the carrots. Top each quart jar with 2 tablespoons onion. Be sure to keep 1¼ inches of headspace in each jar.

5. Ladle the warm spiced broth into the jars, leaving 1 inch of headspace. Remove any air bubbles and add additional broth if necessary to maintain the 1 inch of headspace.

6. Wipe the rim of each jar with a warm washcloth dipped in distilled white vinegar. Place a lid and ring on each jar and hand tighten.

7. Place jars in the pressure canner, lock the pressure canner lid, and bring to a boil on high heat. Let the canner vent for 10 minutes. Close the vent and continue heating to achieve 11 PSI for a dial gauge and 10 PSI for a weighted gauge. Process quart jars for 1 hour 30 minutes and pint jars for 1 hour 15 minutes.

Recipe Tip: If you are interested in preserving in pints, simply fill each pint jar with ½ garlic clove, ½ bay leaf, 1 cup corned beef, ¼ cup potatoes, ¼ cup carrots, a piece or two of cabbage, and 1 tablespoon onion. The headspace remains the same. Pint jars are a perfect personal-size corned beef dinner to take with you for lunch, or enjoy it as a quiet meal at home.

CHICKEN CURRY WITH VEGETABLES

MAKES APPROXIMATELY 7 QUARTS OR 14 PINTS
PREP: 20 MIN • COOK: 20 MIN • CANNER: 1 HR • PROCESSING: 1 HR 30 MIN/1 HR 15 MIN
TOTAL: 3 HR 10 MIN/2 HR 55 MIN

The flavors of this meal are outstanding! This recipe can be used as a meal starter or simply heat a jar and serve it over rice or Thai noodles. I personally enjoy combining breast and thigh meat in this dish, however feel free to use the cut of meat you'd like to see on the end of your fork.

2 tablespoons olive oil

1 large onion, sliced (2 cups)

6 garlic cloves, minced

5 tablespoons red Thai curry paste

1 teaspoon coarse sea salt

½ teaspoon ground black pepper

5 boneless, skinless chicken breasts, cut into 2-inch pieces

10 boneless, skinless chicken thighs, cut into 2-inch pieces

8 cups Chicken Broth (page 104)

3 cups organic coconut milk

4 cups peeled and diced tomatoes

3 cups carrots, peeled and cut into 1-inch-thick rounds

¼ cup lime juice

2 teaspoons dried basil

1. In a large stockpot, combine the oil, onion, garlic, curry paste, salt, and pepper and sauté over medium-high heat until the onion is translucent, about 5 minutes. Add the chicken pieces and cook for 8 to 10 minutes or until the chicken browns on all sides.

2. In a large bowl, whisk together the Chicken Broth and coconut milk. Add the mixture to the stockpot and mix well to coat the chicken pieces and vegetables. Add the tomatoes, carrots, lime juice, and basil. Mix well and bring to a boil for 5 minutes.

3. Using a slotted spoon, fill each hot jar three-quarters full with chicken and vegetables. Ladle the hot curry liquid over the mixture, leaving a generous 1 inch of headspace. Remove any air bubbles and add additional liquid if necessary to maintain the headspace.

4. Wipe the rim of each jar with a warm washcloth dipped in distilled white vinegar. Place a lid and ring on each jar and hand tighten.

5. Place jars in the pressure canner, lock the pressure canner lid, and bring to a boil on high heat. Let the canner vent for 10 minutes. Close the vent and continue heating to achieve 11 PSI for a dial gauge and 10 PSI for a weighted gauge. Process quart jars for 1 hour 30 minutes and pint jars for 1 hour 15 minutes.

Ingredient Tip: There are so many different varieties, colors, and spice levels of curry. Yellow curry paste is the most mellow. Red curry paste is moderate in heat, while green curry is very hot. This recipe takes a middle-of-the-road approach with red curry paste, but choose what you prefer to eat.

Ingredient Tip: Like milk from a corn kernel, coconut milk is not a dairy product and can be successfully pressure canned. If you are not a fan of coconut, feel free to omit it from the recipe and increase the Chicken Broth by 2 cups.

CHAPTER NINE

PRESSURE CANNING TO FILL YOUR PANTRY

IF A NATURAL OR MAN-MADE DISASTER strikes your community, you might not have access to food, water, and electricity for a while. By taking steps now to store emergency food and water supplies, you can reduce the effect of any such disaster on your family. It is important to have enough food and water on hand to survive for at least 2 weeks in the event of a disaster. This chapter gives insight into how to prepare for a disaster; because "disaster" doesn't necessarily mean a large-scale event, it can be far more personal, something as serious as losing a job, having a death in the family, taking a cut in wages, or experiencing a downturn in the economy.

Preparing for Disaster

Having a ready-made food supply is critical in times of disaster, and in extreme cases, it is often the difference between life and death. Ready-made food means it requires no water, heat, or refrigeration and can be eaten immediately without any preparation. Pressure canning gives us the ability to preserve low-acid foods that provide us with protein, carbohydrates, and other nutrients not found in acidic foods. These nutritious foods are critical in times of disaster and essential to having a well-rounded, fully-stocked pantry.

This chapter also teaches you various tips to save money as you build your food supply. While the focus is on pressure canning, I also touch on food preservation as a whole, including successful long-term storage techniques and emergency essentials to keep in your pantry. Preparedness isn't just for preppers—it's for everyone.

PROPER STORAGE

Preserved foods: Keep all stored food, including home-canned goods, in a dry, cool location out of direct or indirect sunlight. The ideal storage temperature is between 50°F to 70°F, with no exposure to direct or indirect sunlight. Choose a location that is free from humidity and vast temperature fluctuations. If storing in a basement, be sure to elevate the jars from dirt or cement floors, due to excessive moisture. Also, do not stack the jars during storage.

Perishable foods: Wrap breads, cookies, crackers, and other perishable foods in plastic bags and keep them in sealed containers.

Dried and dehydrated foods: Store dehydrated foods in glass screw-top jars and/or airtight containers. Fill 5-gallon buckets with airtight twist-lock lids with flour, dried beans, rice, sugar, dehydrated milk flakes, etc. Use food-safe moisture and oxygen absorbers to extend the storage life of dehydrated and dried bulk foods to prevent food spoilage.

WHAT SHOULD I STOCKPILE?

You will often hear me say, *if you won't eat it, don't can it!* This holds true when deciding what to store in your pantry. To start, you must create a list. Otherwise, your pantry just holds foodstuff because there is no plan in mind. A list prevents you from making reckless purchases and poor choices when canning foods that waste time, money, and precious pantry space.

The goal is to store foods you eat regularly and that require no refrigeration, preparation, or cooking. When creating your list of ready-made food and essentials, ask yourself these 5 questions.

1. **Will it get eaten?** If there is a huge discount on SPAM® at your local grocer, but you know full well your spouse cannot stand the stuff and your doctor has you on a strict low-sodium diet, there's no need to rush out and buy 10 cases. Besides, would you want to eat SPAM® morning, noon, and night for two weeks straight? I'd be tired of eating the same thing, even if it was chocolate cake. The bottom line is this: If you do not eat it in your home on a regular basis, do not pressure can it or purchase it to stockpile. Stick to things you know and like to eat.

2. **Are my choices healthy?** During a disaster when we may not have access to all of the privileges we are used to, it is especially important to keep ourselves healthy, especially if the disaster is severe enough that medical aid is limited. If you or your family has diet restrictions or health ailments, be sure your food choices reflect this. As much as we might love pie filling and jam and salty treats like pickles, these foods do not provide our bodies

with enough sustenance to retain proper health. Be sure to include meats, tomato-based sauces, soups, and a colorful variety of vegetables, too.

3. **Is my supply well rounded in the five food groups?** While pressure-canned beans are a great source of protein and inexpensive to preserve, you cannot eat an all-bean diet and expect to retain good health. Be sure to include home-canned soups, fruits, fermented items, vegetables in water, and a variety of meat and bean dishes. Your food storage supply should also have things like oil, salt, grains, dried beans, and evaporated milk.

4. **Did I provide food for comfort?** Mental health is just as important as physical health during times of disaster. Comfort foods and sweet treats can temporarily boost your mental state. I purposely preserve and store foods reminiscent of good times and fond memories. For instance, a store-bought jar of chipped beef brings me back to my childhood, when I enjoyed it for Saturday breakfasts on toast. Apple and blueberry pie fillings remind me and my kids of the fun we had making hobo pies around the campfire. I covet my jars of Beef Burgundy (page 158), so I know that including some in my emergency supply will definitely put a smile on my face in the midst of hardship.

5. **What if someone gets sick?** There are so many obvious reasons to stay healthy, yet it is even more imperative that you do so during times of disaster. Diseases, bacteria, and viruses can run rampant during times of power outages, flooding, and major winter storms. Food is our first line of defense. Pressure can an extra batch or two of Chicken Soup (page 106), meat and bone stocks, and hearty stews to help boost the immune system and provide the

body with natural anti-inflammatory agents. Water bathe and ferment cordials, elderberry jam, fruit and herb elixirs, and extra jars of sauerkraut, which is full of probiotics.

CALCULATE YOUR FAMILY'S FOOD SUPPLY

Did you know the average person consumes 1,996 pounds of food each year? That's almost one ton! The USDA reported these findings in 2014. Granted, we do not think of food in terms of weight per se, so let's quantify that figure in terms of jars.

Each quart jar contains about 4 cups (32 ounces) of food, and each pint jar contains about 2 cups (16 ounces) of food. Half-pints or jelly jars contain about 1 cup of food, or 8 ounces.

Annual consumption in weight is 1,996 pounds, or 31,936 ounces.

Annual consumption in jars totals 998 quart jars or 1,996 pint jars.

That's 250 quarts every 3 months or 83 quarts each month per person.

Now, not everything we consume is home-canned, but you get the picture. We eat a lot!

Use the handy chart on pages 190 and 191 to assess the amount of food consumed by your family, so you know how much you need to preserve to build your food supply (page 190). This chart indicates the individual serving size of each food group. It is then up to you to determine how much is consumed by each person in your family based on their habits. Once that's sorted out, extend the math to determine what amount is needed in cups and quarts each week, then annually, to feed your family. Feel free to photocopy this chart. Use this chart in tandem with your garden and canning calendar each year.

CANNED FOOD STORAGE PLAN FOR MY FAMILY

| KIND OF FOOD | RECOMMENDED SERVING SIZE | WEEKLY SERVINGS PER PERSON | | NUMBER OF PEOPLE IN FAMILY/ HOUSEHOLD |
		RECOMMENDED SERVINGS	ACTUAL SERVINGS	
Example for a Family of 4				
Formulas				
Fruits	½ cup	12	12	4
My Family's Plan				
Fruits (apples, peaches, plums, pears)	½ cup	12		
Juices (apple, berry, grape, tomato)	1 cup	7		
Tomatoes, Vegetables, Beans, and Legumes (tomatoes, beets, beans, carrots, corn, peas, pumpkin, squash)	1 cup	8		
Meat and Seafood (red meat, poultry, meals in a jar, fish)	½ cup	14		
Soups, Stews	1 cup	2		
Pickles, relishes, and ketchup	—	½ cup		
Fruit spreads (jam, preserves, honey)	—	¼ cup		
Sauces (tomato)	½ cup	2		

FAMILY SERVINGS PER WEEK	FAMILY CUPS PER WEEK	FAMILY QUARTS PER WEEK	WEEKS SERVED PER YEAR	FAMILY CANNED QUARTS PER YEAR TOTAL
Actual servings per person multiplied by number of family members who eat that food	Family servings per week multiplied by recommended serving size	Family cups per week divided by 4		Family quarts per week multiplied by weeks served per year
12 × 4 = 48	48 × ½ cup = 24 cups	24 cups ÷ 4 = 6 quarts	36 weeks	216 canned quarts per year

MANAGING COST

The thought of building a separate emergency food supply can be intimating and can appear costly, preventing people from taking time to do so. Here are some tips I use to control cost so I can be prepared without breaking the bank.

Buy in bulk (but only when it makes sense). Yes, I am that dork in the store with a calculator and notepad in hand, because I know that not all bulk purchases save money. Do the math. Divide the cost per unit on a bulk item and compare it to a smaller size. Sometimes purchasing two of a small size yields more product and costs less.

Frequent farm stands and farmers' markets. Taking a drive out to a local farm stand has saved me so much money compared to shopping at a chain grocery store. When you shop at a grocery store, you bear the cost of distribution, marketing, staff, and overhead. When you make the trip out to a farm location or farmers' market, there are fewer overhead costs, and therefore a cheaper price tag.

Shop with intention. Create a list of what your family consumes regularly. Next, create a list of what you currently have in your pantry. Compare the lists to create your shopping list, and stick to it when you're at the store. Do not peruse the aisles or meander aimlessly throughout the store, and certainly be mindful of marketing ploys while shopping. Sticking to the list helps control your spending.

Purchase canning lids almost every time you shop. New canning lids are a vital necessity for the long-term preservation of food. Because lids are a single-use product, serious home canners need a constant supply of them on hand. I purposely spread the cost out over the course of a year by purchasing a box of regular-mouth and a box of widemouthed lids every time I'm at the grocery store. If I did not get in the habit of doing so, I would be faced with a hefty cost at the start of every canning season. I would much rather increase each shopping trip by $5 than pay over $100 all at once every spring.

PROPER FOOD ROTATION AND SHELF LIFE

Labeling each jar lid with the month and year it was canned and the name of the food preserved helps you properly rotate your food supplies. It is imperative to rotate foods being stored, so the oldest foods are eaten first. For this reason, front-loading pantry shelves are ideal; you can then rotate food on a first-in first-out basis, placing

---

FORGOTTEN ESSENTIALS

Nutritional supplements: It is important to stock your pantry and emergency supply closet with vitamins, minerals, and protein supplements to ensure that you receive proper nutrition. While ready-made food is packed with nutrients, some are lost during the canning process. Make up for the nutrient loss by adding store-bought products to your emergency supply.

Heat: In the event of a power outage, many stoves will not work. While ready-made food can be eaten from the jar, some, like dehydrated and freeze-dried foods, require heat and water to be consumed. A portable butane burner with at least 14 butane canisters should be part of your pantry essentials. Having 14 canisters on hand will ensure a canister for each day of your 2-week emergency supply. Also, having an ample supply of butane will allow you to water bathe and pressure can during the disaster to preserve any perishable foods in your refrigerator or freezer that might spoil when the power is out.

Salt and sugar: While these two can be dangerous to our bodies in excess, causing a variety of health problems, salt is essential and is required for survival. Sugar, while not essential, can provide us with short-term energy and temporarily increase glucose levels.

the newest food in the rear and keeping the oldest foods in front. Consuming the oldest foods first cuts down on food waste.

Home-canned foods have a long shelf life, often upwards of 3 to 5 years. While it is best to consume your home-canned goods in the first year, you do not need to discard the food if it goes past the one-year mark. As long as the lids stayed sealed and the jars were stored under the proper conditions, you may enjoy eating your home-canned goods for years. However, do not store a bunch of emergency food in jars and then forget about them. Make it a point to inspect your emergency food supply twice a year. If any jars are approaching the one-year mark and you have recently canned the same food item, swap out the jars. Eat the older food first and place the recently canned food item in your emergency supply. For more on shelf life, see page 32.

CANNING WATER

It is important to stockpile water in your pantry in case of a disaster. There are two types of water required for storage, potable and nonpotable water. Potable water is sterilized water suitable for drinking and cooking, while nonpotable water is used for flushing toilets, washing hands, and watering your garden. An example of nonpotable water at your home would be water captured in rain barrels.

Reuse plastic milk jugs, 2-liter soda bottles, or any 3- and 5-gallon containers with good sealing lids to store nonpotable water. Potable drinking and cooking water cannot be stored for a long time in plastic. Glass is the most sterile method of storage for potable drinking water. Follow these instructions to preserve potable water in quart jars.

Canned Potable Water

1. Fill a large stockpot halfway with water. Bring to a full rolling boil over high heat. Reduce the heat and simmer for 15 minutes.

2. Ladle the hot water into hot quart jars, leaving ½ inch of headspace. If desired, add one drop of bleach to each quart for extra safety, or you may skip this step.

3. Wipe the rim of each jar with a warm, wet washcloth dipped in distilled white vinegar. Place a lid and ring on each jar and hand tighten.

4. Place jars in the pressure canner, lock the pressure canner lid, and bring to a boil over high heat. Let the canner vent for 10 minutes. Close the vent and continue heating to achieve 6 PSI for a dial gauge and 5 PSI for a weighted gauge. Process the quarts for 8 minutes.

Tip: You can do this every time you pressure can a recipe. If you happen to have leftover space in your canner, fill quart jars full of boiled water and process them right along with the foods in the canner. Before you know it you will have stockpiled a good supply of drinking and cooking water. Store jars of preserved water just as you would food.

ALTITUDES OF CITIES IN THE UNITED STATES AND CANADA

UNITED STATES			
State	City	Feet	Meters
Arizona	Mesa	1,243	379
	Phoenix	1,150	351
	Scottsdale	1,257	383
	Tucson	2,389	728
California	Fontana	1,237	377
	Moreno Valley	1,631	497
Colorado	Aurora	5,471	1,668
	Colorado Springs	6,010	1,832
	Denver	5,183	1,580
Georgia	Atlanta	1,026	313
Idaho	Boise	2,730	832
	Idaho Falls	4,705	1,434
Iowa	Sioux City	1,201	366
Kansas	Wichita	1,299	396
Montana	Billings	3,123	952
	Missoula	3,209	978
Nebraska	Lincoln	1,176	358
	Omaha	1,090	332
	Henderson	1,867	569
Nevada	Las Vegas	2,001	610
	Reno	4,505	1,373
New Mexico	Albuquerque	5,312	1,619
	Santa Fe	7,260	2,213
North Carolina	Asheville	2,134	650

UNITED STATES			
State	City	Feet	Meters
North Dakota	Bismarck	1,686	514
Ohio	Akron	1,004	306
Oklahoma	Oklahoma City	1,201	366
Pennsylvania	Pittsburgh	1,370	418
South Dakota	Rapid City	3,202	976
Texas	Amarillo	3,605	1,099
	El Paso	3,740	1,140
	Lubbock	3,256	992
Utah	Provo	4,551	1,387
	Salt Lake City	4,226	1,288
Washington	Spokane	1,843	562
Wyoming	Casper	5,150	1,570

CANADA			
Province	City	Feet	Meters
Alberta	Calgary	3,600	1,100
	Edmonton	2,201	671
Ontario	Hamilton	1,063	324
Manitoba	Brandon	1,343	409
Saskatchewan	Regina	1,893	577
	Saskatoon	1,580	482

THE DIRTY DOZEN AND CLEAN FIFTEEN™

A nonprofit environmental watchdog organization called Environmental Working Group (EWG) looks at data supplied by the US Department of Agriculture (USDA) and the Food and Drug Administration (FDA) about pesticide residues. Each year it compiles a list of the best and worst pesticide loads found in commercial crops. You can use these lists to decide which fruits and vegetables to buy organic to minimize your exposure to pesticides and which produce is considered safe enough to buy conventionally. This does not mean they are pesticide-free, though, so wash these fruits and vegetables thoroughly.

These lists change every year, so make sure you look up the most recent one before you fill your shopping cart. You'll find the most recent lists, as well as a guide to pesticides in produce, at EWG.org/FoodNews.

DIRTY DOZEN™

Apples
Celery
Cherries
Cherry tomatoes
Cucumbers
Grapes
Nectarines
Peaches
Spinach
Strawberries
Sweet bell peppers
Tomatoes

In addition to the Dirty Dozen, the EWG added two types of produce contaminated with highly toxic organophosphate insecticides:

Kale/Collard greens
Hot peppers

CLEAN FIFTEEN™

Asparagus
Avocados
Cabbage
Cantaloupe
Cauliflower
Eggplant
Grapefruit
Honeydew melon

Kiwifruits
Mangos
Onions
Papayas
Pineapples
Sweet corn
Sweet peas (frozen)

MEASUREMENT CONVERSION TABLES

VOLUME EQUIVALENTS (LIQUID)

US STANDARD	US STANDARD (OUNCES)	METRIC (APPROXIMATE)
2 tablespoons	1 fl. oz.	30 mL
¼ cup	2 fl. oz.	60 mL
½ cup	4 fl. oz.	120 mL
1 cup	8 fl. oz.	240 mL
1½ cups	12 fl. oz.	355 mL
2 cups or 1 pint	16 fl. oz.	475 mL
4 cups or 1 quart	32 fl. oz.	1 L
1 gallon	128 fl. oz.	4 L

OVEN TEMPERATURES

FAHRENHEIT (F)	CELSIUS (C) (APPROXIMATE)
250°	120°
300°	150°
325°	165°
350°	180°
375°	190°
400°	200°
425°	220°
450°	230°

VOLUME EQUIVALENTS (DRY)

US STANDARD	METRIC (APPROXIMATE)
⅛ teaspoon	0.5 mL
¼ teaspoon	1 mL
½ teaspoon	2 mL
¾ teaspoon	4 mL
1 teaspoon	5 mL
1 tablespoon	15 mL
¼ cup	59 mL
⅓ cup	79 mL
½ cup	118 mL
⅔ cup	156 mL
¾ cup	177 mL
1 cup	235 mL
2 cups or 1 pint	475 mL
3 cups	700 mL
4 cups or 1 quart	1 L

WEIGHT EQUIVALENTS

US STANDARD	METRIC (APPROXIMATE)
½ ounce	15 g
1 ounce	30 g
2 ounces	60 g
4 ounces	115 g
8 ounces	225 g
12 ounces	340 g
16 ounces or 1 pound	455 g

GLOSSARY

air bubble remover tool: The opposite end of a headspace measure tool used to release trapped air in jars packed with foods. It is also used to tamp down food in jars to pack more in. This tool can also be the handle of a wooden spoon, a small silicone spatula, or a chopstick.

ascorbic acid: Another name for vitamin C. A water-soluble vitamin that is used in food preparation to minimize browning of some vegetables and fruits. Often used together with citric acid, which is derived from lemon or lime juice, in commercially prepared blends to treat fruits to prevent browning.

bacteria: Microorganisms found in the air, soil, and water. Harmful bacteria can survive in low-acid environments and produce toxins that can be deadly. For this reason, low-acid foods are pressure canned to enable heating to a minimum of 240°F, a temperature that kills these bacteria.

blanch: The process of placing a food item in boiling water or steam for a short period of time. Blanching is always followed by an ice-water bath to quickly cool the food item and prevent further cooking. This process is used to inactivate enzymes in foods, as well as to loosen the skin or peel of some fruits and vegetables.

boil: Bringing a liquid to the temperature in which bubbles continuously break its surface. At sea level, the boiling point is 212°F, while at altitudes above 1,000 feet, this is achieved at a lower temperature.

boil, full rolling: Boiling that cannot be stirred down.

botulism: A deadly form of food poisoning caused by the bacterium *Clostridium botulinum*. These spores are present in the soil and air around us, but are able to activate only when there is a lack of oxygen and low acid levels. For this reason, it is highly important to process low-acid foods properly, for the recommended length and temperature, to kill the spores that produce this toxin.

bouquet garni: A bouquet garni is a bundle of herbs usually tied together with string and mainly used to flavor soups, stocks, casseroles and various stews.

brine: A solution used in the pickling process. Typically contains salt and water, although other ingredients such as spices or sugar can also be included.

canning liquid: Any liquid used in canning to cover food products in the jar. This can be water, broth, syrup, or juice. The liquid aids in heat penetration in the jar, as well as preventing foods from darkening.

cassoulet: Cassoulet is a rich, slow-cooked casserole originating in the south of France, containing meat, pork skin, and white beans. The dish is named after its traditional cooking vessel, the *cassole*, a deep, round, earthenware pot with slanting sides.

cheesecloth: A woven cloth designed for kitchen use. Used to strain stocks, drain juice from fruits, and form a spice bag to hold whole spices during cooking.

chinois: A chinois is a conical sieve with an extremely fine mesh. It is used to strain custards, purées, soups, and sauces, producing a very smooth texture. It can also be used to dust food with a fine layer of powdered ingredients.

chutney: A sweet and sour condiment made from fruits or vegetables, vinegar, and spices.

citric acid bath: The blend of ½ cup bottled lemon juice with 8 cups water used to prevent fruit from browning during preparation.

ClearJel®: Also known as Canning Gel, it is a thickening agent made from corn that has been mechanically processed into a fine powder. It retains its viscosity when heated to high temperatures and when reheated after cooling and does not impede heat transfer during processing. Commercially available and approved by the USDA for use in home canning.

enzyme: A protein found in foods that begins the process of both ripening and decomposition. Enzymes can change the texture, color, and flavor of fruits and vegetables. Food preservation methods deactivate these enzymes to permit long-term storage of foods.

food mill: A mechanical kitchen tool used to purée soft foods. A food mill separates the skins and seeds of the fruits or vegetables on its top, and the puréed food is collected below.

headspace: The space at the top of a canning jar that is left unfilled. Headspace varies based on the food type and is essential for creating a proper lid seal.

headspace measuring tool: A tool created specifically for home canning to properly measure the free oxygen left in the interior of the jar after it is filled with food. It is notched to rest on the rim of the jar with etched inches measurements.

hot pack method: Using preheated, hot food to fill jars prior to processing. Filling jars with preheated food expels air from the fibers of the food and allows food to be packed more tightly.

lemon juice: The juice extracted from lemons. In home canning recipes, it is used to ensure the proper acidic pH level. Because the acid in fresh lemons is variable, it is important to use bottled lemon juice when the recipe specifies it to ensure the safety of the finished product. When fresh lemon juice is called for, either bottled or fresh can be used.

pressure canner: A tall pot with a locking lid, rack, and a pressure regulating mechanism. Used to process low-acid foods. The only kitchen appliance for canning that reaches 240°F and higher, the temperature needed to kill harmful bacteria.

syrup: A blend of sugar and water created in a variety of thicknesses used to preserve fruit to help keep the fruit's color and provide a sweet flavor.

venting: A required process in pressure canning during which the vent is left open for a specified length of time while the canner's contents increase in heat. This allows cool air to escape the canner and each jar.

vinegar, apple cider: A vinegar produced from apples that has a tart, fruity flavor. Cider vinegar has a golden color and may darken a recipe. Always use vinegar with 5 percent acidity when using cider vinegar for canning.

vinegar, distilled white: A standard type of vinegar produced from grain alcohol. It is clear and colorless, making it suitable for a lot of different canning projects, as it does not compete with the colors or flavors of the foods. Always use vinegar with 5 percent acidity when canning.

water bath canner: A large pot and lid fixed with a rack to keep jars lifted away from the direct heat. The pot must be deep enough to hold jars that are covered with upwards of 3 inches of water and has room to boil rapidly.

whole, or cut, fruits in a syrup: Best for berries (blackberries, blueberries, currants, raspberries, strawberries); tree fruits (apples, apricots, nectarines, peaches, pears, plums); tropical fruits (guava, mango, passion fruit, pineapple); grapes; peppers (bell peppers and chiles).

RESOURCES

NCHFP.uga.edu—The National Center for Home Food Preservation is your source for methods of home food preservation.

NCHFP.uga.edu/publications/usda/INTRO_Home-Canrev0715.pdf—A guide created by the USDA in 2009 and later revised in 2015 to assist those who were new to home canning.

TheSurvivalMom.com—A resource for all the "prepper" moms keen to increase their family's level of preparedness for emergencies and crises of all shapes and sizes.

AroundTheCabin.com—A resource that teaches self-reliance, survival, primitive skills, prepping and food preservation, homesteading, life hacks, and critical thinking.

HappyPreppers.com/37-food-storage.html—A free guide on how to stock your prepper pantry.

USDA Plant Hardiness Zone Map (http://planthardiness.ars.usda.gov)—For region-specific information about growing a variety of plants.

REFERENCES

Barefoot, Susan, Adair Hoover, E.H. Hoyle, Clemson University, and Pamela Schmutz. "Common Canning Problems." Clemson University. http://www.clemson.edu/extension/hgic/food/food_safety/preservation/hgic3050.html

Devereaux, Diane (blog). "The Benefits of Pressure Canning." Accessed June 23, 2017. https://canningdiva.com/the-benefits-of-pressure-canning/

Devereaux, Diane (blog). "Three Main Elements to Safe Canning Practices." Accessed June 26, 2017. https://canningdiva.com/three-main-elements-to-safe-canning-practices/

Devereaux, Diane (blog). "The Importance of Proper Headspace When Home Canning." Accessed July 10, 2017. https://canningdiva.com/knowing-proper-headspace/

Encyclopaedia Britannica. "Biography of Nicolas Appert." Accessed May 4, 1999. https://www.britannica.com/biography/Nicolas-Appert

How Much Is It. "How Much Does A Whole Chicken Cost?" Accessed February 7, 2018. https://www.howmuchisit.org/whole-chicken-cost/

Looking at the Science on Raw versus Cooked Foods. Part 2E. "Effects of cooking on vitamins." Accessed September 23, 2012. http://www.beyondveg.com/tu-j-l/raw-cooked/raw-cooked-2e.shtml

Mallillin, A.C., T.P. Trinidad, R. Raterta et al. "Dietary Fibre and Fermentability Characteristics of Root Crops and Legumes." *The British Journal of Nutrition* 100, no. 3 (2008): 485–488. Cambridge. Accessed September 2008.

National Presto Industries, Inc. "Parts of a Typical Pressure Canner." Last modified 2014. https://gopresto.com/recipes/canning/Parts.pdf

National Presto Industries, Inc. "Pressure Canning Basics." 2018. https://gopresto.com/recipes/canning/index.php

National Presto Industries, Inc. "Presto Testing Unit #81288." ADW07-5239D. 2018. https://nchfp.uga.edu/educators/Presto%20Testing%20Unit%20ADW07-5239C.pdf

Nestle Professional Nutrition Magazine. "Nutro Pro®." Vol. 2. Accessed June 2006. https://www.nestleprofessional.us/sites/g/files/gfb131/f/media/nutripro_magazine_healthy_cooking_methods.pdf

Raab, Carolyn A. "Canning Seafood." A Pacific Northwest Extension Publication, Oregon State University, Washington State University and University of Idaho. PNW 194. Revised by Jeanne Brandt. Last modified November 2016. http://extension.oregonstate.edu/fch/sites/default/files/documents/pnw_194_canningseafood.pdf

Reynolds, Susan and Paulette Williams. "So Easy to Preserve." Bulletin 989. Cooperative Extension Service, the University of Georgia. Fifth Edition revised by Elizabeth Andress and Judy Harrison. 2006. http://www.clemson.edu/extension/hgic/food/food_safety/preservation/hgic3050.html

Sara Garduno Diaz. You Are What You Ate. (blog) "The Effects of Cooking on Nutrition". Accessed 2001. University of Leeds, United Kingdom. http://www.leeds.ac.uk/yawya/science-and-nutrition/The%20effects%20of%20cooking%20on%20nutrition.html

United States Department of Agriculture Food Safety and Inspection Service. "Clostridium botulinum." Accessed January 2010. https://www.fsis.usda.gov/wps/wcm/connect/a70a5447-9490-4855-af0d-e617ea6b5e46/Clostridium_botulinum.pdf?MOD=AJPERES

United States Department of Agriculture Economic Research Service. "Average daily intake of food by food source and demographic characteristics, 2007–10." Accessed June 27, 2014. https://www.ers.usda.gov/Data/FoodConsumption/

United States Department of Health and Human Services, U.S. Department of Agriculture. "Dietary Guidelines for Americans." Accessed 2018. https://health.gov/dietaryguidelines/2015

William Reed Business Media Ltd. "Tomatoes: Cooked Better Than Raw?" Accessed April 22, 2002. Last modified July 19, 2008. https://www.foodnavigator.com/Article/2002/04/23/Tomatoes-cooked-better-than-raw#

RECIPE INDEX

INDEX

ACKNOWLEDGMENTS

I must first acknowledge and deeply thank my amazing kids for putting up with a messy kitchen for weeks while creating these recipes and for my taking over the kitchen table to write. Many nights we ate dinner on TV tables to accommodate this project. Caleb and Audrey, I thank you both for your ability to roll with the punches and for giving me unconditional love and support.

To my loving mumma who helped me craft the perfect lentil soup recipe and who took my late-night calls and attentively listened to me ramble on about the newest culinary creation that had captured my full attention. Mom, you are my true inspiration in the kitchen. Thank you for putting a paring knife in my hand when I was 3 years old.

Many heartfelt thanks to my amazing sister, Deborah. Thank you for all of your enthusiasm for this project and feedback when tasting my recipes. Deb, you have been my truest companion and strongest shoulder to lean on when I got overwhelmed. Thank you for pouring a mean glass of wine and for getting us gabbing and laughing so my stress just melts away. I am so blessed to call you sister and friend.

And where would I be without my foodie bestie, Jeff Hage? Words cannot express the level of gratitude I have for our friendship. It is rare to find someone who appreciates food and family as much as I do. I will always cherish the countless memories we have made trying new foods, and bourbons, together. Many thanks for making time to help me test recipes in my kitchen for this book.

Last, but certainly not least, I must acknowledge and thank my editor and new friend, Salwa Jabado. We just clicked from day one. You truly made this an amazing experience to which I will always compare every new work. Thank you for challenging me and for helping me look at my words through the eyes of a new canner. A washcloth and tomato will never be the same after this.

ABOUT THE AUTHOR

DIANE DEVEREAUX is The Canning Diva®, a nationally syndicated food preservation expert, television presenter, instructor, mother of two, and author of *Canning Full Circle: From Garden to Jar to Table*. Devereaux has bridged the generational gap of traditional canning methods for over a decade, teaching the art and craft of home canning to busy families across America.

Follow The Canning Diva®:

CanningDiva.com

facebook.com/CanningDiva

instagram.com/CanningDiva

twitter.com/CanningDiva

pinterest.com/CanningDiva

youtube.com/channel/UCBz4TS4jS7DrUr4iwKeO8fA